social suppers
jason atherton

I dedicate this book to two little people in my life – my beautiful daughters, Keziah and Jemimah, who love me regardless of what I do, how many hours I work and no matter how far away from them I am. They are my shining lights, my drive, my inspiration and simply the love of my life. Girls: I love you more than you will ever know.

social suppers
jason atherton

First published in Great Britain in 2014 by
Absolute Press, an imprint of Bloomsbury Publishing Plc

Absolute Press
Scarborough House
29 James Street West
Bath BA1 2BT
Phone 44 (0) 1225 316013
Fax 44 (0) 1225 445836
E-mail office@absolutepress.co.uk
Website www.absolutepress.co.uk

Text copyright © Jason Atherton, 2014
Photography copyright © John Carey, 2014

Publisher Jon Croft
Commissioning Editor Meg Avent
Art Director and Designer Matt Inwood
Project Editor Alice Gibbs
Editor Imogen Fortes
Photographer John Carey
Home Economy and Recipe Testing
Emily Quah and Nicole Herft
Props Stylist Jo Harris
Indexer Zoe Ross

The rights of Jason Atherton to be identified as the author of this work have been asserted by him in accordance with the Copyright Designs and Patents Act 1988.

All rights reserved. No part of this publication may be reproduced, stored in a retrieval system or transmitted in any form or by any means, electronic or otherwise, without the prior permission of Absolute Press.

A catalogue record of this book is available from the British Library

ISBN: 9781472904249

Printed in China by C&C Offset

A note about the text
This book was set using Baskerville, a serif typeface designed in 1757 by John Baskerville (1706–1775) in Birmingham, England. It is classified as a 'transitional' typeface, in appearance bridging the gap between the old-style faces of William Caslon and the modern styles of Giambattista Bodoni and Firmin Didot.

Bloomsbury Publishing Plc
50 Bedford Square, London WC1B 3DP
www.bloomsbury.com

Bloomsbury is a trademark of Bloomsbury Publishing Plc

Cook's notes
• All spoon measures are level unless otherwise stated:
1 teaspoon = 5ml spoon; 1 tablespoon = 15ml spoon.
• All herbs are fresh and all pepper is freshly ground black pepper unless otherwise suggested.
• Egg sizes are specified where they are critical, otherwise use large organic or free-range eggs.
• If you are pregnant or in a vulnerable health group, avoid those recipes that contain raw egg whites or lightly cooked eggs.
• Oven timings are for fan-assisted ovens. If you are using a conventional oven, increase the temperature by 15°C (1 gas mark). Individual ovens can deviate by as much as 10°C from the setting, either way. Get to know your oven and use an oven thermometer to check its accuracy.
• Timings are provided as guidelines, with a description of colour or texture where appropriate, but the reader should rely on their own judgement as to when a dish is properly cooked.

CONTENTS

6 FOREWORD BY THOMAS KELLER
8 INTRODUCTION

10 STARTERS

80 MAIN COURSES

166 DESSERTS

214 BASICS

230 INDEX
239 ACKNOWLEDGEMENTS

FOREWORD
BY THOMAS KELLER

When I first met Jason Atherton in London, the first thing I noticed was his approachability and warmth, layered with a boundless energy that was both affable and curious.

My *chef de cuisine* of The French Laundry at the time, Eric Ziebold, and I chose to dine at Jason's restaurant for its reputation. It was a wonderful experience – to our delight Jason took care of us that day and made a lasting impression.

A few years later, when I had the chance to taste Jason's food at Pollen Street Social for the first time, I saw this warmth and energy, refined and infused with innovative flavour profiles. Jason's cuisine at Pollen Street Social and around the world takes the simple flavours of home – and homes around the world – and elevates them in dishes mastered with skill and technique.

I know that it takes courage to cook simple food, and that is one way the great chefs are separated from the good ones. Jason is one of the greats. He's the best of both worlds. He has the prowess of a Michelin-starred chef with accolades from every corner of the globe, but he is also the person you want to be preparing your Sunday supper.

In *Social Suppers*, Jason invites us into his home for one such dinner. From starters, main courses and desserts to learning the basics, he uses his incredible technique and approachable nature to walk you through each step. With dishes like fried eggs with black pudding, capers and anchovies; Mrs. Tee's wild mushrooms on toast with bacon jam (named for his mushroom forager); and bone marrow, gentleman's relish and onions on toast (so popular on his Hong Kong restaurant's menu that they can't remove it); you'll experience recipes that have a strong foundation and yet take playful risks in ways that will surprise and delight.

I have known Jason for ten years, and throughout his ascent to success he has maintained a humility that is admirable. Jason is more than the praise he has garnered, and through his recipes in *Social Suppers*, you will sense that. He represents the next generation of chefs and the future of food.

As he says, when you're a cook, 'you've got power in your hands – to entertain people, to impress people, to win over friends, family, lovers, whatever you want to do.' When we experience Jason's food, we gladly relinquish our power and turn it over to a person who nourishes us at the table and beyond.

Thomas Keller, The French Laundry
February 2014

INTRODUCTION

During my life as a chef I have been very fortunate to have travelled to many different countries. Just the thought of travel gives me butterflies in my stomach – thinking about the styles of dishes I may encounter, the new recipes and cuisines I will discover, and the chefs I may meet and learn from.

Travelling is one of life's great luxuries. So when I was asked by my business partners in Asia, Mrs. Oei and Peng and Geoff, whether I would like to expand into Singapore with a new restaurant it was a big 'YES'. It meant for the first time I could combine my love of travel and cooking in one restaurant. Esquina was born in Chinatown in Singapore with the talented Andrew Walsh. Seven restaurants later – spanning Hong Kong, Shanghai and Singapore – I sometimes think I have the best job in the world.

When I am on a long-haul flight or just in a coffee shop grabbing some precious moments alone, I will write down all of the dishes that I would love to cook to share with my friends and family at home: food which I know is going to taste great and evoke memories of my travels for me. In this book are those dishes: recipes inspired by my restaurants from all around the world and by the food I have experienced while travelling to so many different countries. But you don't have to travel far to have these memories and inspirations – I have also included dishes that are based right on my doorstep in Britain yet still have great meaning for me. I have recreated all the recipes for you to try in your own home. Some you will be familiar with and others not, but I urge you to taste them all.

It might sound obvious, but the recipes in this book are all about flavours. When you cook anything – from a Michelin-starred dish to a simple salad – the thing that needs to come first, above everything else, is the flavour. I know from cooking these dishes time and again that the flavours harmonize beautifully, but you can add your own flair to these recipes; you don't need to tie yourself to everything exactly as it's written here – so be creative and let these recipes inspire you to make great food that you love.

These dishes are perfect for family and friends to share. I would love this book to inspire you to cook and I hope that you can use the joy of food and wine to bring your nearest and dearest back around the table to experience love, joy and laughter together.

Happy cooking.

Jason Atherton

STARTERS

STARTERS

14/ SPANISH BREAKFAST **16/** FRIED EGGS WITH BLACK PUDDING, CAPERS AND ANCHOVIES **18/** POTATO AND PARSLEY SOUP WITH BLACK PUDDING AND CHEDDAR TOASTIES **21/** RABBIT CONFIT WITH CELERIAC CREAM SOUP AND RABBIT FLOSS

22/ BURRATA AND FIGS WITH TRUFFLE HONEY **25/** SPRING VEGETABLE TARTINE WITH CREAMED BURRATA **26/** GOAT'S CHEESE WITH PEAS, BROAD BEANS, MINT AND SERRANO HAM **28/** MRS. TEE'S WILD MUSHROOMS ON TOAST WITH BACON JAM **29/** BABY VIOLET ARTICHOKES WITH DATTERINI TOMATOES AND BROAD BEANS **31/** TOMATO TARTARE **32/** GARLIC-ROASTED PINK FIR APPLE POTATOES WITH PARSLEY AND BRAVA SAUCE **33/** GRIDDLED CORN ON THE COB WITH PARMESAN AND CHILLI

34/ MIXED BEETROOT SALAD WITH GOAT'S CHEESE MOUSSE AND PINE NUT DRESSING **37/** WINTER VEGETABLE SALAD WITH GOAT'S CURD **38/** AVOCADO, BABY GEM, ORANGE AND SAUTÉED BABY CARROT SALAD **41/** ROQUEFORT AND ICEBERG SALAD WITH WARM CROUTONS AND ALSACE BACON **42/** ROAST CAESAR SALAD WITH WHITE ANCHOVIES **44/** SEARED TUNA SALAD WITH MISO AUBERGINES AND SHERRY DRESSING

45/ TUNA TARTARE D.I.Y. **46/** CONFIT TUNA WITH PIPERADE AND CHIVES **47/** SALMON 'CRUDO' WITH PICKLED CUCUMBER AND WASABI AND AVOCADO PURÉE **49/** SPANISH TOMATO BREAD WITH SARDINES **50/** PASTRAMI OF SEA BASS WITH GAZPACHO GARNISH **51/** BEETROOT-CURED SEA TROUT WITH ROAST BEETROOT AND HORSERADISH CREAM **55/** KOHLRABI, APPLE, WHISKY WALNUT AND SEA TROUT SALAD **56/** SCALLOP CEVICHE WITH PICKLED FENNEL AND LEMON CONFIT **59/** RAZOR CLAMS WITH CHORIZO, CORIANDER AND CHILLI **60/** CRAB AND ASPARAGUS SALAD WITH RADISHES **63/** GOAT'S-CHEESE-STUFFED COURGETTE FLOWERS WITH APPLE AND CORIANDER CRAB SALAD **64/** CRAB MAYONNAISE WITH BITTER LEAVES ON TOAST **65/** LANGOUSTINES WITH PICKLED VEGETABLES AND PEAS **66/** FINE DE CLAIRE OYSTERS WITH VIETNAMESE DRESSING

69/ ROASTED CEPS, PISTOU OF GREEN VEGETABLES AND PAPRIKA OCTOPUS **70/** SALT AND PEPPER SQUID WITH SQUID INK AÏOLI **72/** SEA URCHIN, GOAT'S CHEESE AND PEPPERS ON TOAST **73/** SALAD OF QUAIL, CANDIED LEMON, PEAR AND SOURDOUGH CRUMB **75/** LITTLE SOCIAL STEAK TARTARE WITH QUAIL'S EGG AND RADISH SALAD **76/** CRISP LAMB'S TONGUE WITH MINT GRIBICHE **77/** FRIED OX TONGUE WITH MUSHROOMS AND PEAS **78/** BONE MARROW, GENTLEMAN'S RELISH AND ONIONS ON TOAST

SPANISH BREAKFAST

My mother used to say that you should never start the day with an empty stomach, and I couldn't agree more. Breakfast is my favourite meal of the day and I love the idea of incorporating egg dishes in every meal. This dish unites all my Spanish favourites: potatoes, poached eggs, a tomato brava sauce and crisp chorizo. One mouthful and I'm instantly transported to Spain.

SERVES 4

For the brava sauce
2 tablespoons light olive oil
1 small banana shallot, peeled and finely diced
1 large garlic clove, peeled and chopped
2 tablespoons tomato purée
500g plum tomatoes, peeled, deseeded and chopped
1 small onion, peeled and diced
1 small cooking chorizo (about 75g), diced
1 teaspoon paprika
1 tablespoon sherry vinegar
sea salt and freshly ground black pepper

For the crisp chorizo and poached eggs
100g chorizo, thinly sliced on the angle
1 teaspoon white wine vinegar or cider vinegar
4 large eggs

To finish and serve
3 tablespoons olive oil
250g potatoes, peeled and cut into 1.5cm dice
200g chorizo, cut into 1.5cm dice
½ teaspoon paprika
2 banana shallots, peeled and sliced into rings
a few sprigs of thyme, leaves stripped
a knob of butter
1 tablespoon finely chopped flat-leaf parsley, to garnish

To make the brava sauce, heat a tablespoon of the oil in a heavy-based pan over a medium heat. Add the shallot and stir well. Sweat the shallot for 6–8 minutes, stirring occasionally, until it is translucent. Stir in the garlic and tomato purée. Cook for another 2–3 minutes, then stir in the chopped tomatoes. Bring to a simmer and cook gently for 10–15 minutes, until the mixture has thickened and reduced by half. Take the pan off the heat.

In another heavy-based pan, heat the remaining tablespoon of oil and sweat the onion for 8–10 minutes, stirring occasionally, until soft. Add the chorizo and increase the heat slightly. Fry for another couple of minutes until the chorizo releases its orangey-red oils. Add the paprika and stir for another minute. Deglaze the pan with the vinegar, scraping the bottom of the pan with a wooden spoon to release all the flavours. Let the liquid bubble away until the pan is quite dry. Finally tip in the tomato mixture from the other pan. Stir well and simmer until the mixture has thickened to a sauce consistency. Season well with salt and pepper.

To make the crisp chorizo, preheat the oven to 180°C/Gas Mark 4. Arrange the slices on a baking tray and bake for about 6–8 minutes until they are golden brown. Remove from the oven. The chorizo will crisp as it cools.

To poach the eggs, bring a tall pan of water to the boil. Lower the heat to a simmer and add the vinegar. Crack an egg into a small cup or ramekin. Swirl the water with a spoon to create a whirlpool. Lower each egg into the centre of the whirlpool, one at a time. Poach for 3 minutes until the egg whites are cooked but the yolks are still runny. Remove the eggs from the pan with a slotted spoon and gently place on a plate lined with kitchen paper. Just before serving, warm them through in a pan of gently simmering water.

To finish, heat the oil in a heavy-based pan over a medium heat. Add the diced potatoes and a pinch of salt and pepper. Sauté the potatoes for 6–8 minutes until they begin to soften. Tip in the diced chorizo and paprika. Fry for 4–5 minutes, until the chorizo releases its oils. Stir in the shallots and thyme leaves and fry for another 5 minutes, stirring occasionally, until the shallot is just tender and golden brown. Add the butter and toss the potatoes until evenly coated with the foaming butter.

To serve, spoon the brava sauce on to the base of warmed, shallow bowls. Spoon the shallot, chorizo and potato mixture over the sauce then top with the poached eggs. Garnish each plate with the crisp chorizo slices and a sprinkling of chopped parsley. Serve while still hot.

STARTERS

FRIED EGGS WITH BLACK PUDDING, CAPERS AND ANCHOVIES

I absolutely love eggs – whether they are boiled, fried, poached, scrambled or cooked in a custard. Many chefs may not agree, but I think something as simple as a perfectly fried egg can take pride of place on a fine dining menu. As with any key ingredient, use the best eggs you can afford. I insist on free-range eggs but do go organic if your purse strings allow. This dish may be simple but it just works when you've got four great ingredients balancing each other in terms of taste and texture.

SERVES 2

1–1½ tablespoons light olive or vegetable oil
100g black pudding, halved
4 large eggs
1 tablespoon capers, chopped
4 anchovy fillets in oil, drained and chopped
sea salt and freshly ground white pepper

Heat a little oil in a small non-stick frying pan over a medium heat. Add the black pudding and fry for about 6–10 minutes, turning over halfway, until golden brown and just cooked through. Remove the pieces to a plate lined with kitchen paper and keep in a warm place.

Add a little more oil to the pan if necessary, then break the eggs into the pan. Season the eggs with a little salt and white pepper, to taste. Cook gently until the egg whites are set but the yolks are still runny in the centre.

Serve the fried eggs with the black pudding and scatter over the chopped capers and anchovies. Serve immediately.

POTATO AND PARSLEY SOUP WITH BLACK PUDDING AND CHEDDAR TOASTIES

This is a dish that Phil Carmichael, my head chef and partner at Berners Tavern, came up with. Each of us went through the '70s and '80s with our Breville toasters and, amazingly, we still use our toasters today. This simple soup and sandwich combo is a little nod to those retro years.

SERVES 4

For the soup
700g Desiree potatoes, peeled and thinly sliced
50g unsalted butter
750ml Vegetable or Chicken Stock (see pages 218–219)
150ml double cream
5–6 tablespoons Parsley Purée (see page 227)
300g black pudding, cut into cubes, to serve
extra-virgin olive oil, to finish
sea salt and freshly ground black pepper

For the black pudding and Cheddar toasties
25g unsalted butter
200g black pudding, chopped
1 banana shallot, peeled and finely chopped
4 large garlic cloves, peeled and finely chopped
a small bunch of curly or flat-leaf parsley (thick stalks removed), finely chopped
8 thick slices of white bread
4 slices of Cheddar

Place the potatoes in a colander and rinse under cold running water to remove the excess starch. Drain and pat dry with a clean tea towel. Melt the butter in a large heavy-based pan placed over a low heat and add the potatoes and some salt and pepper. Cover the potatoes with a cartouche – a damp circle of baking parchment cut to the width of the pan. Sweat the potatoes over a low heat for about 10 minutes. Remove the cartouche, pour in the stock, stir well and bring to a simmer. Simmer for another 10 minutes until the potato is very soft.

Carefully transfer the soup to a blender until it comes halfway up the sides of the blender (you may need to do this in two batches). Put the lid on and drape a folded kitchen towel over it. Holding down the lid, blend the soup until smooth. Pour in the cream and blend again to mix. Pour the soup into a clean saucepan, stir in the parsley purée, then taste the soup and adjust the seasoning to your liking. If you find the soup too thick, let it down with a little boiling water. Reheat before serving.

For the toasties, melt the butter in a heavy-based pan over a medium heat. As it begins to foam, add the black pudding. Fry for 4–5 minutes, stirring occasionally, until golden brown all over. Stir in the shallot and garlic and sauté for another 6–8 minutes until the shallots are tender. Season to taste, stir in the parsley, then take the pan off the heat. Leave to cool completely.

Preheat the oven to 180°C/Gas Mark 4. To assemble a toastie, lay a slice of Cheddar on a slice of bread, then spread a layer of black pudding mixture over the cheese. Sandwich with another slice of bread. Continue assembling the sandwiches until you've used up the black pudding mixture. The sandwiches can be made a few hours in advance and chilled, wrapped well with cling film.

Just before you are ready to serve, toast the sandwiches using a panini press, or grill them on a hot griddle pan, pressing down with the back of a spatula as you toast each side. Once toasted place in the oven for 5 minutes or until the filling is warm and the cheese has melted.

Meanwhile, heat a non-stick frying pan until hot. Add the cubes of black pudding and toss until golden all over.

Ladle the soup into bowls, top with the fried black pudding cubes and drizzle over a little oil. Slice the toasties into quarters and serve alongside.

STARTERS

RABBIT CONFIT WITH CELERIAC CREAM SOUP AND RABBIT FLOSS

When I travelled in South-east Asia, I was intrigued by their technique of making floss out of meat, poultry and even fish. Basically, the meat is dehydrated or wok-fried until it is crisp and finely shredded. We've taken the same idea and made floss using rabbit. It provides a lovely contrast of textures when served with celeriac soup and confit rabbit.

SERVES 6

For the rabbit confit and floss
5 rabbit legs
1 tablespoon sea salt
1–1½ litres duck (or goose) fat, melted

For the soup
2 tablespoons olive oil, plus extra to finish
2 large celeriacs, peeled and chopped
1 onion, peeled and chopped
750ml rabbit stock (or Chicken Stock, see page 218)
400ml double cream
a small handful of finely chopped chives or flat-leaf parsley, to garnish
sea salt and freshly ground black pepper

Preheat the oven to 120°C/Gas Mark ½. Put the rabbit legs into a deep ovenproof dish in which the rabbit legs fit snugly. Season with the sea salt then pour in enough duck fat to cover the legs. Place the dish into the oven and gently cook for 1½ hours or until the meat is tender.

Meanwhile, make the celeriac soup. Heat the olive oil in a large ovenproof pan. Add the chopped celeriac and onion with some salt and pepper. Sweat the vegetables over a medium heat, stirring occasionally, for about 10 minutes, until the vegetables are tender. Pour in the stock, topping up with boiling water as necessary to cover the vegetables. Simmer for about 20 minutes until the celeriac is soft. Add the cream and season well to taste. Blend the soup using a hand-held stick blender (or a regular blender) until it is smooth and creamy. Reheat before serving.

When the rabbit confit is ready, remove from the oven and leave to cool slightly. Reduce the oven temperature to 100°C/Gas Mark ¼. Once cool enough to handle, take the rabbit legs out of the fat (save it for roast potatoes or another dish) then pull the rabbit meat away from the bones. Set aside the meat from 3 of the legs and finely shred the remaining half. Spread out the shredded meat evenly on a wide baking tray. Place into the low oven and let the meat dehydrate for 45 minutes to one hour or until it dries out and turns crisp. Remove from the oven and leave to cool.

Just as you are ready to serve, heat 1–2 tablespoons of the confit duck fat in a wide frying pan. When hot, fry the reserved confit rabbit with a little salt and pepper until evenly golden brown. Take the pan off the heat.

To serve, neatly place the seared rabbit meat into the middle of the warmed soup bowls. Arrange small piles of the rabbit 'floss' on top of the meat. Carefully pour the celeriac soup into each bowl but do not allow it to come up to the level of the rabbit floss. Sprinkle with chopped chives, drizzle with olive oil and serve immediately.

BURRATA AND FIGS WITH TRUFFLE HONEY

This has to be one of the easiest starters you can make for a dinner party! It was only four years ago that I started to use burrata in my cooking. I say cooking, but in fact, a good-quality burrata requires very little done to it. Like buffalo mozzarella, burrata simply needs a couple of well-chosen accompaniments, such as sweet figs and truffle honey, to contrast with its rich, creamy texture.

SERVES 4

4 ripe figs
1 tablespoon truffle honey (or regular clear honey), plus extra to drizzle
1 tablespoon good-quality aged balsamic vinegar, plus extra to drizzle
1 teaspoon olive oil, plus extra to drizzle
knob of butter
4 blanched hazelnuts
8 thin slices of baguette
4 x 200g burrata cheeses, drained and patted dry
sea salt and freshly ground black pepper

Cut two figs into quarters and the remaining two into 6 wedges each. Put the figs into a bowl and season with a little salt and pepper. Drizzle over the honey, vinegar and olive oil. Gently toss the figs to ensure that every piece is coated with the dressing. Set aside.

Melt the butter in a small frying pan and tip in the hazelnuts. Roast them over a medium heat, tossing frequently, until they are evenly golden. Transfer to a small plate lined with kitchen paper to absorb the excess butter. Leave to cool.

When you are about ready to serve, preheat the oven grill to the highest setting. Arrange the baguette slices in a single layer on a baking tray then drizzle a little olive oil over each slice. Sprinkle over a little salt then grill for about a minute until golden brown and crisp. Turn the slices over, drizzle with a little more oil and grill for another minute. Do not leave them unattended as the bread can burn easily. Remove and set aside.

Season the burrata with salt, pepper and a drizzle of olive oil.

To assemble, spoon the figs on to four individual serving plates in neat piles, then drizzle a little balsamic vinegar around them. Place the burrata alongside the figs, add two slices of toasted baguette to each plate, then grate a hazelnut over each burrata. Serve immediately.

STARTERS

SPRING VEGETABLE TARTINE WITH CREAMED BURRATA

Since travelling to the South of France a long time ago, I have been crazy about tartines. Open-faced sandwiches have full impact as the bread acts like a plate on which beautiful ingredients are presented. Here, creamed burrata is spread on toast to form a base for gorgeous spring vegetables. It's a simple and stunning dish that you can serve as a starter or alongside a bowl of spring vegetable soup for a light lunch.

SERVES 4

100g fresh peas (or use frozen but thaw them first)
100g fresh broad beans (or use frozen but thaw them first)
8 asparagus tips
10 breakfast radishes
200g cherry tomatoes, halved
1 spring onion, trimmed and thinly sliced on the diagonal
80ml Basic Vinaigrette (see page 222)
4 slices of sourdough
300g burrata
extra-virgin olive oil
50g aged Comté cheese,
a small handful of chervil, leaves only, to garnish
a small handful of chives, finely chopped, to garnish
a small handful of wild rocket, to garnish
sea salt and freshly ground black pepper

Bring a large pan of salted water to the boil and have ready a large bowl of iced water. Blanch the peas, broad beans and asparagus separately until they are bright green and just tender; the peas and broad beans will take 2 minutes; the asparagus will take a minute longer. As soon as each vegetable is cooked, remove it with a slotted spoon and plunge it into the iced water immediately to stop the cooking. Once cooled, drain the vegetables and remove the tough outer skins from the broad beans.

Slice the radishes as thinly as possible using a mandolin or a sharp knife. Place them in a bowl of iced water to keep them crisp.

Put the cherry tomatoes and spring onions in a bowl. Tip in the blanched peas, broad beans and asparagus, then add the vinaigrette, season with salt and pepper and toss well.

A few minutes before you are ready to serve, toast the sourdough. Meanwhile, drain the burrata and put into a large bowl with a pinch of salt and pepper. Beat the cheese with a spatula until it is creamy and smooth. Spread the burrata evenly over the toasted sourdough slices then place these on a serving plate. Spoon over the dressed vegetables. Drain the radishes and pat dry before arranging on top of the tartines. Drizzle over a little olive oil and sprinkle with a little salt and pepper, to taste. Shave the Comté over the tartines, then garnish with a sprinkling of chervil, chives and wild rocket leaves. Serve at once.

GOAT'S CHEESE WITH PEAS, BROAD BEANS, MINT AND SERRANO HAM

This is one of the tapas dishes included on the spring menu at 22 Ships, our tapas bar in Hong Kong. I simply love the combination of peas, broad beans and mint during spring and early summer when these ingredients are in their prime. Such amazing ingredients need little more than thin slices of salty Serrano ham to provide a bit of contrast in taste and texture.

SERVES 4

For the goat's cheese mousse
250g soft, creamy goat's cheese
40g goat's curd
sea salt and freshly ground black pepper

For the shallot dressing
1½ tablespoons olive oil
1 banana shallot, peeled and finely diced
½ red chilli, deseeded and finely chopped
2 teaspoons finely grated fresh ginger
5 tablespoons Yuzu Wasabi Dressing
   (see page 223)

For the peas and broad beans
200g frozen peas
200g frozen broad beans
small handful of mint leaves, chopped

To serve
100g Serrano ham slices

First, make the goat's cheese mousse. Put all the ingredients into a bowl and whisk until light and smooth. Taste and adjust the seasoning. Cover with cling film and chill (for a professional touch, you can spoon the mixture into a piping bag before chilling).

For the shallot dressing, heat the oil in a small pan and add the shallot, chilli and ginger. Stir frequently over a medium–low heat for 6–8 minutes until the shallots are soft and translucent. Season lightly with salt and pepper. Transfer the mixture to a bowl and leave to cool before mixing with the yuzu and wasabi dressing.

Preheat the oven to 200°C/Gas Mark 6. Lay out the Serrano ham slices in a single layer on a baking sheet lined with silicone or baking parchment. Top with another piece of parchment, then weigh down with another baking sheet to keep the ham slices flat. Bake for about 10 minutes or until the ham is golden brown and crisp. Remove from the oven and take off the baking parchment. The ham slices will continue to crisp up as they cool.

Meanwhile, bring a pan of salted water to the boil and have ready a bowl of iced water. Blanch the peas and broad beans separately; the peas will take around 2–3 minutes; the broad beans 3–4 minutes. As soon as each is ready, remove from the pan using a slotted spoon and immediately refresh in the iced water to stop the cooking process. Drain well then remove the pale skins from the broad beans.

When ready to serve, mix the peas and broad beans with a few tablespoons of shallot dressing – you need just enough to coat them. Stir through the chopped mint and check the seasoning. Spoon the mixture on to serving plates. Spoon or pipe the goat's cheese mousse around the plate, add the crisp Serrano ham and serve.

STARTERS

MRS. TEE'S WILD MUSHROOMS ON TOAST WITH BACON JAM

Mrs. Tee has been our mushroom supplier for as long as I can remember. She supplies foraged wild mushrooms to most of London's top restaurants. Whenever autumnal mushrooms come into season, the chefs get very excited in the kitchen as Mrs. Tee's team bring in boxes of chanterelles, pied de moutons and my personal favourite, ceps.

This particular dish doubles as a light lunch or a sumptuous, posh breakfast. If serving for breakfast, top the mushrooms with a poached or fried duck egg for the ultimate indulgence.

SERVES 4

For the bacon jam
250g smoked streaky bacon, finely diced
½ Spanish onion, peeled and finely chopped
2 garlic cloves, peeled and finely chopped
200ml apple cider vinegar
125g soft dark brown sugar
3 tablespoons maple syrup
50ml freshly brewed espresso coffee
sea salt and freshly ground black pepper

For the wild mushrooms
300g wild mushrooms, cleaned
2 tablespoons olive oil
1 shallot, peeled and finely chopped
1 garlic clove, peeled and finely chopped
a knob of butter
2 tablespoons chopped flat-leaf parsley

To serve
½ loaf of sourdough, cut into 1cm slices
olive oil, to brush

First, make the bacon jam. Fry the bacon in a dry frying pan for 4–6 minutes until golden brown and crisp. Remove the crisp bacon to a plate with a slotted spoon, leaving the bacon fat in the pan. Add the onion and garlic to the pan and toss to coat in the bacon fat. Cook for 6–8 minutes, stirring occasionally, until the onion is translucent and soft. Add the remaining ingredients to the pan and bring to a simmer. Return the bacon to the pan and give the mixture a stir. Turn the heat to low and simmer gently for about 45 minutes or until it the mixture has thickened to a runny, jammy consistency. Taste and adjust the seasoning with a little salt and pepper. Transfer to a bowl or a sterilised jar and leave to cool. The jam will thicken more as it cools.

Cut or tear the mushrooms into smaller pieces. Heat the oil in a wide frying pan over a medium–high heat. Add the shallot and garlic and cook for 4–6 minutes, until the shallot begins to soften. Add the mushrooms, butter and some seasoning. Stir the mixture then increase the heat to high and fry for 4–6 minutes until the mushrooms are golden brown. Add the chopped parsley then immediately remove the pan from the heat.

Heat the oven grill until hot. Brush the sourdough slices with olive oil then arrange in a single layer on a baking sheet. Pop the sheet under the grill and toast the bread until golden brown around the edges.

To serve, spread some bacon jam on each slice of toast then place on to warmed plates. Top with the sautéed mushrooms and serve at once.

BABY VIOLET ARTICHOKES WITH DATTERINI TOMATOES AND BROAD BEANS

I'm a fan of vegetable dishes and I believe that as a nation we should eat more varieties of vegetables. Even for something as simple as a bean and tomato salad, try to source different types of each vegetable. Baby violet artichokes are a real treat and we'll always get them whenever they come in season. Datterini tomatoes hail from Italy and they are one of the sweetest and juiciest tomatoes I've tried. If you can't get hold of them, use the best vine-ripened tomato you can find.

SERVES 4

500g broad beans, thawed if frozen
½ lemon
12 baby violet artichokes
2 tablespoons olive oil
1 banana shallot, peeled and finely chopped
1 garlic clove, peeled and finely chopped
3 sprigs of thyme
a large pinch of coriander seeds
250ml dry white wine
about 500ml Chicken Stock (see page 218)
12 datterini (or other ripe vine) tomatoes, halved
1 tablespoon extra-virgin olive oil
finely grated zest of ½ lime
1 teaspoon lemon juice
1 tablespoon finely chopped flat-leaf parsley
1 teaspoon finely chopped chives
2 tablespoons unsalted butter
sea salt and freshly ground black pepper

Bring a pot of salted water to the boil and have ready a large bowl of iced water. Blanch the broad beans for a minute then drain and refresh in the iced water to cool them down quickly. Drain again and squeeze out the beans and discard the pale skins. Set aside.

Squeeze the juice from the lemon half into a large bowl of cold water. Trim the stem of each artichoke so that they are about 2.5cm in length. Snap off the outer leaves until you reach the tender light green ones, then peel the stems and trim the ends again to neaten the shape. Cut the artichokes in half lengthways and scoop out the furry choke in the middle with a melon baller or a spoon. As each one is ready, quickly submerge the prepared artichoke in the acidulated water, as they oxidise and brown quite quickly.

Heat the olive oil in a wide pan over a medium–high heat. Drain and pat the artichokes dry with a clean kitchen towel then add them to the pan, cut side down. Sauté the artichokes for 2 minutes on each side until lightly golden brown. Add the shallot, garlic and thyme and toss well. Sweat the vegetables for a couple of minutes before adding the coriander seeds and wine. Let the wine bubble away until the pan is quite dry, then pour in enough chicken stock to cover the vegetables. Season well with salt and pepper. Let the stock simmer for about 10–15 minutes until the artichokes are just tender and they offer no resistance when you pierce them with a knife. You may need to add a little more stock to the pan if it looks quite dry, but ideally, the stock would have cooked down to a shiny glaze by the time the artichokes are ready.

Add the broad beans and tomatoes to the artichokes and toss to mix. Cook for a few minutes, just until the beans and tomatoes are warmed through, then remove the pan from the heat. Add the remaining ingredients and stir until well mixed. Divide between warmed plates and serve.

TOMATO TARTARE

This vegetarian starter began its life when we launched Pollen Street Social in 2011. I'm a big fan of Mediterranean food and this was a way to take the ingredients and flavours of a classic Provençal tomato salad and present it in the form of a meat-free tomato tartare. We always make this dish at the height of summer when ripe, juicy and flavourful tomatoes are plentiful.

SERVES 4

150g heritage tomatoes, preferably different colours and sizes, halved or quartered depending on size
6–8 basil leaves, roughly torn into small pieces
1 red onion, sliced into rings
olive oil, to serve

For the tomato paste
12 plum tomatoes
1 tablespoon olive oil
2 shallots, finely chopped
1 garlic clove, crushed
1 teaspoon thyme leaves
sea salt and freshly ground black pepper

For the sourdough croutons
olive oil
2 slices slightly stale sourdough, crusts removed and cut into 1cm cubes

For the tapenade
250g pitted black olives, finely chopped
1 tablespoon capers, rinsed
1 garlic clove, crushed
2–4 tablespoons olive oil
juice of 1 lemon

Start by making the tomato paste. Bring a large pan of water to the boil. Blanch the tomatoes for 10 seconds, then drain thoroughly. Remove the skin and cut the tomatoes into quarters. Heat the olive oil in a frying pan over a medium heat, add the shallot and garlic, and sauté gently until softened but not coloured. Add the thyme and cook for a further minute. Remove from the heat, stir in the tomatoes, season to taste and leave to cool.

For the croutons, heat a thin film of olive oil in a frying pan over a medium–high heat. Toss in the bread cubes and fry until golden and crisp. Drain on kitchen paper and leave to cool.

For the tapenade, place the olives, capers, garlic and 2 tablespoons of the olive oil in a food processor. Pulse until combined and smooth, then add lemon juice, seasoning and more olive oil, to taste.

To serve, spoon a layer of the tomato paste on to serving plates. Divide the heritage tomatoes between the plates, making sure you mix up the colours or types. Scatter over the croutons, basil and onion rings, then dot small amounts of tapenade over the salad. Drizzle with olive oil and serve.

GARLIC-ROASTED PINK FIR APPLE POTATOES WITH PARSLEY AND BRAVA SAUCE

This is another simple vegetarian tapa that you could serve as a side dish to accompany meat or fish. If you have not come across it, the pink fir apple potato is a tubular, knobbly fingerling potato with reddish skin and a yellow, waxy flesh. It is a rather ancient crop that is having a bit of a comeback in chef circles. Its nutty and buttery flavour is just delicious. If you have no luck sourcing this variety, feel free to use Anya, Jersey Royal or baby new potatoes instead.

SERVES 4 AS A SIDE

750g pink fir apple potatoes, washed
2 tablespoons olive oil
4 garlic cloves, peeled and finely crushed
6 thyme sprigs
a small handful of flat-leaf parsley (thick stalks removed), chopped

For the brava sauce
800g vine-ripened tomatoes
2 tablespoons olive oil
5 shallots, peeled and chopped
1 head of garlic, peeled and chopped
2 bay leaves
2 thyme sprigs, leaves only
1 tablespoon tomato purée
1–2 tablespoons Basic Vinaigrette (see page 222)
75g Tomato Fondue (see page 226)
sea salt and freshly ground black pepper

First, make the sauce. Blanch, peel and deseed the tomatoes then roughly chop them. Heat the oil in a large pan and add the shallots and garlic. Sweat them for 6–8 minutes, stirring frequently, until they are soft but not coloured. Add the bay leaves, thyme and tomato purée. Stir frequently over a medium–high heat for 2 minutes then add the chopped tomatoes. Cook for another 15 minutes until the tomatoes have cooked down and the mixture is not too wet.

Carefully transfer the sauce to a blender and blitz until smooth. Pass it through a fine sieve into a clean saucepan, then stir in the vinaigrette and tomato fondue and season to taste. Reheat just before serving.

Boil the potatoes in well-salted water for 15 minutes until tender when pierced with the tip of a knife. Allow the potatoes to cool in the cooking liquid then drain well. Heat the olive oil in a wide pan, add the potatoes and fry for 4–6 minutes, turning a few times, until the potato skins are golden brown. Add the garlic and thyme and cook for a further 2 minutes. Transfer the potatoes to a warm serving plate then spoon over the brava sauce. Sprinkle with the chopped parsley and serve at once.

GRIDDLED CORN ON THE COB WITH PARMESAN AND CHILLI

I had never eaten corn on the cob this way until I went to New York, eight to ten years ago, and was invited out to a Mexican restaurant called Esquina. To me, it was a revelation and I couldn't believe what I had been missing out on all those years. In Mexico, where corn on the cob is an everyday street food, they coat the grilled corn with mayonnaise, chilli and cotija cheese. Cotija is a crumbly curd cheese that is rather difficult to source in this country. At a pinch, I find that Parmesan works just as well.

SERVES 4
AS A STARTER OR SIDE

4 corn ears, husks removed, cut in half crossways
1 teaspoon mild (or hot) chilli powder, to taste
100g crème fraîche
80g grated Parmesan

Put the kettle on to boil. Put the corn ears into a large pan. Pour in enough boiling water to cover the corn then place the pan over a medium–high heat and cover it with a lid. Simmer for about 5 minutes until the corn is tender. Drain and let the corn dry on a plate lined with kitchen paper.

Meanwhile, heat a griddle pan until hot. Griddle the corn for about 2 minutes on each side until lightly charred (do this in batches if your griddle pan is not wide enough to fit all the corn). While the corn is still hot, lightly dust it with the chilli powder. Using a pastry brush, lightly coat each piece of corn with crème fraîche then sprinkle with the grated Parmesan.

MIXED BEETROOT SALAD WITH GOAT'S CHEESE MOUSSE AND PINE NUT DRESSING

Beetroot and goat's cheese are a great combination and this vegetarian starter is so simple to make. The only 'real cooking' is in baking the beetroot, which essentially means placing whole beetroot on a bed of salt and chucking the whole thing in the oven. The baking process really intensifies the earthy flavour of the beetroot and it is miles away from the boiled and vacuum-packed beetroot you get in supermarkets.

SERVES 4

For the marinated beetroot
3 beetroot (preferably a mix of varieties such as yellow, red and stripy Chioggia beetroot), peeled and finely sliced (ideally using a mandolin)
80ml light olive oil
2 tablespoons white wine vinegar
2 tablespoons clear honey
1 tablespoon caster sugar
a few sprigs of thyme, leaves only
1 garlic clove, peeled and finely chopped
1 teaspoon sea salt

For the baked beetroot
400g baby beetroot, preferably with leaves
1–2 tablespoons sherry vinegar
sea salt

For the pine nut dressing
50g pine nuts
2 tablespoons Cabernet Sauvignon or red wine vinegar
50ml extra-virgin olive oil

For the goat's cheese mousse
250g soft, creamy goat's cheese
35g goat's curd (or more goat's cheese)
1 tablespoon whole milk
freshly ground black pepper

First, prepare the marinated beetroot. Stack a few beetroot slices and use a 4–5cm round pastry cutter to stamp out neat discs. Put the rounds into a bowl and the trimmings into a saucepan. Repeat with the rest of the beetroot slices. Mix together the remaining ingredients to make a marinade then pour this over the beetroot discs. Cover and chill for at least two hours, preferably overnight.

For the baked beetroot, preheat the oven to 200°C/Gas Mark 6. Trim the tops and roots from the beetroot, chop the trimmings and add them to the other trimmings in the saucepan. Keep all the beetroot leaves, wash well with water and place in the refrigerator until needed. Put the beetroot in the middle of a large sheet of foil, drizzle over the vinegar, then sprinkle with a generous pinch of salt. Loosely wrap the foil around the beetroot and place on a roasting tray. Bake for 50–60 minutes or until tender when pierced with a knife. Unwrap the beetroot and leave to cool slightly. Peel them while they're still warm then slice each one into halves or quarters depending on their size. Set aside.

Meanwhile, pour in just enough water to cover the beetroot trimmings in the pan then bring to the boil. Lower the heat and simmer for 20 minutes until soft. Transfer to a blender and blitz until smooth. Strain this through a fine sieve into a clean saucepan, pressing down on the pulp with the back of a ladle to extract as much juice as possible. Boil the beetroot juice until it has reduced to a syrupy glaze. Take the pan off the heat and leave to cool.

Meanwhile, make the dressing. Toast the pine nuts in a dry frying pan over a medium heat until lightly golden and fragrant. Transfer to a bowl and add the reduced beetroot juice, vinegar and olive oil. Stir to combine and season with salt to taste.

Finally, make the goat's cheese mousse. Put all the ingredients into a bowl and whisk until light and smooth. Taste and adjust the seasoning. Cover with cling film and chill.

To serve, arrange the baked beetroot around each serving plate then neatly spoon or pipe the goat's cheese mousse around them. Arrange the marinated beetroot slices and beetroot leaves around the plate then drizzle over the pine nut dressing. Serve immediately.

STARTERS

SOCIAL SUPPERS

WINTER VEGETABLE SALAD WITH GOAT'S CURD

As a chef, I often find vegetarian recipes much more interesting than protein-heavy dishes, as it is more challenging to make a few inexpensive vegetables shine on their own, particularly if we use humble and often unattractive root vegetables. As a nation, I truly believe that we should eat more vegetables – it is outrageous that about 20 per cent of our amazing home-grown vegetables go to waste every year! In the winter, this roast vegetable dish can proudly take its place as a main course for weekend lunches.

SERVES 4

rock salt
8 golden or red baby beetroot, topped and tailed
8 golden or red beetroot, topped and tailed
4 globe artichokes
squeeze of lemon juice
4 sprigs of thyme
100ml white wine vinegar
1 teaspoon white peppercorns
400g baby carrots, peeled and tops trimmed
6 small baby fennel, trimmed and halved
8 baby leeks, trimmed
60g unsalted butter
1 tablespoon olive oil
150–200ml Shallot Vinaigrette (see page 222)
160g goat's curd or soft goat's cheese

Preheat the oven to 160°C/Gas Mark 3.

Scatter a layer of rock salt over a roasting tray and place the beetroot on top. Roast for about 1 hour until tender. There should be little resistance when you pierce the beetroot with the tip of a small knife or skewer. Transfer the hot beetroot to a large bowl, immediately cover with cling film and leave to cool slowly. (The steam will make it easier to remove the skins of the beetroot.) Once cooled, peel the beetroot and set aside. (If cooking in advance, cover and chill until ready to serve.)

Cut off most of the top crowns of the artichokes. Trim the outer leaves and cut off most of the stem. With a paring knife (a small round-bladed knife), trim off the tough skin around the artichoke hearts and then scoop out the furry chokes with a teaspoon. Squeeze a little lemon juice into a large bowl of cold water. Place the artichoke hearts in the acidulated water to prevent them from browning.

Bring about a litre of water to the boil in a non-metallic pan. Add the thyme, vinegar and peppercorns followed by the artichoke hearts. Cover the pan and simmer for about 20 minutes until the hearts are tender. Take the pan off the heat and leave to cool completely. Once cool, drain and quarter the artichokes. Put them in a covered container and chill if preparing ahead.

Bring another pan of salted water to the boil and have ready a large bowl of iced water. Blanch the baby carrots and allow these to cook for 2 minutes before adding the fennel and leek. Cook the vegetables for a further 4 minutes over a medium heat until they are just tender. Drain and refresh in iced water then drain again. Dry the cooked artichoke hearts, carrots, fennel and leeks on a large tray with kitchen paper.

Heat the butter and olive oil in a large frying pan. Add the blanched vegetables in batches until lightly roasted on all sides. Dress with two-thirds of the shallot vinaigrette and toss the vegetables to coat. Season to taste. Neatly place the salad on a serving platter. Toss the roast beetroot with a little shallot vinaigrette and arrange them on the platter. Garnish with the goat's curd and drizzle over any remaining vinaigrette before serving.

AVOCADO, BABY GEM, ORANGE AND SAUTÉED BABY CARROT SALAD

This is a really great citrus salad that has everything going for it: creamy avocado, zingy orange segments, fresh and crunchy Baby Gem leaves, and tender baby carrots. In the winter you can use clementines or grapefruits instead of oranges (or even Seville oranges when they start to arrive). In the early spring, try making this with gorgeous blood oranges.

SERVES 4

3 oranges
1 lime
1 tablespoon coriander seeds
1 tablespoon cumin seeds
75ml extra-virgin olive oil
16 young carrots with tops, about 600g
a large knob of unsalted butter
1 tablespoon olive oil
2 ripe avocados
1 Baby Gem lettuce, base trimmed and leaves separated
3–4 tablespoons Basic Vinaigrette (see page 222)
a handful of coriander leaves
sea salt and freshly ground black pepper

First, segment the oranges. Cut off the skins and white pith from 2 of the oranges then cut out the orange segments in between the membranes. Juice the remaining orange and the lime and pass the juice through a fine sieve.

Put the coriander and cumin seeds into a dry pan, place it over a high heat and heat the seeds until they are fragrant and lightly toasted. Tip the spices into a bowl and allow to cool before grinding them to a coarse powder using a pestle and mortar. Set aside half the ground spice and mix the rest with the orange and lime juice, olive oil and some salt and pepper to taste, to make a spiced dressing.

Trim off the stalks of the young carrots and save the tender leaves for garnish. Heat the butter and oil in a pan until hot. Add the carrots and a bit of seasoning and toss to coat in the melted butter. Sauté over a medium heat for 7–10 minutes until the carrots are lightly golden brown and tender. Transfer the carrots to a plate lined with kitchen paper.

Peel and stone the avocados then cut them into eighths. Place these into a bowl along with the carrots, orange segments and spiced dressing. Toss gently to coat.

Select six of the nicest-looking lettuce leaves and cut them in half. Trim the rest of the leaves into neat oval pieces. Dress the lettuce with the vinaigrette.

To serve, arrange the orange pieces, avocado, carrots and lettuce leaves on individual serving plates. Garnish with the coriander and carrot leaves and sprinkle with the reserved ground spice. Serve immediately.

STARTERS

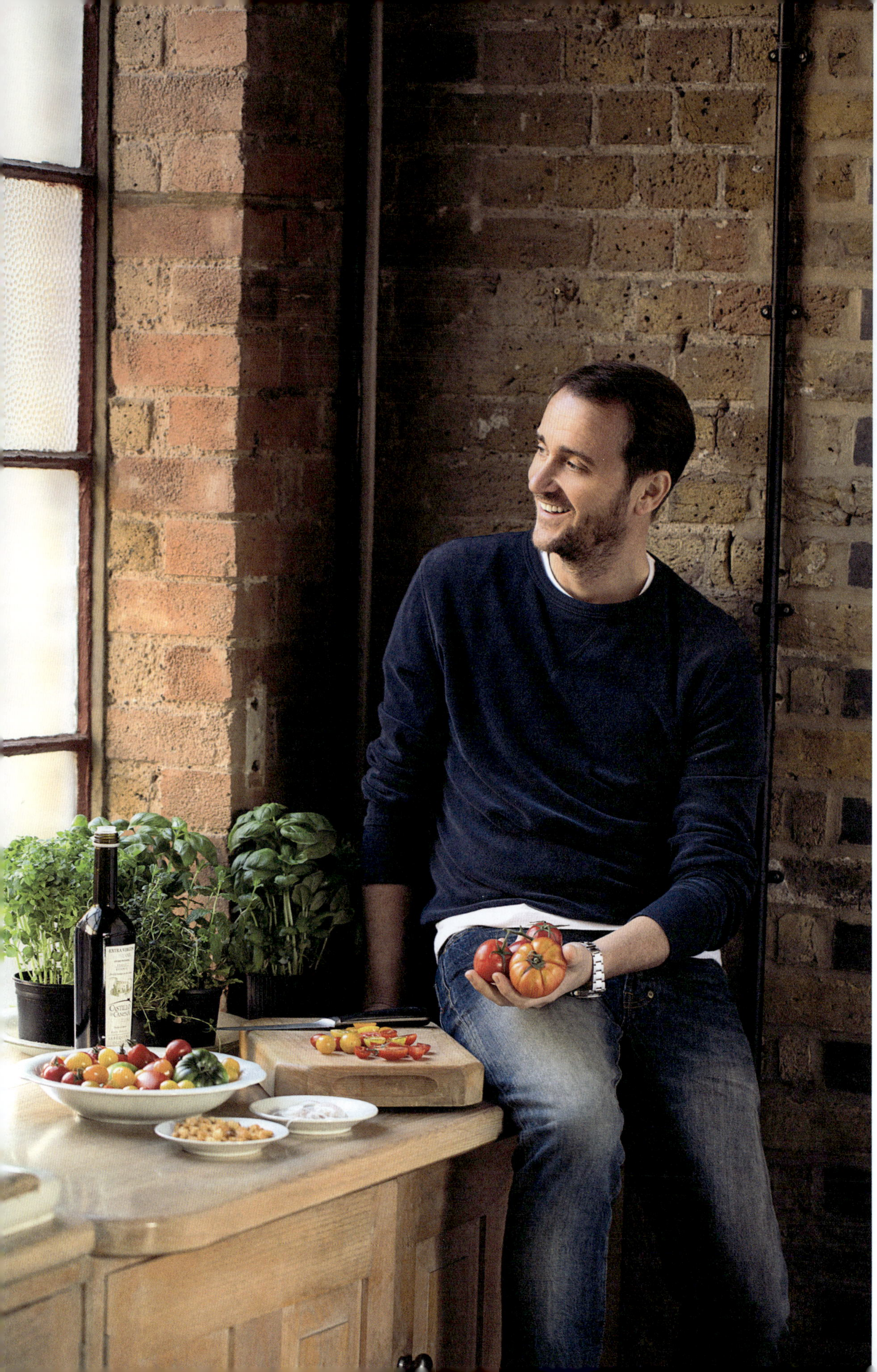

ROQUEFORT AND ICEBERG SALAD WITH WARM CROUTONS AND ALSACE BACON

Roquefort was the first blue cheese I fell in love with. The savoury salty kick really appeals to my palate and I often use it as a way to dress and flavour robust salads. Similar to a Caesar salad, I'm teaming Iceberg lettuce with Roquefort, crunchy croutons and Alsace bacon, an ingredient I grew to love during my time spent in this region of France.

SERVES 4

2 tablespoons unsalted butter
100g streaky bacon, preferably Alsace country-style bacon, diced
1 head of English Iceberg lettuce, washed and cut into thin wedges

For the blue cheese dressing
100g Roquefort
50g Stilton
1 tablespoon clear honey
150g crème fraîche
30ml Vegetable Stock (see page 219) or hot water

For the warm croutons
¼ loaf of brown sourdough, crusts removed
3 tablespoons unsalted butter
2 sprigs of thyme
sea salt

First, make the dressing. Crumble the Roquefort and Stilton into the bowl of a small food processor. Add the honey and crème fraîche and blend until smooth. With the motor running, trickle in the vegetable stock until you get a creamy dressing consistency. Transfer to a bowl and set aside.

For the croutons, tear the bread into rough 2cm pieces. Place the butter and thyme sprigs in a pan and heat until the butter starts to foam. Add the bread pieces to the foaming butter and stir until the croutons become crisp and golden in colour. Season with salt and then tip the croutons on to a baking tray lined with kitchen paper. Keep warm in a low oven.

Carefully wipe off the breadcrumbs from the frying pan with kitchen paper and return to the heat. Add the butter and diced bacon and fry for 4–6 minutes until evenly golden brown and crisp, tossing once or twice.

Arrange the lettuce wedges on individual chilled plates. Drizzle some blue cheese dressing over the lettuce and scatter over the warm croutons and crisp bacon.

ROAST CAESAR SALAD WITH WHITE ANCHOVIES

Here, we've given the ubiquitous Caesar salad a slight twist by roasting the lettuce and garnishing it with some fresh marinated anchovies. This is something that we made back in the days when I worked with Marco Pierre White in a restaurant called Canteen, by Chelsea Harbour. The salad was never taken off the menu because it was a constant sell-out. It's a lovely dish to have in anyone's cooking repertoire.

SERVES 4

For the croutons
1 small baguette
150g unsalted butter
4 garlic cloves, peeled and lightly crushed
2 sprigs of thyme, leaves only

For the salad
8 wafer-thin slices of pancetta
8 quail's eggs
8 fresh white anchovies (boquerones)
4 heads of Little Gem lettuce
a knob of unsalted butter, for roasting (optional)
Parmesan shavings, to garnish
sea salt and freshly ground black pepper

For the Caesar dressing
3 medium egg yolks
4 anchovy fillets in oil, drained
3 garlic cloves, peeled and roughly chopped
2 tablespoons white wine vinegar or cider vinegar
75g grated Parmesan
200ml light olive or vegetable oil

First, make the croutons. Put the baguette in a freezer bag and freeze for 30–60 minutes, until firm. Meanwhile, melt the butter in a small saucepan over a medium heat. Add the garlic, thyme leaves and a pinch each of salt and pepper. Take the pan off the heat and leave the butter to cool and infuse.

Preheat the oven to 200°C/Gas Mark 6. Take the bread out of the freezer and slice it as thinly as possible. Brush the slices with the infused butter and arrange in a single layer on one or two large baking sheets. Bake for 5–8 minutes until completely dry and crisp. Remove and leave to cool.

For the salad, arrange the pancetta slices in a single layer on a baking tray and place another baking tray on top. Bake for 10–12 minutes or until the pancetta is crisp and golden brown. Set the pancetta aside to cool completely, still sandwiched between the trays as this keeps the pancetta flat.

To cook the quail's eggs, lower them into a pan of simmering water and cook for 2½ minutes. Remove and refresh the eggs in a bowl of iced water to cool them down. Peel the eggs and set aside. Cut them in half just before serving.

Put all the ingredients for the Caesar dressing, except for the oil, into a food processor. Blend to a thick and smooth paste. With the motor running, slowly trickle in the oil; the mixture will start to emulsify and thicken to the consistency of mayonnaise. If you find the dressing too thick, blend in a little warm water to let it down. Season to taste.

Half an hour before you are ready to serve, wash the lettuces, cut each in half and place them, cut side up, on a baking tray. Either run a blowtorch over the cut sides to scorch and 'roast' the lettuce or roast in a pan, as follows. Heat a frying pan to a high heat until smoking. Add a knob of butter and the lettuce halves and cook for one minute to roast them well on one side. Place two lettuce halves on each plate then top each half with a slice of pancetta, a crouton and a white anchovy. Neatly arrange the quail's eggs and dressing on each plate. Sprinkle over the Parmesan shavings and a little seasoning to taste. Serve immediately.

STARTERS

SEARED TUNA SALAD WITH MISO AUBERGINES AND SHERRY DRESSING

Andrew Walsh, my head chef at Esquina, our tapas bar in Singapore, created this dish, having been inspired by Asian flavours and ingredients. In our Asian restaurants, we always try to include yellowtail tuna in our menus because the quality of the fish there is so fresh and amazing. Because the tuna is quickly seared and served rare, do make sure to ask your fishmonger for sashimi-grade tuna loin.

SERVES 4

400g very fresh tuna, from the loin
60ml soy sauce
25ml balsamic vinegar
4 tablespoons vegetable oil, plus extra for cooking
25ml sesame oil
1 tablespoon Dijon mustard
100g mixed salad leaves
a handful of crisp shallots (available from Asian grocers or see page 118)

For the sherry dressing
½ shallot, peeled and finely chopped
1 tablespoon sherry vinegar
3 tablespoons olive oil
a pinch of caster sugar
sea salt and freshly ground black pepper

For the miso aubergines
2 aubergines
vegetable oil, for frying
2 teaspoons toasted sesame seeds
60g red miso
1 tablespoon mirin
25ml sake
30g caster sugar
a dash of sesame oil

Cut the tuna into four even-sized pieces. Stir the soy sauce, vinegar, oils and mustard together in a bowl. Add the tuna and toss to coat. Cover the bowl with cling film and chill for at least 30 minutes to allow the fish time to marinate. Remove from the refrigerator about 15–20 minutes before cooking to allow the fish to come to room temperature.

Next, make the sherry dressing. Combine the shallots and vinegar in a bowl and leave to infuse for about 15 minutes. Whisk in the oil and season to taste with salt, pepper and a pinch of sugar.

Cut the aubergines in half lengthways, keeping the stem end on. Score the cut side in a diamond pattern as close as possible to the skin but without cutting through it. Heat a thin layer of vegetable oil in a large frying pan. Then add the aubergines to the pan, cut side down, and fry for about 2–3 minutes until lightly golden brown. Flip the aubergine halves over and fry the other sides for another 2 minutes until they begin to soften. Remove from the pan and place them on a plate lined with kitchen paper to drain.

Preheat the grill to the highest setting. Arrange the aubergine halves, cut side up, on a baking tray lined with baking parchment. Except for the sesame seeds, mix together all the remaining ingredients to make a miso sauce. Brush this generously over the aubergine halves then pop the tray under the hot grill. Grill for 2–4 minutes until the miso glaze starts to bubble. Remove the tray from the grill and keep in a warm spot while you sear the tuna.

Heat a frying pan with a little vegetable oil over very high heat. Drain the tuna from the marinade and pat dry with kitchen paper. Add to the hot pan and fry the fish for 30 seconds on each side. Remove from the pan and leave to cool slightly.

In a large bowl, toss the salad leaves with a little sherry dressing then place neat handfuls on individual serving plates. Slice the seared tuna thickly and arrange them on each plate. Spoon over a little sherry dressing then sprinkle a few crisp shallots over the tuna and salad. Sprinkle the miso aubergines with the sesame seeds then place one on each plate. Serve immediately.

TUNA TARTARE D.I.Y.

This is loosely based on a dish cooked by Daniel Humm of Eleven Madison Park, one of the 'must try' restaurants in New York City. Last time I was there, Daniel served this amazing carrot tartare in which all the accompaniments for the dish were brought out to the table to be assembled by the diner. When we set up our restaurant in Hong Kong, I wanted to include a tuna version of his tartare dish as a little homage to Daniel.

SERVES 4

For the tuna tartare
500g sashimi-grade tuna loin
a handful of chives, finely chopped
4–5 tablespoons toasted sesame seeds
juice of 4 or 5 limes, plus 1 whole lime, cut into wedges
4–5 teaspoons wasabi paste
4–5 tablespoons soy sauce
4–5 tablespoons sesame oil
5–6 tablespoons olive oil
sea salt

For the Vietnamese relish
50ml sesame oil
8 garlic cloves, peeled and finely chopped
5 banana shallots, finely chopped
2 tablespoons finely grated ginger
4 red chillies, deseeded and finely chopped
1 teaspoon palm sugar (or soft brown sugar)
4 teaspoons mirin
250ml rice wine vinegar
125ml soy sauce
50ml fish sauce
25ml lime juice
2 tablespoons chopped coriander

First, prepare the Vietnamese relish. Put the sesame oil, garlic, shallots, ginger and chillies into a small saucepan and place over a medium–low heat. Add the palm sugar and give the mixture a stir. Cook for 6–8 minutes, stirring occasionally, until the shallots are tender. Add the mirin and rice wine vinegar and let the mixture simmer for 10 minutes until the liquid has reduced down to a jammy consistency. Add the soy sauce and let it simmer until reduced by half. Tip in the fish sauce and lime juice and take the pan off the heat. Transfer the relish to a serving bowl and leave to cool. Add the chopped coriander before serving.

Trim the tuna and cut it into neat cubes, about 5mm wide. Divide the tuna between serving plates or shallow bowls. Put each remaining ingredient into separate ramekins or small bowls and bring to the table. Pass the ingredients around the table and encourage your guests to assemble and dress their plates of tuna.

CONFIT TUNA WITH PIPERADE AND CHIVES

Confit tuna has a wonderfully succulent texture, but at a pinch you could make this lovely starter with good-quality tinned tuna. For a vegetarian alternative, replace the tuna with creamy goat's cheese or sharp pecorino and top with a sprinkling of toasted pine nuts.

SERVES 4

400g very fresh tuna
4 bay leaves
a few sprigs of thyme
3 tablespoons black peppercorns
finely grated zest of 2 lemons
about 400ml olive oil
sea salt and freshly ground black pepper

For the piperade

3–4 tablespoons olive oil
1 small onion, peeled and thinly sliced
1 red onion, peeled and thinly sliced
6 garlic cloves, peeled and sliced
285g piquillo peppers, chopped
4 ripe tomatoes, preferably San Marzano, deseeded and cut into 1cm dice
a pinch of smoked paprika
small bunch of flat-leaf parsley, leaves only, finely chopped

To serve

4 long slices of ciabatta
1 garlic clove, halved
extra-virgin olive oil, to brush
small handful of chives, finely chopped

Note: You will need a food thermometer for this recipe.

Prepare the confit tuna a day before you intend to serve the dish. Find a saucepan into which the tuna will fit snugly. Put the bay leaves, thyme, peppercorns, and lemon zest into the pan, then pour over the oil. Gently heat the oil to just below boiling point (95–99°C). Rub the tuna with a little salt then lower it into the pan. If necessary, top up with a little more hot oil if the tuna is not fully submerged, then remove the pan from the heat. Once cooled, cover the pan and chill overnight.

The next day remove the tuna from the oil and break it into bite-sized chunks.

To make the piperade, heat a heavy-based frying pan until hot. Add the olive oil and stir in the onions. Sauté for 8–10 minutes, stirring occasionally, until the onions are tender and beginning to colour. Tip in the garlic, peppers, tomatoes and paprika. Season well then stir and cook gently for about 10 minutes until the tomatoes have just softened. Spread the mixture on to a wide plate and leave to cool slightly. Transfer to a clean chopping board and roughly chop the vegetables further. Put into a bowl, stir in the parsley and adjust the seasoning to taste.

A few minutes before you are ready to serve, toast the ciabatta. Heat a griddle pan until hot. Rub the ciabatta slices with the garlic. Brush over a little extra-virgin olive oil and griddle for 1–2 minutes on each side, until nicely toasted. Place each toasted ciabatta slice on to a warmed serving plate. Spoon a generous layer of piperade over each, then scatter over the flaked confit tuna. Sprinkle over the chopped chives and a little pinch of salt and pepper. Serve immediately.

SALMON 'CRUDO' WITH PICKLED CUCUMBER AND WASABI AND AVOCADO PURÉE

'Crudo' means 'raw' in Italian, so this dish is essentially raw salmon served with crunchy marinated cucumbers and smooth avocado purée, which has a lovely creaminess. This version has a wasabi kick, which goes perfectly with the oily salmon.

SERVES 4

500g sashimi-grade skinless and boneless salmon fillet
65ml extra-virgin olive oil
1 tablespoon orange juice
1 tablespoon lime juice
1 tablespoon Japanese yuzu (or fresh lemon) juice
1 tablespoon rice wine vinegar
½ garlic clove, peeled and finely crushed
sea salt and freshly ground black pepper

For the pickled cucumber
½ cucumber, thinly sliced
3 tablespoons chilli garlic sauce
1 tablespoon light soy sauce
2 tablespoons sesame oil
1½ tablespoons white wine vinegar
135ml mirin

For the avocado and wasabi purée
2 ripe avocados
juice of 1 lime
1 teaspoon wasabi paste

To serve
1 Granny Smith apple
a handful of baby purple shiso leaves (or a mixture of small mint and basil leaves)
Chilli Oil, to drizzle (see page 221) (optional)

First, prepare the pickled cucumber. In a large bowl, stir together the chilli garlic sauce, light soy sauce, sesame oil, vinegar and mirin. Add the cucumber slices and toss until all the slices are evenly coated with the marinade. Cover the bowl with cling film and refrigerate for a few hours, preferably overnight.

Neatly slice off any grey flesh from the top of the salmon fillet, then wrap the fillet in cling film and freeze for 15–20 minutes to allow it to firm up. Meanwhile, make the avocado and wasabi purée. Halve the avocados and remove the stones. Scoop out the flesh into the bowl of a food processor. Add the lime juice, wasabi paste and a pinch of salt. Blend until the mixture is smooth then pass it through a sieve. Transfer to a bowl, cover and chill until ready to use.

Mix together all the remaining ingredients for the salmon to make a citrus marinade, seasoning well to taste. Once the salmon has firmed up, remove the cling film and slice it thinly. Place the salmon slices in a shallow bowl and spoon over the marinade. Leave to marinate for a few minutes while you prepare the rest of the salad.

Cut the apple into quarters, removing the core, then slice as thinly as possible. (Use a mandolin if you have one.) Drain the pickled cucumber slices and pat them dry with kitchen paper. Arrange the salmon slices on to individual plates then arrange 6–7 slices of pickled cucumber on top. Dot the avocado and wasabi purée around the fish then garnish with the apple slices and shiso leaves. Finally, drizzle over the chilli oil, if using, and serve.

SOCIAL SUPPERS

SPANISH TOMATO BREAD WITH SARDINES

This is a modern take on the meals that my dad used to serve me as a young lad. Whenever he had to knock up a meal, it was always either beans on toast or sardines on toast. For some reason, I adored the beans and loathed the sardines, even though they were both tinned. It was only in my adult years that I discovered the joys of freshly marinated sardines. The fact that sardines are cheap, sustainable, delicious and full of healthy oils is an added bonus.

SERVES 4

2 pieces of ciabatta or baguette (about the length of the sardines) sliced through the middle
1 garlic clove, halved
olive oil, to drizzle
a small bunch of mixed herbs (such as flat-leaf parsley, dill, chervil and tarragon), leaves only
a handful of frisée leaves
1–2 tablespoons Basic Vinaigrette (see page 222)

For the tomato sauce
100ml olive oil
2 shallots, peeled and finely chopped
2 garlic cloves, peeled and finely chopped
3 sprigs of thyme, leaves only
25g tomato purée
20ml sherry vinegar
4 ripe plum tomatoes, roughly chopped
juice of 1 lemon, to taste

For the sardines
1–2 tablespoons olive oil
8 butterflied sardines (ask your fishmonger to remove the back bones of the fish but keep them whole)
sea salt and freshly ground black pepper

To make the tomato sauce, heat the oil in a heavy-based saucepan over a medium heat. Add the shallots, garlic and thyme and stir well. Sweat the vegetables for 6–8 minutes until soft then add the tomato purée. Increase the heat slightly and stir-fry for a couple of minutes. Add the sherry vinegar, stir well and cook until the vinegar has almost cooked off and the pan is quite dry. Tip in the chopped tomatoes and cook for another 10–15 minutes until the tomatoes are soft and the mixture has thickened slightly. Transfer the mixture to a blender and blitz to a smooth sauce. Pass the sauce through a fine sieve into a clean saucepan. Taste and adjust the seasoning with salt, pepper and lemon juice. Reheat before serving.

When you are ready to serve, heat a griddle or frying pan over a medium heat. Rub the cut sides of the bread with the garlic clove then drizzle over a little oil. Toast the bread for about 2 minutes on each side until golden brown around the edges.

To cook the sardines, heat the oil in a wide frying pan over a medium–high heat until hot. Season the sardines and fry, skin side down, for 2–3 minutes until the skin is crisp and the fish is more than halfway cooked. Flip them over to fry the other side for 1–2 minutes until firm and just cooked through.

To serve, dress the mixed herbs and frisée leaves with a little vinaigrette. Place a slice of toasted bread on each warmed serving plate then spoon over a layer of tomato sauce. Lay the sardines on top then garnish with the salad. Serve at once.

PASTRAMI OF SEA BASS WITH GAZPACHO GARNISH

I first started making a salmon pastrami dish back in 1994, when I was working as a sous chef for Oliver Peyton and Stephen Terry at Coast restaurant. It was awesome and very modern at the time. Through the years, I've applied the same technique with various types of fish, such as sea bass, and I've also discovered that the flavours of the cured fish go really well with gazpacho. In this particular dish, I've taken the key ingredients and flavours of a gazpacho but instead of blitzing them all into a soup, they form a beautiful garnish for the sea bass pastrami.

SERVES 2

250g sea bass fillets, skin on (choose the thickest fillets possible)
15g coarse sea salt
1 teaspoon black peppercorns, lightly crushed
2 teaspoons soft dark brown sugar
½ teaspoon coriander seeds, lightly crushed
½ teaspoon paprika
2 garlic cloves, peeled and finely chopped
2 tablespoons lemon juice

For the gazpacho garnish
1 plum tomato
8 pitted black olives
½ small ripe avocado
a squeeze of lemon juice
1 tablespoon extra-virgin olive oil

Run your fingers over the sea bass fillets to check for any pin bones and remove them with a pair of kitchen tweezers. Except for the lemon juice, mix all the remaining ingredients together in a small bowl to make a dry rub. Brush the fillets all over with the lemon juice then coat them with the spice rub. Place in a wide bowl or a baking tray, cover with cling film and refrigerate for 48 hours. When ready, the fish will feel firm and will have released some of their juices. If they do not feel firm enough, leave to cure in the spice rub for another 12 hours.

Wash the spice rub off the fish fillets then pat dry with kitchen paper. Carefully remove the skins from the fillets, then slice them thinly on a diagonal, as you would a fillet of smoked salmon. Arrange the fish neatly on a serving platter (or on individual serving plates), cover with baking parchment and chill for a few hours if preparing ahead.

Prepare the gazpacho garnish a few minutes before serving. Quarter the tomato, remove the seeds, then chop the flesh into small pieces, no larger than 1cm. Chop the black olives to about the size of the chopped tomato. Peel, stone and dice the avocado, again to about the same size as the tomato, then squeeze over a little lemon juice to stop it from browning. Add the olive oil to the bowl and gently toss all the ingredients together. Spoon the mixture over the sea bass pastrami and serve.

BEETROOT-CURED SEA TROUT WITH ROAST BEETROOT AND HORSERADISH CREAM

This dish is on our menu at Berners Tavern and it features the classic British combination of cured fish with horseradish, watercress and beetroot. You can use salmon instead of sea trout, but I'm a big supporter of our amazing British farmed sea trout, which offers fantastic taste and value.

SERVES 4

500g skinless sea trout fillets (choose the thickest fillets you can find)
75g watercress, leaves only, to serve
3 tablespoons Basic Vinaigrette (see page 222), to serve

For the beetroot cure
250g beetroot, peeled and cut into rough chunks
250g rock salt
½ teaspoon fennel seeds
handful of tarragon, leaves only
125g caster sugar

For the roasted beetroot
75g rock salt
12 baby beetroot

For the horseradish cream
30g fresh horseradish, peeled and cut into small chunks
100ml whipping cream

Remove any pin bones from the sea trout fillets with a pair of kitchen tweezers and set aside.

Put all the ingredients for the beetroot cure in a food processor. Blitz until the mixture is a smooth, wet paste. You may need to stop the processor once or twice to scrape down the sides as you do this. Spread a thin layer of the beetroot cure on a baking tray and place the trout on it. Cover the fish fillets with the rest of the cure then cover with cling film. Chill and allow it to marinate in the refrigerator for at least 48 hours, then wash off the beetroot cure and pat the fish dry with kitchen paper. Cover and chill again until you are ready to serve.

To roast the baby beetroot, preheat the oven to 160°C/Gas Mark 3. Spread the rock salt over a baking tray and place the beetroot on top. Roast for about 1 hour until the beetroot is tender to the core when you pierce it with a small knife. Transfer the hot beetroot to a large bowl and cover with cling film. When cool enough to handle, peel the skins. Cut the beetroot into halves, or quarters if large. Set aside.

To make the horseradish cream, put the horseradish in a small food processor and blend until it's as fine as possible. In a separate bowl, whip the cream to medium peaks. Gradually fold the horseradish into the cream, tasting as you go, until you are happy with the flavour of the cream. Blitz the cream again until thickened and check the seasoning.

To serve, thinly slice the cured sea trout on the diagonal. Arrange the fish, roasted beetroot and a neat tablespoonful of horseradish cream on serving plates. Dress the watercress leaves with the vinaigrette and arrange on each plate. Serve immediately.

Beetroot Cured Sea Trout with Roast Beetroot and Horseradish Cream, page 51

STARTERS

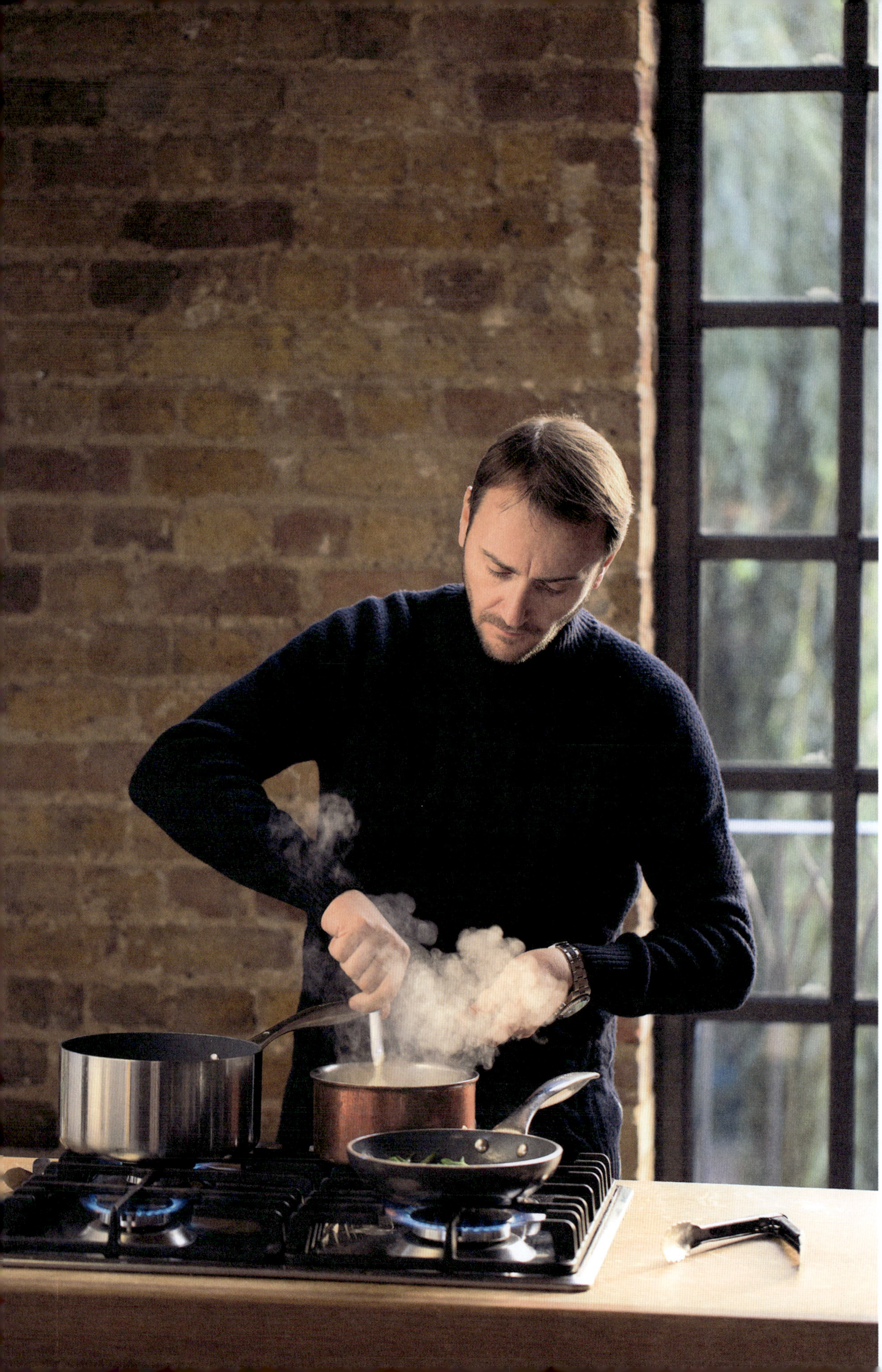

KOHLRABI, APPLE, WHISKY WALNUT AND SEA TROUT SALAD

At first glance, this seems to be an odd combination of flavours, but I urge you to give it a try because it is gorgeous. Sea trout is an oily fish and it pairs beautifully with the sweet and crisp apple and kohlrabi. The whisky walnut was something that we've recently experimented with. Our bar manager at Pollen Street Social, Gareth Evans, always keeps a tall jar of walnut-infused whisky (or rum) to make his exquisite cocktails. We took the leftover soaked walnuts, coated them in sugar and caramelised them to give a praline-like coating. They make a wonderful garnish for quite a number of our restaurant dishes.

SERVES 4

4 trout fillets, about 100g each
500ml olive oil
a few garlic cloves
finely grated zest of 1 lemon
a few sprigs of thyme
sea salt

For the candied whisky walnuts
150g soft light brown sugar
50ml whisky
150g walnuts

For the salad
½ lemon
1 kohlrabi
1 red apple, such as Royal Gala
1 Granny Smith apple
50g Roquefort
150g Mayonnaise (see page 224)
2 fresh walnuts, to garnish (optional)

First, confit the trout. Feel the trout fillets with your fingers and remove any pin bones you come across with a pair of kitchen tweezers. Combine the oil, garlic, lemon zest and thyme in a wide pan. Warm the oil over a medium heat until little bubbles start to appear at the bottom of the pan. The oil should not be too hot – about 50°C. Remove the pan from the heat and lower the trout fillets into the oil. Leave the fish in the warm oil for 10 minutes, occasionally spooning the oil over any piece of trout that is not fully submerged in the oil. After 10 minutes, lift the trout fillets from the oil and drain on a tray lined with kitchen paper.

For the whisky walnuts, line a baking tray with a sheet of baking parchment. Put the sugar and whisky into a saucepan and place it over a medium–high heat. Give the mixture a stir to encourage the sugar to dissolve. Leave the syrup to boil until it starts to colour and caramelise. Cook for 1–2 minutes, then tip in the walnuts and take the pan off the heat. Continue to stir until the walnuts are well coated with the caramel. Evenly spread the nuts and caramel on the lined tray with a heatproof spatula. Leave to cool completely.

For the salad, squeeze the lemon juice into a large bowl of cold water. Peel the kohlrabi and slice it into thin batons. Add this to the acidulated water to prevent it from browning. If you wish, peel the skins of the apples (I leave them with their skins) and remove the core. Dice the apples and add them to the bowl.

Next, make the dressing. Crumble the Roquefort into a bowl and add the mayonnaise. Whisk or beat the mixture until smooth and season to taste.

To assemble the dish, place a trout fillet on each serving plate and sprinkle with a little sea salt. Add a spoonful of blue cheese mayonnaise on the side. Drain the apple and kohlrabi pieces and pat dry with kitchen paper. Toss them with a little blue cheese mayonnaise and place neat piles on each plate. Garnish the salads with the candied whisky walnuts. Finally, shave a little fresh walnut over each plate, if using, and serve immediately.

STARTERS

SCALLOP CEVICHE WITH PICKLED FENNEL AND LEMON CONFIT

This is straight out of the repertoire of my flagship restaurant, Pollen Street Social. I adore tender raw scallops, and in this recipe their sweetness is accentuated by the lemon and fennel marinade.

SERVES 4

12 large scallops, cleaned and roe removed, cut in half horizontally
100ml Yuzu Wasabi Dressing (see page 223), plus extra to drizzle
sea salt and freshly ground black pepper
Confit Lemon Strips (see page 230), to garnish (optional)
reserved fennel fronds or dill sprigs, to garnish

For the pickled fennel
125ml muscatel or sherry vinegar
100ml white wine vinegar
100g caster sugar
1 star anise
1 cinnamon stick
3 cloves
1 teaspoon mustard seeds
1 large fennel bulb, preferably with fronds

First, make the pickled fennel. Put everything except the fennel into a small saucepan and place over a medium heat. Stir to melt the sugar. Once the sugar has dissolved, take the pan off the heat and leave to cool.

Bring a pan of salted water to the boil and have ready a bowl of iced water. Trim the base of the fennel and reserve the fronds for garnish. Very finely slice the bulb or shave it using a mandolin. Blanch the sliced fennel for 1 minute, then drain and refresh in the iced water. Drain well again and then add the fennel to the pickling liquid. Let the flavours infuse for at least 30 minutes. (If making in advance, put the blanched fennel in a sterilised jar then pour over the pickling liquid, to cover. Seal and keep refrigerated until ready to use.)

Place the scallops in a bowl and pour over the yuzu wasabi dressing then season with a little pinch of salt and pepper. Cover the bowl with cling film and let the scallops marinate in the refrigerator for about 20 minutes.

When ready to serve, place 6 scallop halves on each serving plate. Drizzle over a little wasabi dressing. Top each scallop with a few confit lemon strips and a few slices of pickled fennel then garnish with the reserved fennel fronds or sprigs of dill. Sprinkle over a little sea salt and freshly ground pepper and serve.

STARTERS

SOCIAL SUPPERS

RAZOR CLAMS WITH CHORIZO, CORIANDER AND CHILLI

When I was setting up my restaurant in Shanghai, I asked to be taken to the wet market, and what an eye-opening experience it was! The market had everything, from snakes to live fish to geoduck clams. Out of the corner of my eye, I saw an unassuming, tiny basket of live razor clams set at the base of the fish stall. It reminded me of our beautiful Scottish versions, and at that very instant I made up my mind to include razor clams on our menu. This particular dish has its roots in Spain, but we've included a bit of fresh Asian zing in the form of chillies and coriander.

SERVES 4

16 live razor clams
2 tablespoons olive oil
8 small chorizo dulce, sliced
25g unsalted butter
1 red chilli, peeled, deseeded and chopped
2 garlic cloves, peeled and finely chopped
125ml dry white wine
a small handful of coriander leaves, chopped
warm crusty bread, to serve
sea salt and freshly ground black pepper

Wash the razor clams in cold running water to remove any grit. Give each one a light tap and discard any that do not open when tapped.

Heat the olive oil in a wide pan over a medium heat. Add the chorizo slices and fry for about 2 minutes on each side until they are golden brown and the oil is stained a lovely reddish-orange colour. Increase the heat slightly then add the butter, followed by the chilli, garlic and white wine. Bring to the boil. Tip in half the clams, give the mixture a stir and cover the pan with a lid. As soon as the clams open their shells, which will take about a minute, remove them with a slotted spoon or a pair of kitchen tongs. Repeat with the second batch of clams. Leave the pan on a medium heat to reduce the liquid by half. Season to taste with salt and pepper.

As soon as the clams are cool enough to handle, remove the flesh with your hands and reserve the shells. Cut off any dark bits, which will be tough and may contain grit. Discard any razor clams that have not opened. Arrange the shells on a warmed serving platter or bowl. Return the razor clams to the pan to reheat slightly in the sauce. Stir in the coriander then remove the pan from the heat. Spoon the razor clams and the sauce over the shells and serve immediately with warm crusty bread.

CRAB AND ASPARAGUS SALAD WITH RADISHES

When asparagus comes into season, I like to include it in as many dishes as possible because I think it is one of the best vegetables we grow in this country. I've travelled the length and breadth of the world, and from my experience, no other country can rival our home-grown asparagus. The advice I would give is to make sure you peel the bottom half of any large asparagus to remove the woody skins. Having to chew on these can instantly take away the enjoyment of eating asparagus. In this recipe, the asparagus is simply blanched and served with creamy, flaky crabmeat and crisp, peppery radishes. Although we prepare our own crabs at the restaurants, feel free to use ready-prepared white crabmeat to save time.

SERVES 4 OR 5

For the salad
24–30 asparagus spears, trimmed
120g radishes (use a mixture of red and black radishes if you can find them)
1 Granny Smith apple
juice of 1 lemon, or to taste
200–250g white crabmeat
a handful of coriander leaves, roughly chopped
a handful of chervil leaves, roughly chopped
80ml Basic Vinaigrette (see page 222)
extra-virgin olive oil
sea salt and freshly ground black pepper

Bring a pan of salted water to the boil and have ready a bowl of iced water. Blanch the asparagus for 2–3 minutes, until tender. Drain and immediately refresh the asparagus in the iced water to stop the cooking process. Once cool, drain again and spread the spears out on a tray lined with kitchen paper. Cover and chill until ready to serve.

Trim and thinly slice the radishes using a sharp knife or a mandolin. Put the radish slices in a bowl of iced water to keep them crisp. Peel, core and cut the apple into fine dice. Put the diced apple into a bowl of cold water with half the lemon juice to keep it from turning brown. Pick over the crabmeat to ensure there are no bits of shell left in it. Mix the coriander and chervil with the crabmeat in a large bowl. Drain the diced apple and add to the crab mixture, along with a little more lemon juice. Add two thirds of the vinaigrette and season well to taste. Gently toss the mixture.

When you are ready to serve, dress the asparagus with the remaining vinaigrette. Spoon the crab salad on to individual plates then top with the asparagus. Drain the radish slices then toss with a little extra-virgin olive oil and some salt and pepper. Garnish each salad with the radish slices and serve immediately.

STARTERS

SOCIAL SUPPERS

GOAT'S-CHEESE-STUFFED COURGETTE FLOWERS WITH APPLE AND CORIANDER CRAB SALAD

This is my take on a dish that Ben Tish (of Salt Yard restaurant) made for me once. The combination of deep-fried courgette flowers with goat's cheese and honey dressing is just divine. I'm serving my version with a refreshing apple and coriander crab salad; the two together is my idea of an ideal summer starter.

SERVES 4

For the stuffed courgette flowers
2 shallots, peeled and finely chopped
2 tablespoons olive oil
200g soft goat's cheese (such as Sairass) or fresh goat's curd
80–100ml double cream
a small bunch of chives, chopped
8 courgette flowers
2 large egg yolks
280ml–300ml ice-cold water
190g store-bought tempura batter
vegetable oil, for deep-fat frying
sea salt and freshly ground black pepper

For the lemon and honey dressing
1 heaped tablespoon clear honey
2 tablespoons sherry vinegar
2 teaspoons soy sauce
2 tablespoons lemon juice
2 tablespoons plum sake
80ml grapeseed oil
2 tablespoons finely chopped shallots
1 teaspoon finely chopped chives

For the apple and coriander crab salad
1 Granny Smith apple
a squeeze of lemon juice
250g white crabmeat
a small handful of coriander, leaves only, chopped
3–4 tablespoons Basic Vinaigrette (see page 222)

For the courgette flowers, sweat the shallots with the olive oil in a heavy-based pan placed over a low–medium heat. Season with salt and pepper and cook gently, stirring occasionally, for about 6–8 minutes until the shallots are soft and translucent. Take the pan off the heat and leave to cool completely.

Meanwhile, make the dressing. Combine the honey, vinegar, soy sauce, lemon juice and sake in a bowl. Gradually whisk in the grapeseed oil until the mixture has emulsified. Taste and adjust the seasoning with salt and pepper to your liking. Stir in the shallots and set aside. Just before serving, stir in the chopped chives.

Next, prepare the salad. Peel and cut the apple into small dice then place into a bowl of cold water mixed with a squeeze of lemon juice. Pick through the white crabmeat and discard any leftover bits of shell. Add the coriander to the crabmeat. Just before serving, drain the diced apple and add to the crabmeat. Set aside.

To stuff the courgette flowers, put the goat's cheese and double cream into a large bowl and whisk until the mixture is smooth and creamy. Fold in the chopped chives and the sweated shallots. Put the mixture into a piping bag. Gently pull apart the petals and remove the stamen from each flower. Carefully fill the cavity of each courgette flower with the cheese mixture. Gently press and twist the tips of the petals to secure the filling.

Half-fill a heavy-based pan with vegetable oil. Heat the oil over a medium–high heat until it reaches a temperature of 190°C. The oil is hot enough when a small piece of bread sizzles immediately when dropped into it.

While the oil is heating, make the batter for the stuffed courgette flowers. Lightly beat the egg yolks in a cold mixing bowl. Then add the ice cold water and very lightly mix it together with a fork. Tip in all the tempura batter and mix it again with the fork until you get a lumpy batter. Deep-fry the stuffed courgette flowers in batches. To do this, dip the courgette flowers into the batter and then lower them into the hot oil. Deep-fry for 3–4 minutes, turning halfway, until they are evenly golden brown. Remove and drain on a tray lined with several layers of kitchen paper. Keep warm while you fry the rest.

To serve, toss the crab salad with the vinaigrette. Serve with the hot courgette flowers and drizzle over the lemon and honey dressing.

CRAB MAYONNAISE WITH BITTER LEAVES ON TOAST

On my travels I've eaten different crabs from various parts of the world, but I still feel that our British brown crabs have the best taste and texture. If you think in terms of how much meat you can get from each crab, they are certainly good value. This lovely starter is a gorgeous way to showcase the sweetness and flakiness of white crabmeat.

SERVES 4

250g white crabmeat
80g Mayonnaise (see page 224)
juice of 1 small lemon
1 tablespoon chopped chives, plus extra to garnish
1 tablespoon chopped chervil, plus extra leaves to garnish
1 tablespoon chopped tarragon, plus extra leaves to garnish
2½–3 heads of mixed radicchio (such as pink radicchio, radicchio di Castelfranco and radicchio Trevisano)
1 wild baby red radicchio ('grumolo rosso', or a small regular radicchio)
1–2 tablespoons olive oil
½ baguette, thinly sliced
6 tablespoons Shallot Vinaigrette (see page 222)
sea salt and freshly ground black pepper

Pick through the crabmeat and discard any bits of shell or cartilage you come across. Place in a large bowl and mix with the mayonnaise, lemon juice and chopped herbs. Taste and adjust the seasoning as necessary.

Separate the leaves from the radicchio then wash and dry them with a salad spinner. Set aside.

When you are about ready to serve, heat a thin layer of oil in a wide frying pan placed over a medium–high heat. Fry the slices of baguette for 1–2 minutes on each side until golden brown around the edges. Remove from the pan to a plate lined with kitchen paper to soak up any excess oil.

Dress the radicchio leaves with the shallot vinaigrette and season to taste with salt and pepper. Arrange the leaves in neat piles on individual serving plates. Scatter over a few herb leaves then divide the crab mayonnaise between the plates. Place the toasts alongside and serve immediately.

LANGOUSTINES WITH PICKLED VEGETABLES AND PEAS

Langoustines are a real luxury because they're so expensive, but I think their flavour and texture are superb, even superior to lobsters and scallops. If you can't afford langoustines, try substituting other shellfish such as crayfish or prawns. This is a great summer dish and you can pretty much prepare the whole dish in advance. The vegetables can be pickled and kept in Kilner jars in the refrigerator. And since the dish is served cold or at room temperature, you can also blanch the langoustines and peas ahead of serving.

SERVES 4

12 extra-large langoustines, or 20 smaller ones
550g sugar snap peas, trimmed
120ml cold Dashi Stock (see page 221); alternatively use Brown Fish or Chicken Stock (see page 218)
extra-virgin olive oil
1 tablespoon light soy sauce
1 tablespoon mirin
a squeeze of lemon juice
1 quantity of Pickled Radishes (see page 75)
sea salt and freshly ground black pepper

If your langoustines are alive, put them into the freezer for about an hour to desensitise them and render them unconscious.

Bring a large pot of salted water to the boil and have ready a large bowl of iced water. Blanch the sugar snap peas for 3 minutes until they are just cooked but still retaining a crunch. With a slotted spoon, remove them to the bowl of iced water. Once they have cooled, drain them and pat dry with kitchen paper. Weigh out 150g of blanched sugar snap peas and place these into the bowl of a food processor. Slice the remaining sugar snap peas on the diagonal.

Return the pot of salted water to the boil. (If using live langoustines, push the tip of a sharp, heavy knife through the centre of each langoustine head to kill it instantly.) Place the langoustines into the boiling water and cook for 3 minutes. To check if they are cooked, look underneath the langoustines. The meat beneath the translucent shell should have turned to an opaque white colour. Drain the langoustines and spread them out in a single layer on a large tray to cool. As soon as they are cool enough to handle, remove the flesh from the shells. To do so, pull the tail away from the head and claws. Pinch the tail between finger and thumb to break the shell and then pull out the meat. (If you find this tricky, use a pair of kitchen scissors to carefully cut along the bottom shell, trying not to break up the delicate meat, then pull out the meat from the shell.) Remove any dark intestinal veins you come across. (You can save the head and shells to make a bisque, if you wish.)

For the sauce, put the 150g of blanched sugar snap peas, dashi and a dash of extra-virgin olive oil into the bowl of a food processor. Blend until smooth then add the soy sauce, mirin and lemon juice. Blend again then taste and adjust the seasoning with a little salt and pepper as necessary. Strain the mixture through a sieve into a bowl.

To serve, put the langoustine meat, sliced sugar snap peas and pickled radishes into a large bowl and dress with a drizzle of extra-virgin olive oil and a pinch each of salt and pepper. Toss well to coat. Spoon a layer of sugar snap pea sauce on to individual plates then neatly pile the langoustine and vegetable mixture on top. Drizzle a little more extra-virgin olive oil around each plate. Serve immediately.

FINE DE CLAIRE OYSTERS WITH VIETNAMESE DRESSING

Good seafood really doesn't get simpler than this: freshly shucked oysters with a mind-blowing Vietnamese dressing. The dressing is one of my all-time favourites – a truly universal vinaigrette that I use with everything: from grilled meats and fish to tofu and vegetable salads. You can prepare the Vietnamese dressing a day in advance. Make sure you get good-quality fresh oysters. All you have to do is to wait for your guests to arrive before shucking the oysters.

SERVES 4

24 very fresh fine de claire oysters (or any seasonal oyster)
1 quantity of Vietnamese Dressing (see page 223)
2 red chillies, deseeded and finely chopped
a handful of small coriander leaves
2 limes, cut into wedges, to garnish

For the crisp ginger
5cm piece of fresh ginger, peeled and thinly sliced
vegetable oil, for frying
sea salt and freshly ground black pepper

First, fry the ginger. Stack the ginger slices and slice into matchsticks. Heat 5cm of vegetable oil in a wok or saucepan over a medium heat. Fry the ginger slices until golden brown and crisp. You may need to adjust the heat as the ginger can turn from golden brown to black very quickly. Remove with a slotted spoon and drain on a plate lined with several layers of kitchen paper to absorb the excess oil. Leave to cool. If making in advance, store the cooled ginger in small jars or airtight containers.

Put a layer of crushed ice on a serving platter. Shuck the oysters just before ready to serve. To do this, hold an oyster in a folded tea towel with one hand, with the flat shell upright and level. With the other hand, insert an oyster knife into the hinge of the shell, then wriggle it from side to side to cut through the hinge muscle. Push in the knife and twist it to lift up the top shell, making sure you don't spill the flavourful oyster juice as you do so. Hold the knife flat and run it along the base of the oyster to release the flesh from the bottom shell. Pick out any bits of broken shell then rest the oyster on the bed of ice. Repeat with the remaining oysters.

Spoon a little Vietnamese dressing over each oyster then top with the chopped chilli, coriander leaves and crisp ginger. Serve immediately, with the lime wedges.

STARTERS

SOCIAL SUPPERS

ROASTED CEPS, PISTOU OF GREEN VEGETABLES AND PAPRIKA OCTOPUS

Having lived and worked in Spain, it is firmly entrenched in my mind that octopus should always be served with paprika. I just love the smoky flavour it lends cephalopods. Go to any good Spanish tapas bar and I'm pretty sure you'll find tender paprika octopus dressed with just a little lemon juice and good olive oil. We've taken it one step further by serving it with nutty cep mushrooms and a vibrant green vegetable pistou.

SERVES 4

For the octopus
750g octopus tentacles (or the tentacles from 1 octopus)
1 tablespoon olive oil
½ onion, peeled and chopped
2 bay leaves
1 star anise
1 leek, cut into large chunks
3 celery stalks, cut into large chunks
a knob of butter
sea salt and freshly ground black pepper

For the pistou of green vegetables
3 tablespoons olive oil
2 courgettes, trimmed and roughly chopped
1 garlic clove, peeled and finely chopped
1 teaspoon pine nuts
a small handful of basil leaves
a small handful of flat-leaf parsley
25g Parmesan, finely grated
a squeeze of lemon

For the smoked paprika dressing
80g Confit Shallots (see page 229)
100ml Basic Vinaigrette (see page 222)
1 teaspoon smoked paprika

For the roasted ceps
150g cep mushrooms, cleaned and thickly sliced
2 tablespoons olive oil

First, braise the octopus. Heat the olive oil in a large pan or pot over a medium heat. Add the onion and sweat for 4–6 minutes, stirring occasionally, until the onion begins to soften. Add the octopus and all the remaining ingredients except the butter to the pan, then pour in enough water to cover the octopus by 5cm. Season the water with a generous pinch of salt. Bring to the boil then lower the heat and simmer for 30–45 minutes, until the octopus is tender. Lift out the tentacles with a pair of kitchen tongs and leave to cool slightly.

When cool enough to handle, rub the skins off the octopus then cut the tentacles into 2cm pieces.

For the pistou, heat a tablespoon of the olive oil in a wide frying pan over a high heat. Add the courgettes and fry for 5 minutes, until soft. Remove the pan from the heat. Put the garlic and pine nuts into a food processor and blend for a few seconds. Add the basil, parsley, Parmesan and courgettes, and blend again. Finally, add the remaining olive oil and lemon juice and blend to a coarse, wet paste. Taste and adjust the seasoning.

Mix all the dressing ingredients and set aside.

To cook the ceps, heat the oil in a wide frying pan over a high heat. Add the ceps and some seasoning and fry for about 8–10 minutes, turning them over once, until they are golden brown and any moisture released by the mushrooms has cooked off. Add the knob of butter to a hot pan and sauté the octopus quickly until golden and warmed through.

To serve, arrange the octopus and ceps on serving plates, dot with the pistou, drizzle with the paprika dressing and serve immediately.

SALT AND PEPPER SQUID WITH SQUID INK AÏOLI

I've always had this dish on a menu in some shape or form in one of my restaurants around the world. It is a delicious crowd-pleaser. I have no pretension of having invented the dish – I just love to cook it. Adding squid ink to the aïoli turns the sauce jet black, which looks really striking on the plate. It is also a nice way to use up every edible bit of squid in a single dish.

SERVES 4 OR 5

450g baby squid, defrosted if frozen
1 teaspoon Szechuan peppercorns
1 teaspoon fine sea salt
1 teaspoon freshly ground black pepper
½ x 150g packet tempura batter
5 heaped tablespoons plain flour
groundnut oil, for deep-frying

For the squid ink aïoli
2 garlic cloves, peeled and finely crushed
2 medium egg yolks
a small pinch of saffron threads
75ml olive oil
75ml vegetable oil
1 teaspoon white wine vinegar, or to taste
20g sachet of squid ink (available from good fishmongers)

To serve
1 green chilli, finely sliced into rounds
2 limes, cut into wedges
coriander leaves, to garnish
coarse sea salt, to sprinkle

First, make the squid ink aïoli. Put the garlic, egg yolks and saffron into a food processor and blitz to a thick paste. Put both oils into a measuring jug. With the motor running, trickle the oils into the food processor and blend until all the oil has been incorporated and you get a thick sauce. (If the sauce splits, transfer it to a jug then add another egg yolk or two to the food processor. Blitz until thick then slowly blend in the split sauce.) Season the sauce with the vinegar and some salt and pepper, to taste. Finally blend in the squid ink. Transfer to a bowl, cover and chill until ready to use.

Wash the squid well and pat dry with kitchen paper. Set aside the squid tentacles and slice the body pouches into rings. Again, pat the squid dry with kitchen paper. Lightly toast the Szechuan peppercorns in a small dry pan. When fragrant, grind them with the salt using a pestle and mortar. Sift this into a large mixing bowl, then add the black pepper and tempura mixture. Make the batter according to the packet instructions. Put the flour into a shallow bowl and season with the salt and pepper. Dip the squid in the flour, then the batter.

Heat the oil in a deep-fat fryer or other suitable deep, heavy pan to 180°C. Deep-fry the squid rings and tentacles in batches in the hot oil for 1–1½ minutes until lightly golden and crisp. (Make sure you don't overcrowd the pan or the temperature of the oil will drop.) Remove with a slotted spoon, carefully shake off the excess oil, drain on kitchen paper and keep warm while you deep-fry the rest of the squid. Sprinkle the deep-fried squid rings and tentacles with a little coarse salt. Divide between warm plates and scatter over the sliced chilli and coriander leaves. Serve at once with lime wedges and the squid ink aïoli.

STARTERS

SEA URCHIN, GOAT'S CHEESE AND PEPPERS ON TOAST

This dish comes from Commune Social, my tapas bar in Shanghai, but I must admit that I first came across the unlikely combination of sea urchin and goat's cheese at a small restaurant in Washington, D.C. You wouldn't expect it but the pairing really works. Sea urchin has a slightly sweet and savoury essence of the sea, which marries well with the tangy creaminess of goat's cheese. Together with some sweet roasted peppers, this is my idea of posh cheese on toast.

SERVES 4

200g very fresh sea urchin roe (ask your fishmonger to prepare it for you)
50g goat's curd (or soft, creamy goat's cheese)
50g softened butter
20ml sherry vinegar
zest and juice of 1 lemon
2 teaspoons Confit Shallots (see page 229)
1 teaspoon finely chopped garlic
1 loaf of ciabatta (about 200g), sliced, or 8 slices of ciabatta, about 1cm thick
extra-virgin olive oil, to brush and finish
300g Piquillo peppers, drained
a handful of coriander cress (or mustard cress), to garnish
3–4 lime leaves, very finely sliced, to garnish (optional)
sea salt and freshly ground black pepper

Keep the sea urchin roe well chilled to keep it as fresh as possible.

In a medium bowl, lightly beat the goat's curd with the butter, sherry vinegar, lemon zest, confit shallots and garlic. Season to taste with salt, pepper and lemon juice. If making ahead, cover the bowl with cling film and chill until ready to use.

Just before you are ready to serve, heat a griddle pan until hot. Brush the bread slices with olive oil and grill for 1–2 minutes on each side until nicely toasted. Sprinkle with a little sea salt and keep warm.

Brush off or tip out any breadcrumbs from the griddle pan and return to the heat. Pat the peppers dry with kitchen paper then lay them on the hot griddle. Grill for 2–3 minutes until lightly charred. Remove to a plate.

To assemble the dish, thickly spread each piece of toast with the goat's curd butter, then arrange the grilled piquillo peppers on top. Lay 2 or 3 sea urchin pieces on top of the peppers then garnish with the coriander cress and lime leaf strips, if using. Finish off with a drizzle of extra-virgin olive oil and serve at once.

SALAD OF QUAIL, CANDIED LEMON, PEAR AND SOURDOUGH CRUMB

This is a lovely warm salad ideal for the colder months of the year. Quail is delicious but the delicate flesh can dry out easily. To ensure that the meat stays succulent, we lightly poach the whole bird in stock, then carve out the breasts and legs to finish roasting just before serving. I'm not using the quail's legs for this particular dish, but do freeze them to use another day. A good way to enjoy them is with parsnip purée and some pan-roasted purple sprouting broccoli.

SERVES 4

500ml Chicken Stock (see page 218)
½ head of garlic
a few sprigs of thyme
4 oven-ready quail
1 tablespoon olive oil
25g unsalted butter

For the anise dressing
1 large egg yolk
juice of ½ lemon
1 teaspoon fennel pollen (available from specialist online suppliers) (optional)
2 tablespoons Pernod (or other anise-flavoured liqueur)
175ml rapeseed oil
sea salt and freshly ground black pepper

For the salad
3 lemons
60ml Pernod (or other anise-flavoured liqueur)
30g caster sugar
2 heads of Bibb lettuce, washed and leaves separated
1 firm but ripe pear
¼ teaspoon sea salt
½ teaspoon fennel pollen (optional)

To serve
¼ teaspoon fennel pollen (optional)
½ quantity of sourdough breadcrumbs (see page 139 and follow instructions for the parsley breadcrumbs, but omitting the parsley)

For the quail, bring the chicken stock, garlic and thyme to the boil in a medium pan. Reduce to a simmer and add the quail. Poach the birds for 3 minutes, turning them once if the stock doesn't completely cover them, then remove them from the stock with a slotted spoon and place them on a plate lined with kitchen paper. Once they are cool enough to handle, carve out the legs and breasts. (Save the legs for another dish.)

Make the anise dressing while the quails are poaching. Put the egg yolk, lemon juice, fennel pollen (if using) and Pernod into a blender or food processor and blend for about 30 seconds. With the blender on a low–medium speed, slowly trickle in the oil to create an emulsion. Once all the oil has been incorporated, add a little salt and pepper to taste. Transfer the dressing to a jar or bottle, cover and refrigerate until ready to use. If making in advance, shake the dressing well before using.

For the salad, segment the lemons. To do so, slice off the top and bottom of the lemon. Stand the lemon upright on a chopping board. Cut off the remaining peel on the sides, following the curve of the fruit and taking care to remove the white pith as well. Holding the fruit over a sieve set on top of a bowl, cut out each lemon segment and remove any pips. Squeeze out the juice from the core of the segmented lemon then discard the pulp.

Put the Pernod and sugar into a small saucepan and stir over a medium–high heat to dissolve the sugar. Take the pan off the heat just before the mixture begins to boil. Immediately pour this over the lemon segments and leave to cool and for the flavours to infuse.

To finish cooking the quail breasts, heat a thin layer of oil in a wide frying pan until hot. Add the breasts, skin side down, and fry for 1–2 minutes until the skin is golden brown and crisp. Flip the breasts over and add the butter to the pan. Baste the foaming butter over the breasts several times and fry for another minute or two. Remove the breasts to a plate lined with kitchen paper to drain off the excess oil and butter.

To assemble the salad, tear any large leaves of lettuce into smaller pieces and place in a large bowl. Remove the core from the pear and slice it into thin wedges. Add to the lettuce leaves and toss with half of the anise dressing. Arrange the lettuce, pear and marinated lemon segments on individual serving plates. Slice the quail breasts on an angle and arrange them on each plate. Spoon over the remaining dressing. Mix the fennel pollen (if using) with the sourdough breadcrumbs and sprinkle over each salad. Serve immediately.

SOCIAL SUPPERS

LITTLE SOCIAL STEAK TARTARE WITH QUAIL'S EGG AND RADISH SALAD

I believe that every bistro should have a good steak tartare dish on its menu and this recipe is one that Cary Docherty, my chef-partner at Little Social, put together. It's been popular ever since we opened the doors of the restaurant. It is essential to use good-quality steak, but you can also make the tartare using off cuts or leftover trimmings from other tender steak dishes. Simply freeze these trimmings until you have enough to assemble the dish.

SERVES 4

80g tomato ketchup
1 tablespoon Dijon mustard
25ml Worcestershire sauce
2–3 drops Tabasco sauce
25g cornichons, finely chopped
25g capers (preferably Spanish Liliput capers), finely chopped
small handful of flat-leaf parsley (thick stalks removed), chopped
240g beef fillet (or sirloin), trimmed of any fat and sinew, finely diced
sea salt and freshly ground black pepper

For the pickled radishes
100g caster sugar
100ml white wine vinegar
125ml muscatel vinegar
1 star anise
1 cinnamon stick
3 cloves
1 teaspoon mustard seeds
200g radishes (preferably a mixture of round and breakfast radishes)

To serve
8 thin slices of sourdough
extra-virgin olive oil
4 quail's eggs, shells washed
a handful of mixed salad leaves

First, make the pickled radish. Put all the ingredients except for the radishes into a saucepan and slowly bring to the boil, stirring to dissolve the sugar. Let it boil for a few minutes then turn off the heat and allow to cool, leaving the flavours to infuse. When cooled, strain through a fine sieve into a bowl and discard the spices.

Meanwhile, wash the radishes in cold water. Trim and thinly slice the round radishes. If you have breakfast radishes, cut these into halves or quarters. Put all but two of the radishes in the cooled pickling liquid and leave to infuse while you prepare the beef. Reserve the raw radishes for the garnish.

For the tartare, combine all the ingredients except the steak in a large bowl. Stir thoroughly, then add the diced beef and mix well. Taste a little and adjust the seasoning with a little more salt and pepper, if necessary.

Toast the sourdough slices and lightly brush or drizzle them with extra-virgin olive oil. Neatly arrange the steak tartare in mounds on four serving plates. Use a very sharp knife to carefully cut off the top of a quail's egg then place it upright on a mound of tartare. Repeat with the remaining eggs. Dress the salad leaves and raw radishes with a little olive oil, season with salt and pepper and arrange on the plate. Serve with the toast slices and the pickled radishes.

CRISP LAMB'S TONGUE WITH MINT GRIBICHE

It is often more challenging and rewarding to cook with the less utilised parts of an animal. If you've never cooked with the tongue of an animal, a good place to start would be with smaller, more manageable lamb's tongues. You need to get past the way they look and move on with the recipe. Prepared the right way, I promise you'll end up with wonderfully tasty, tender morsels of meat coated with crunchy breadcrumbs. The accompanying mint gribiche sauce is the icing on the cake.

SERVES 4

4 lamb's tongues
½ Spanish onion, peeled and sliced
½ head of garlic
2 sprigs of rosemary
1 tablespoon sea salt, plus extra to sprinkle
2 large eggs
60ml whole milk
120g plain flour
120g panko breadcrumbs
vegetable oil, for deep-frying

For the mint gribiche
1 medium egg yolk
1 teaspoon Dijon mustard
1 teaspoon white wine vinegar
300ml vegetable oil
juice of ½ lemon, to taste
a pinch of caster sugar, to taste
2 hard-boiled medium eggs, finely chopped
3 tablespoons gherkins, finely chopped
1 tablespoon small capers, finely chopped
2 tablespoons finely chopped shallots
3 tablespoons chopped mint leaves

Put the lamb's tongues, onion, garlic, rosemary and salt into a large pan and pour in enough cold water to cover. Bring to the boil then reduce the heat to low and skim off any froth and scum that rise to the surface. Simmer for 2½ hours, until the tongues are tender and they offer no resistance when you pierce them with a knife. Remove the pan from the heat and let the tongues cool in the cooking stock.

To make the mint gribiche, whisk the egg yolk, mustard and vinegar together in a large bowl. Very slowly trickle in the oil, whisking continuously to emulsify the sauce. Once all the oil has been incorporated, whisk in the lemon juice, salt and sugar to taste. Fold through the chopped eggs, gherkins, capers, shallot and mint.

Once the tongues have cooled, remove them from the cooking stock and peel off the layer of coarse outer skin. Place the peeled tongues on a plate or tray, cover with cling film and chill for about an hour or so, which will make them firm and easier to slice.

Remove the tongues from the refrigerator and cut them into quarters lengthways. In a small bowl, whisk together the eggs and milk to make an egg wash. Place the flour and breadcrumbs into separate bowls. Coat the tongues in flour, patting off any excess, then dip in the egg wash, then roll them in the breadcrumbs.

Place about 20cm of vegetable oil into a large pan and place it over a medium–high heat. When the oil is hot, about 180°C, fry the breaded tongue pieces in batches. The oil should sizzle immediately as you lower each piece into the pan. Fry the tongues for 4 minutes, until golden brown and crisp, turning over halfway. Remove them with a slotted spoon and drain on a tray lined with several layers of kitchen paper. Lightly sprinkle the fried pieces with sea salt while they are still hot. As you cook each batch, put the fried pieces in a low oven to keep warm.

Divide the fried lamb's tongues between warmed plates and serve immediately with the mint gribiche.

FRIED OX TONGUE WITH MUSHROOMS AND PEAS

Ox tongue may look intimidating and, let's be honest, downright ugly, but it can be delicious if cooked properly. As with any hardworking muscle, the tongue needs long, slow cooking to tenderise the meat. Once tender, remove the skins, portion out the meat and fry it off. I can assure you that very few people would have any qualms eating it. In this dish, I'm pairing the inexpensive offal with spring peas and morels. A dish fit for a king!

SERVES 4

1 ox tongue
½ Spanish onion, peeled and sliced thinly
3 bay leaves
handful of thyme
a squeeze of lemon juice
6 garlic cloves, peeled and lightly crushed
2 teaspoons sea salt
250ml dry white wine
125g plain flour
vegetable oil, for deep-frying

For the sauce
1 tablespoon unsalted butter
½ red onion, peeled and finely chopped
80ml balsamic vinegar
75g soft dark brown sugar
125ml tomato ketchup
½ teaspoon Tabasco sauce
sea salt and freshly ground black pepper

For the mushrooms and peas
50g unsalted butter
200g morel or oyster mushrooms, cleaned
1 banana shallot, peeled and thinly sliced
1 tablespoon white wine vinegar
200ml Chicken Stock (see page 218)
150g peas, thawed if frozen

Place all the ingredients for the ox tongue (except the vegetable oil and flour) into a large pan or pot and pour in enough cold water to cover the tongue. Bring up to the boil, then reduce to a simmer and skim off the froth and scum at the top of the liquid. Gently simmer the tongue for 3 hours, until tender – it should offer no resistance when prodded with a knife.

Take the pan off the heat and let the tongue cool in the cooking liquid. Lift out the tongue (reserve the cooking liquid) and peel off the coarse outer skin. Trim the base of the tongue to roughly the same diameter as the rest of it so that you are left with a somewhat cylindrical shape. Wrap the tongue tightly in several layers of cling film, twisting the cling film at both ends, then refrigerate overnight to allow the shape to set.

Next, make the sauce. Strain the cooking liquid through a fine sieve into a jug and discard the solids. Measure out 200ml of the liquid. Melt the butter in a small pan and add the red onion and a pinch each of salt and pepper. Sweat the onion for 6–8 minutes, stirring occasionally, until it begins to soften. Add the 200ml cooking liquid, balsamic vinegar, brown sugar, ketchup and Tabasco. Bring the mixture to a simmer and let it cook over a medium heat until the sauce has reduced to a syrupy consistency. Do remember to give the mixture a stir every once in a while to prevent it from catching at the base and burning. When ready, set the pan aside, ready to reheat before serving.

To finish off the tongue, place about 20cm of vegetable oil into a very large pan and heat it to around 180°C. Meanwhile, slice the ox tongue on the diagonal to about 1.2cm-thick slices. When the oil is hot enough, it should sizzle immediately as you lower a slice of ox tongue into the pan. Fry the tongue slices in batches for 3 minutes, flipping them halfway, until golden brown and crisp all over. Remove with a slotted spoon and drain on a tray lined with several layers of kitchen paper. Lightly sprinkle the fried tongue pieces with sea salt as soon as they come out of the pan. Keep warm in a low oven while you cook the mushrooms and peas.

Melt 30g of the butter in a pan placed over a medium heat. Add the mushrooms with a little salt and pepper, then tip in the sliced shallot. Sauté for 8 minutes, stirring frequently, so that the shallots sweat without taking on any colour. Tip in the vinegar and let it boil and reduce until the pan is quite dry. Add the chicken stock and bring to the boil. Let it boil until reduced by two thirds and thickened to a syrupy consistency. Tip in the peas and cook for 3–4 minutes then remove the pan from the heat and stir in the remaining butter.

Divide the fried tongue between warmed plates and spoon the mushrooms and peas alongside. Drizzle a little sauce over each plate and serve immediately.

BONE MARROW, GENTLEMAN'S RELISH AND ONIONS ON TOAST

I invented this dish for our tapas bar in Hong Kong and it has proved so popular that we haven't been able to take it off our menu. We have since included the dish in all our tapas restaurants and bistros at some point or other. I've always loved the pungent savouriness of Gentleman's Relish. Teamed with sourdough toasts, sweet onion jam and unctuous bone marrow, this is a taste sensation!

SERVES 4

4 x 7–8cm veal marrowbones, sawn in half lengthways (ask your butcher to do this)
8 thin slices of sourdough
sea salt and freshly ground black pepper
½ quantity of sourdough breadcrumbs (optional), to serve (see page 140)

For the onion jam
2 tablespoons olive oil
350g onions, peeled and finely sliced
60g caster sugar
50ml sherry vinegar
100ml red wine
50ml port wine

For the gentleman's relish
250ml cider vinegar
85g pitted prunes, chopped
125ml tomato ketchup
65g brown sugar
50ml Worcestershire sauce
4 spring onions, trimmed and finely chopped
3 cloves garlic, peeled and finely chopped
2 anchovy fillets, chopped
3 cloves
1 tablespoon English mustard powder
2 teaspoons ground allspice
a pinch of chilli powder
50ml water

Note: you will need a meat thermometer for this recipe.

First, make the onion jam. Heat the oil in a heavy-based pan and add the onions and a pinch of salt and pepper. Stir occasionally, over a medium–high heat, for 8–10 minutes, until the onions turn golden. Tip in the sugar, vinegar and wines and bring to the boil. Lower the heat and simmer, stirring occasionally, for 30–40 minutes, until the wines have almost reduced completely and the onions have cooked down to a soft and sticky consistency. Taste and adjust the seasoning. Cool then spoon into sterilised jars and seal. (The jam can be kept in the refrigerator for several weeks.)

To make the gentleman's relish, combine all the ingredients in a pan with a generous grating of black pepper. Stir well and simmer over a low heat for about 30 minutes, until the prunes are soft and the mixture has thickened. Transfer to a food processor and blitz until the mixture is very smooth. For a professional finish, push the mixture through a fine sieve into a bowl. Spoon into a sterilised jar, seal and refrigerate. (Any extra relish can be kept in the refrigerator for 2–3 weeks.)

For the roasted bone marrow, preheat the oven to 180°C/Gas Mark 4. Place the marrowbones on a baking tray, season with a pinch of salt and pepper, then roast for about 15–20 minutes or until the marrow reaches a core temperature of 70°C. The marrow should be soft and wobbly but not melting away. Remove from the oven and set aside.

Just before the marrowbones are ready, toast the bread and spoon the onion jam and gentleman's relish into small individual serving bowls. Divide the roasted marrowbones between serving plates, sprinkle the sourdough breadcrumbs, if using, over the top and serve with the onion jam, relish and warm toast.

STARTERS

MAIN COURSES

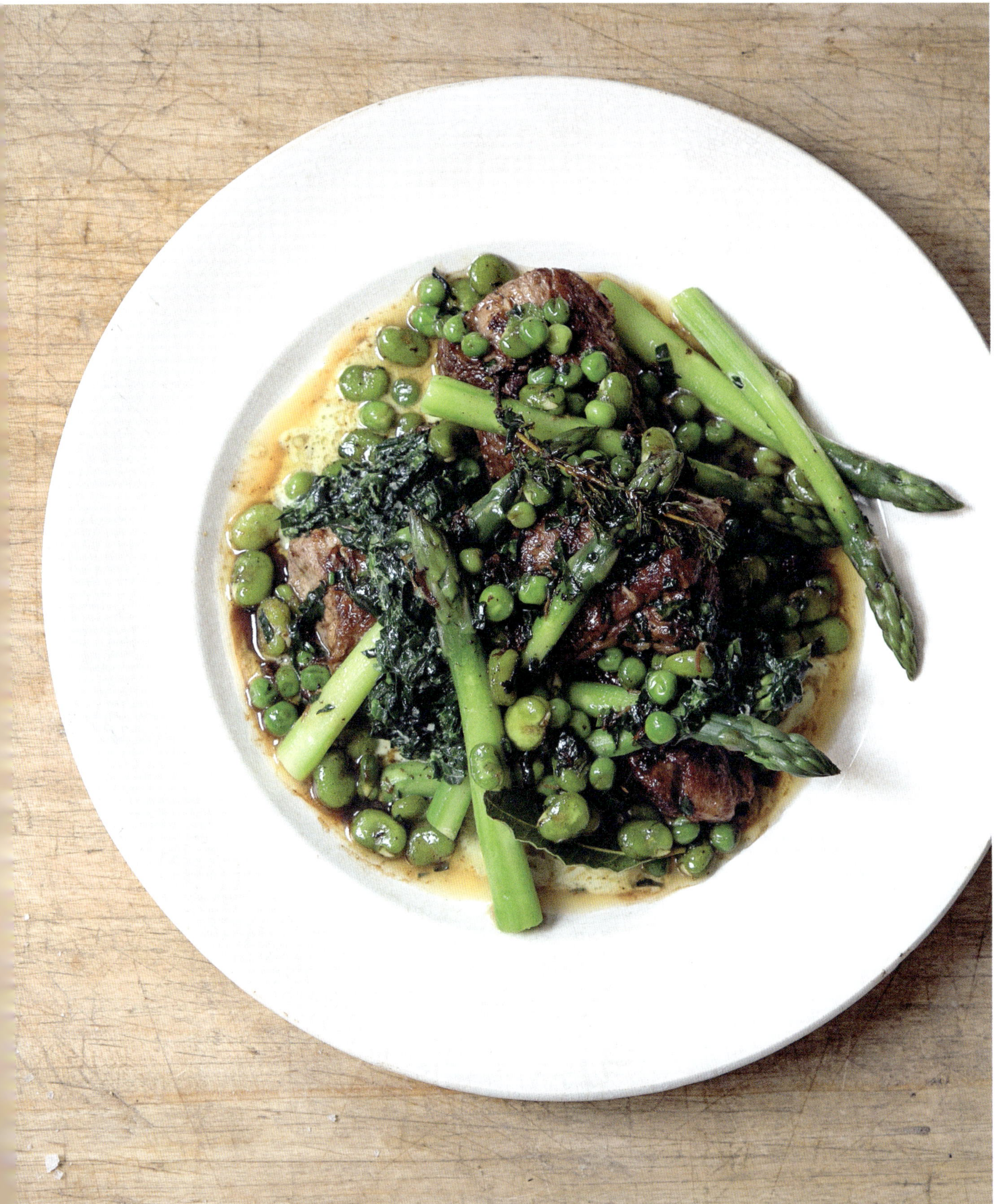

MAIN COURSES

84/ POACHED EGG AND BASIL PIZZA **86/** CEP MUSHROOM PIZZA WITH BALSAMIC ONION CHUTNEY, MASCARPONE AND PARMESAN **89/** RED MULLET PIZZA WITH TAPENADE AND PROVENÇAL ROAST VEGETABLES **90/** SMOKED SALMON, BROCCOLI AND SAIRASS CHEESE PIZZA

92/ HALIBUT WITH PARSLEY POTATOES, MORECAMBE BAY SHRIMPS AND ASPARAGUS **95/** CORNISH COD WITH BRAISED LENTILS AND LARDO DI COLONNATA **96/** ROAST COD WITH BRAISED HARICOT BEANS, CHORIZO AND TOMATO **97/** SPICED POTTED RICE WITH COD **100/** SMOKED HADDOCK, MANCHEGO AND SPRING ONION TORTILLA **101/** SMOKED HADDOCK GRATIN WITH HARICOT BEANS AND GRUYÈRE HERB CRUST **102/** CURRIED MONKFISH WITH SAUTÉED CAULIFLOWER AND BULGUR WHEAT **105/** SEA BREAM WITH MORECAMBE BAY SHRIMPS, SAUTÉED KALE, SAMPHIRE AND MUSTARD VELOUTÉ **106/** BAKED JOHN DORY WITH RED ONIONS, TOMATOES AND ROSEMARY POTATOES **107/** HERB-ROASTED SEA TROUT WITH PINK FIR APPLE POTATOES, SAMPHIRE AND ASPARAGUS SALAD **109/** CHARGRILLED SOLE WITH SCOTTISH COCKLES **110/** CAULIFLOWER AND CRAYFISH RISOTTO **113/** SQUID AND PRAWN BURGER WITH SMOKED TOMATO CHUTNEY **114/** CORNISH FISH STEW WITH GARLIC TOAST AND AÏOLI **116/** PULLED PORK SANDWICHES WITH PICKLED KOHLRABI AND COLESLAW

117/ B.B.L.T. (BELLY, BRIOCHE, LETTUCE & TOMATO) **118/** BRAISED PORK CHEEKS WITH HONEY, SOY AND CRISP SHALLOTS **120/** PORK CHEEKS WITH SOFT POLENTA AND APPLE **121/** BRAISED PORK BELLY WITH CHORIZO AND PEPPER PURÉE AND SPICED ONIONS **123/** SLOW-ROASTED PORK BELLY WITH BLACK PUDDING, CRUSHED POTATOES AND GREEN BEANS **124/** TAMARIND-GLAZED PORK BELLY WITH BRAISED RED CABBAGE AND SAUTÉED MUSHROOMS **126/** HONEY-ROAST HAM HOCK WITH CRISP PIGS' EARS, BLACK PUDDING

AND PICCALILLI 129/ PORK SHANKS WITH HARICOT BEANS
130/ PORK CHOPS WITH HARICOT BEANS AND SPICY TOMATO SAUCE
131/ 'SPANISH-STYLE' ROAST SUCKLING PIG WITH CANDIED PINEAPPLE AND ROAST PEPPERS 134/ CHARGRILLED RIB-EYE STEAKS WITH CHIMICHURRI DRESSING
137/ GARLIC HERB BEEF WITH KOHLRABI REMOULADE AND WATERCRESS
139/ BRAISED OXTAIL WITH PASTA 140/ BRAISED OX CHEEKS, CARROTS, BONE MARROW, SOURDOUGH CRUMBS AND HORSERADISH POMME PURÉE 143/ CÔTE DE BOEUF WITH HERB SALSA, COURGETTE FRITES AND CEPS 144/ MEATBALLS WITH TOMATO SAUCE
147/ LITTLE SOCIAL BURGER WITH SMOKY BACON AND BALSAMIC ONION CHUTNEY
148/ SIMPLE ROAST LEG OF LAMB WITH ROSEMARY RUB AND POTATO DAUPHINOIS
151/ BRAISED LAMB NECK, PEAS, BROAD BEANS, ASPARAGUS AND CREAMED WILD GARLIC
152/ SLOW-ROASTED LAMB SHOULDER WITH AUTUMN VEGETABLES
AND CABBAGE AND MINT PESTO 155/ ROAST RACK OF LAMB WITH SPICED OLIVE JUS AND CREAMY MASHED POTATOES

156/ LOIN OF VENISON WITH BEETROOT AND VENISON SAUCE AND BRAISED CABBAGE
158/ ROAST VENISON AND BEETROOT WITH POACHED PEARS 160/ ROAST ANJOU SQUAB, WITH YAKITORI OF INNARDS, BRUSSELS SPROUTS AND BRAISED RED CABBAGE
162/ ROAST DUCK BREAST WITH MINI ROAST POTATOES, TURNIPS, BEETROOT AND CARROT PURÉE 165/ SPICED ROAST PHEASANT WITH PUMPKIN, BREAD SAUCE AND HOME-MADE GRANOLA

MAIN COURSES

POACHED EGG AND BASIL PIZZA

Of the four pizzas I've included in this book, this is the closest to the traditional Neapolitan pizza, with the exception of a poached egg on top. When you cut into it, the runny yolk oozes out and provides a luscious richness which contrasts with the tangy tomato sauce. On several occasions, I've also served this as a breakfast pizza with a few slices of Parma ham on top.

SERVES 4

1 teaspoon white wine vinegar or cider vinegar
4 large eggs
grated or shaved aged Parmesan, to taste
a handful of small basil leaves
extra-virgin olive oil, to drizzle

For the pizza base
400g Italian 00 flour or strong bread flour
1 teaspoon fine sea salt
2 x 7g sachet dried active yeast (or 25g fresh yeast)
250ml tepid water

For the tomato basil sauce (makes enough for 8 pizzas)
2 tablespoons olive oil
1 Spanish onion, peeled and chopped
6 garlic cloves, peeled and chopped
1 red chilli, deseeded and chopped
1 tablespoon tomato purée
250g plum tomatoes on the vine, roughly chopped
500g passata
1 teaspoon caster sugar, or to taste
a small bunch of basil, roughly chopped
sea salt

Start by making the dough. Sift the flour and salt into the bowl of a stand-alone mixer (with the dough hook attachment) then sprinkle over the yeast. Make a well in the centre. Pour the water into the well then mix on a low speed. (If using fresh yeast, crumble it into a small bowl then stir in the water to dissolve. Leave in a warm spot for 5–10 minutes to activate the yeast. When the mixture begins to foam and expand, add it to the flour mixture.) Increase the speed slightly and knead for a few minutes until you have a smooth, springy dough. Put the dough into a large, lightly floured bowl then dust a little more flour on top. Cover the bowl with a lightly oiled sheet of cling film. Leave in a warm spot for about an hour, until the dough has doubled in size.

Meanwhile, make the tomato sauce. Heat the oil in a large heavy-based pan over a medium heat. Add the onion, garlic and chilli, and stir well. Sweat the vegetables for 6–8 minutes until they begin to soften, stirring occasionally. Add the tomato purée and fry for another minute or two. Tip in the chopped tomatoes, passata, salt, sugar and half the basil. Bring to a simmer and lower the heat. Gently simmer, stirring occasionally, for about 25–30 minutes until the tomatoes are very soft and the mixture has thickened slightly. Note that the sauce makes enough for 8 pizzas but you can freeze the extra and use it for another batch.

Add the reserved basil to the sauce then blend it using a hand-held blender, if you have one; otherwise, use a regular blender or food processor. For a very smooth result, pass the sauce through a fine sieve. If you prefer the sauce thicker, return it to the pan and simmer until reduced to the desired consistency.

Preheat the oven to 220°C/Gas Mark 7. Divide the dough into 4 pieces, then roll them out thinly on a lightly floured surface (they should be about 20cm wide). Lift the dough bases on to a couple of lightly floured baking sheets. Prick the base with a fork – this prevents bubbles from forming on the base. Spread a layer of the tomato sauce over each pizza. Bake for 8–10 minutes until the pizza edges are crisp.

While the pizzas are in the oven, poach the eggs. Bring a tall pan of water to the boil. Lower the heat to a simmer and add the vinegar. Crack the eggs into small ramekins. Swirl the water with a spoon to create a whirlpool. Gently lower the eggs into the centre of the whirlpool, one at a time. Poach for 3 minutes until the egg whites are cooked but the yolks are still runny. Remove the eggs from the pan with a slotted spoon and carefully place on a plate lined with kitchen paper.

When ready, remove the pizzas from the oven and sprinkle with as little or as much Parmesan as you like. Put a poached egg on each pizza, sprinkle over the basil leaves and drizzle with a little extra-virgin olive oil. Slice and serve immediately.

MAIN COURSES

CEP MUSHROOM PIZZA WITH BALSAMIC ONION CHUTNEY, MASCARPONE AND PARMESAN

This is a delicious vegetarian white pizza that I make when wild mushrooms come into season. The sweet nuttiness of fresh cep mushrooms is so satisfying, even die-hard carnivores would not hesitate to devour this pizza. When wild mushrooms are not available, or if you're on a tight budget, ordinary chestnut mushrooms would work just as well. If you have a bottle of truffle oil to hand, drizzle a few drops over the pizza to lift the flavour of the mushrooms.

MAKES 4

2 tablespoons olive oil
400g cep mushrooms (or regular chestnut mushrooms if ceps are not in season), cleaned, trimmed and thickly sliced
2 garlic cloves, peeled and finely chopped
a few sprigs of thyme, leaves only
1 bay leaf
a generous knob of butter
1 quantity of Pizza Dough (see page 229)
1 quantity of Balsamic Onion Chutney (see page 147)
200g mascarpone
175g mozzarella, grated
50g Parmesan shavings
sea salt and freshly ground black pepper

Heat the oil in a heavy-based pan until hot. Add the mushrooms, garlic, thyme, bay leaf and a pinch each of salt and pepper. Fry over a medium–high heat for 4–6 minutes until the mushrooms are golden brown and any moisture released has cooked off. Add the butter to the pan and as it melts and begins to foam, toss the mushrooms to coat.

When you are ready to assemble the pizza, preheat the oven to 220°C/Gas Mark 7. Divide the dough into 4 pieces, then roll them out thinly on a lightly floured surface (they should be about 20cm wide). Lift the dough bases on to a couple of lightly floured baking sheets. Spread a quarter of the onion chutney over each pizza base. Place neat dollops of the mascarpone around the bases then arrange the mushrooms on top. Scatter over the mozzarella and Parmesan. Drizzle each pizza with olive oil and season with salt and pepper. Bake for 8–10 minutes until the pizza edges are golden and crisp. Slice and serve immediately.

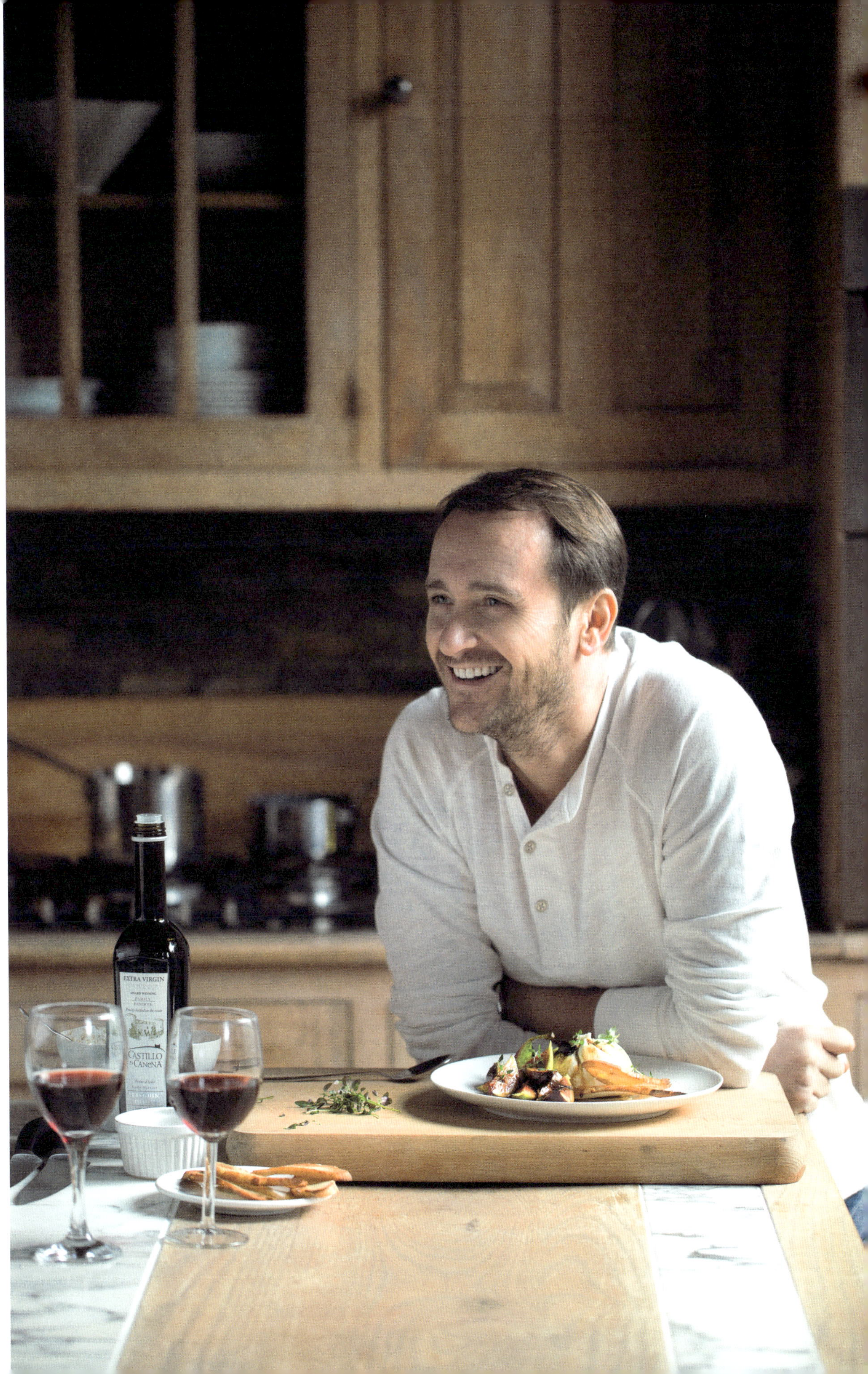
EXTRA VIRGIN
FAMILY
CASTILLO DE CANENA

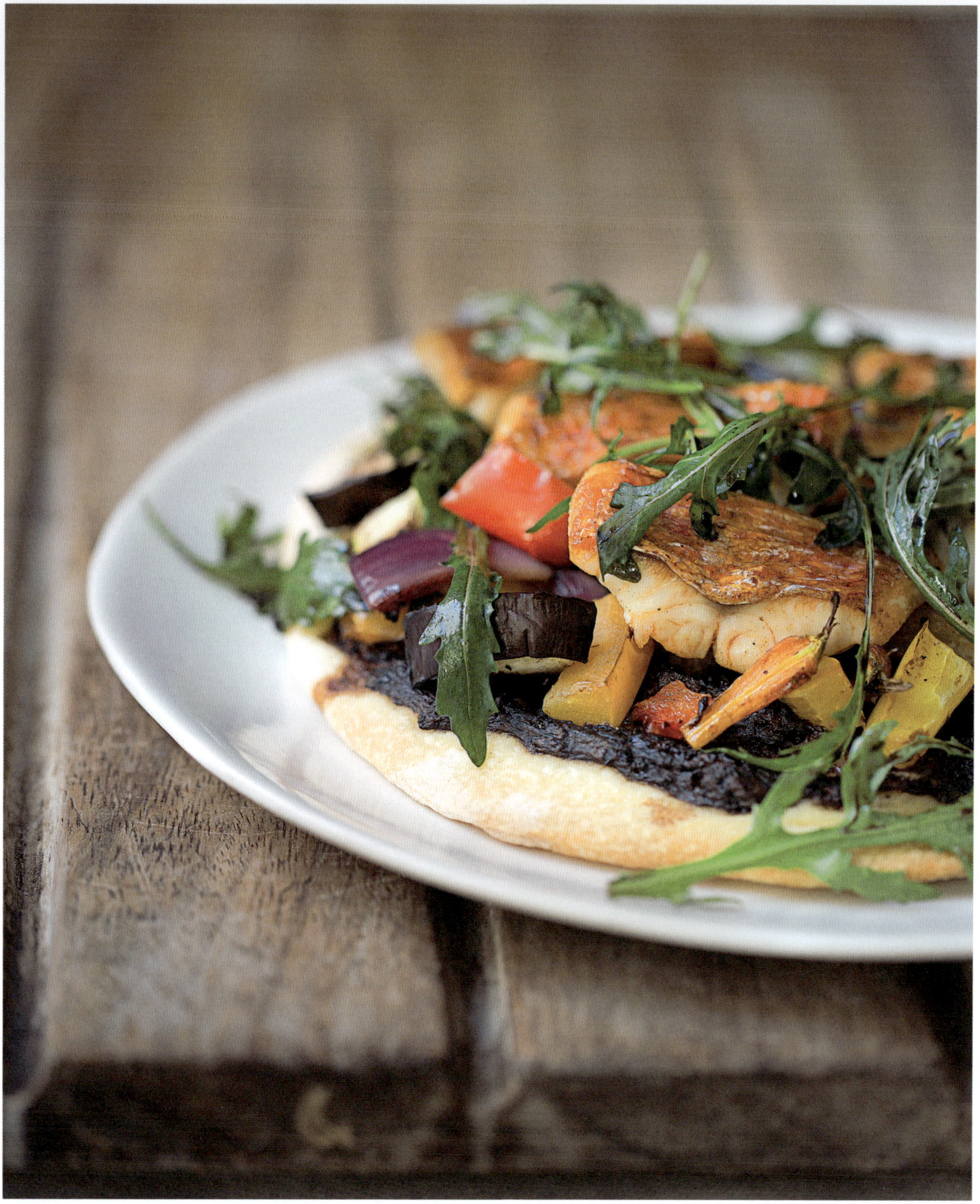

RED MULLET PIZZA WITH TAPENADE AND PROVENÇAL ROAST VEGETABLES

Having worked with Ferran Adrià at el Bulli, I've learnt to set aside any preconceptions and inhibitions when I cook. So when tasked with creating an interesting pizza for one of our restaurants, I took the pizza base as a blank canvas on which I could place all kinds of tasty combinations. This particular pizza has all my favourite Provençal flavours. It isn't really that odd to add olives and roasted vegetables to a pizza and the red mullet takes the place of the usual ham or cheese to create a beautifully light combination.

SERVES 4

5 medium red mullet fillets
100g mixed vegetables (such as baby carrots, red onions, red and yellow peppers, courgettes or aubergines)
4 tablespoons olive oil
2 garlic cloves, finely crushed
2 teaspoons Herbes de Provence
1 quantity Pizza Dough (see page 229)
4 tablespoons Tapenade (see page 225)
4 tablespoons crème fraîche
sea salt and freshly ground black pepper

To serve
2 handfuls of wild rocket
2 tablespoons olive oil
a splash of balsamic vinegar

Run your fingers through every red mullet fillet and remove any pin bones with a pair of kitchen tweezers. Cut each fillet in half lengthways and then in half again crossways. Place on a plate, cover with cling film and chill until ready to cook.

Preheat the oven to 200°C/Gas Mark 6. If using baby carrots, peel and cut them into 1cm dice. Peel and chop the red onions. Trim, deseed and cut the peppers into similar-sized pieces. Similarly, trim and dice the courgettes and aubergines, if you are using them. Put all the vegetables into a large bowl and toss with the olive oil, garlic, herbs and some salt and pepper.

Divide the dough into 4 pieces, then roll them out thinly on a lightly floured surface (they should be about 20cm wide). Lift the dough bases on to a couple of lightly floured baking sheets. Mix the tapenade and crème fraîche together in a small bowl. Thinly spread the mixture on to the pizza bases. Scatter the vegetables over the pizza and bake for 8 minutes until the pizza crust is golden brown and crisp around the edges.

Meanwhile, season the red mullet pieces with salt and pepper. Remove the pizzas from the oven then arrange 5 pieces of the fish on top of each. Return the pizzas to the oven and bake for another 2–3 minutes. Meanwhile, dress the rocket with the olive oil, vinegar and a pinch each of salt and pepper. When ready, garnish the pizzas with the dressed rocket leaves and serve immediately.

SMOKED SALMON, BROCCOLI AND SAIRASS CHEESE PIZZA

Smoked salmon and broccoli may seem like odd pizza toppings; but trust me, they work a treat! Now I'm not a dietitian, but I'd like to think of this as a nutritionally-balanced pizza. A good one for the kids if you can persuade them to try it.

SERVES 4

1 small head of broccoli
1 quantity of Pizza Dough (see page 229)
4 tablespoons Tomato Sauce (see page 226)
200gm Sairass cheese (or ricotta)
12 anchovies in oil, drained
250g smoked salmon

Bring a pan of salted water to the boil and prepare a bowl of iced water on the side. Cut the broccoli into small florets (save the stalk to make soup or use it in another dish). Blanch the broccoli florets for 3–5 minutes until tender and bright green. Drain and refresh in the iced water to stop the cooking process. Once cooled, drain off the broccoli and let it dry on a plate lined with kitchen paper.

Preheat the oven to 230°C/Gas Mark 8. Divide the dough into 4 pieces, then roll them out thinly on a lightly floured surface (they should be about 20cm wide). Lift the dough bases on to a couple of lightly floured baking sheets. If you prefer a thicker crust, let the dough rise a little for about 20 minutes. Thinly spread the tomato sauce on to the pizza bases then drop small dollops of Sairass cheese evenly over each base. Divide the anchovies and broccoli between the pizza bases then bake for about 8–10 minutes until the edges are golden brown and crisp.

Remove the pizzas and immediately drape the smoked salmon slices on top. Serve immediately.

MAIN COURSES

HALIBUT WITH PARSLEY POTATOES, MORECAMBE BAY SHRIMPS AND ASPARAGUS

This is a lovely fish supper to cook in the late summer or early autumn when Morecambe Bay shrimps are in season. They provide an earthy and savoury intensity that really complements the halibut. It is also really easy to cook and the end result is outstanding. Instead of halibut, you could use brill, turbot or any other firm, flat fish.

SERVES 4

2 bunches of asparagus, woody ends removed and peeled
2 tablespoons unsalted butter
4 x 150g halibut fillets
1 tablespoon olive oil
sea salt and freshly ground black pepper

For the potatoes and shrimps
750g baby new potatoes, washed
1 tablespoon unsalted butter
1 tablespoon olive oil
400g Morecambe Bay shrimps or brown shrimps
300ml dry white wine
150ml double cream
2 tablespoons chopped flat-leaf parsley

Preheat the oven to 180°C/Gas Mark 4.

First, prepare the shrimps and potatoes. Put the potatoes into a large pan and cover with cold water. Add a generous pinch of salt and bring to the boil. Boil the potatoes for about 12–16 minutes until tender when pierced with a small knife. Drain well and return to the hot pan to allow them to dry off a little.

For the shrimps, heat the butter and oil in a medium–hot pan. Add the potatoes and sauté for about 3 minutes, then add the shrimps and cook for another 2 minutes. Use a slotted spoon to remove the potatoes and shrimps to a warm plate. Pour the white wine into the pan and let it boil until reduced by half. Pour in the cream and return to the boil. Season to taste with salt and pepper. Just before you are ready to serve, return the shrimps and potatoes to the sauce to warm through then add the parsley and mix well.

Blanch the asparagus in salted boiling water for 2 minutes. Remove and cool in iced water. Drain on kitchen paper. Melt the butter in a frying pan and sauté the asparagus for 2 minutes. Keep it warm while you cook the fish.

Season the halibut fillets with salt and pepper. Heat a frying pan with the olive oil over a high heat until it is hot, then add the fillets to the pan, skin side down. Fry for about 1–2 minutes until golden brown and crisp, then carefully flip the fillets over to cook the flesh side for 2 minutes or until cooked through. Transfer to warmed serving plates and serve with the shrimp and potatoes and sautéed asparagus.

MAIN COURSES

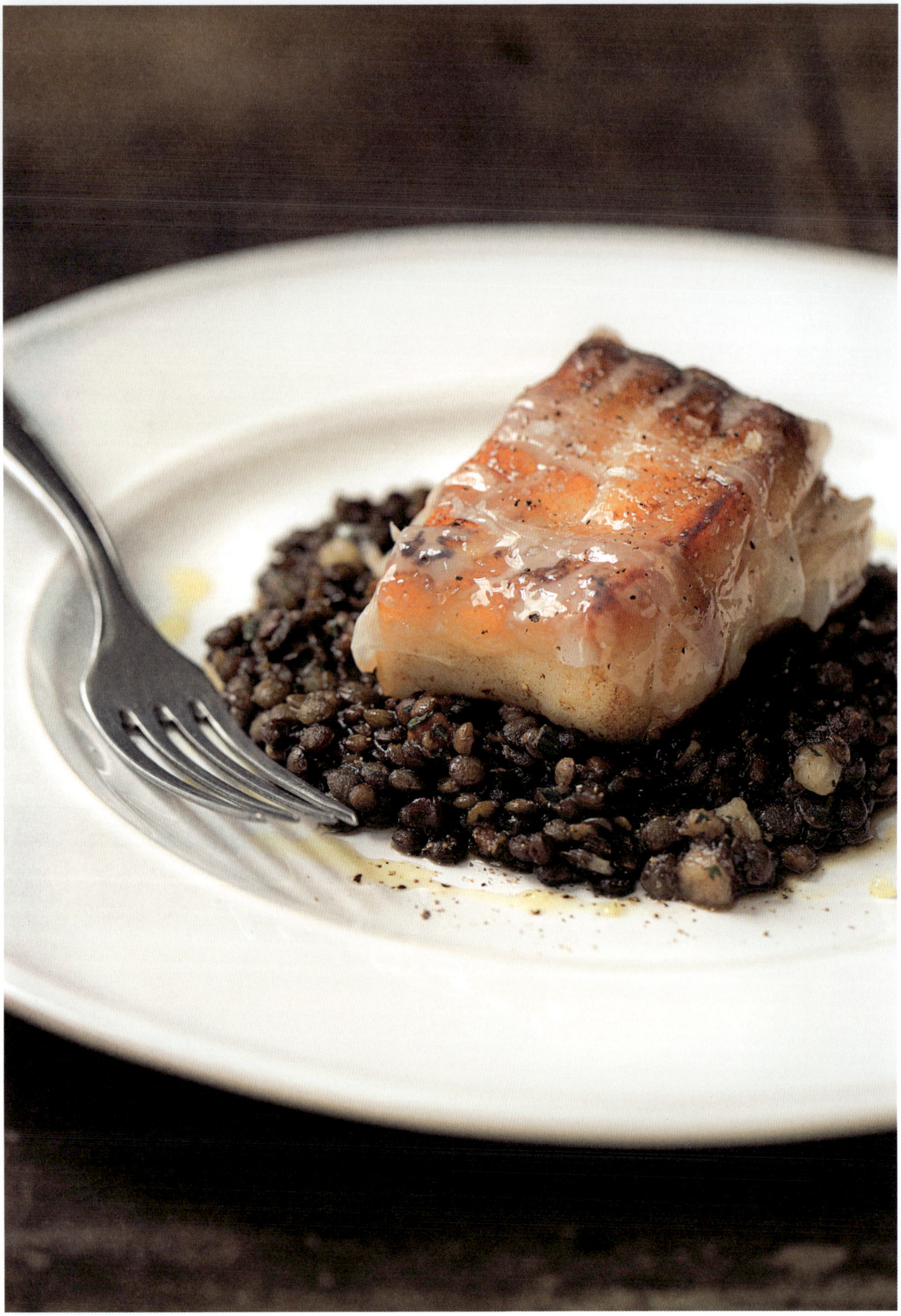

CORNISH COD WITH BRAISED LENTILS AND LARDO DI COLONNATA

Earthy lentils make a good base for roasted fish. This dish is a little more distinctive because I'm infusing both the lentils and cod with lardo di colonnata, a wonderful cured pork back fat from Italy. The best lardo is produced in Colonnata, a small city in the Italian Alps where marble is abundant. The lard is rubbed with salt, herbs and spices before being aged for about 6 months in porous marble basins. In Britain, you can find it at good Italian delis, specialist butchers or online grocers.

SERVES 4

For the cod fillets
4 cod fillets, each about 180g
a squeeze of lemon
1–2 tablespoons olive oil

For the braised lentils
300g Puy lentils
20ml olive oil
100g lardo di colonnata, or fatty pancetta, diced
1 onion, finely diced
2 garlic cloves, crushed
1 celery stalk, trimmed and finely diced
1 carrot, peeled and finely diced
1 leek, trimmed and finely sliced
2 sprigs of thyme, leaves only, chopped
2 sprigs of rosemary, leaves only, chopped
1 litre Chicken Stock (see page 218)
sea salt and freshly ground black pepper

To serve
30g unsalted butter
a small bunch of flat-leaf parsley (thick stalks removed), finely chopped
4 thin slices of lardo di colonnata (optional)

First, prepare the lentils. Soak in plenty of cold water for at least an hour. Heat the olive oil in a heavy-based pan over a medium heat. Add the lardo di colonnata, onion and garlic and sauté for a few minutes, stirring once or twice. Add the remaining vegetables and herbs to the pan and stir well. Gently sweat the vegetables for 5–6 minutes until they begin to soften. Drain the lentils and add them to the pan together with the chicken stock. Bring the stock to the boil then lower the heat. Simmer for 20–30 minutes or until the lentils are tender and have absorbed most of the stock. Season to taste with salt and pepper. Take the pan off the heat.

Run your fingers through the fish fillets and remove any pin bones with a pair of kitchen tweezers. Rub the fillets with lemon juice and a little salt and pepper. Heat a thin layer of olive oil in a wide, non-stick frying pan placed over a medium–high heat. When the pan is hot, add the fish fillets, skin side down, and fry for about 3–5 minutes until the skin is golden brown and crisp and the fish is cooked two-thirds of the way. Turn the fish over and fry the other side for a further 1–2 minutes until the fish is firm and just cooked through.

To serve, reheat the lentils, stirring in the butter and chopped parsley and season to taste. Spoon the lentils on to warm plates. Place the fish on top of the lentils then lay a slice of lardo di colonnata (if using) over each fillet. The lardo will melt with the residual heat of the fish and baste the fillets. Serve immediately.

ROAST COD WITH BRAISED HARICOT BEANS, CHORIZO AND TOMATO

This rustic dish is very loosely based on the French cassoulet, which combines meat (or fish in this instance) with beans and sausages in a rich sauce. To save time, you could make this a one-pot meal. Instead of roasting the cod separately, place the raw fillets on top of the cooked bean and chorizo mixture and stick the whole casserole in the oven. Serve with crusty bread and a green salad for an easy supper.

SERVES 4

4 x 150g cod fillets
1½ tablespoons olive oil

For the braised haricot beans
180g dried haricot beans, soaked overnight in cold water
2 tablespoons olive oil
1 banana shallot, peeled and chopped
3 sprigs of thyme
50g chorizo, diced
60ml dry white wine
300g grape or cherry tomatoes, halved
500ml Vegetable Stock (see page 219)
sea salt and freshly ground black pepper

Start by braising the beans. Drain and rinse the soaked beans under cold running water.

Heat the oil in a heavy-based pan over a medium–high heat. Add the shallot, thyme and chorizo and toss to coat in the oil. Fry for 4–6 minutes, stirring occasionally, until the shallots begin to soften and the chorizo has released its orangey-red oils. Add the wine, then add the tomatoes. Boil the wine for a few minutes then pour in the stock and beans and return to a simmer. Season well with salt and pepper. Cover the pan with a lid and gently simmer for about 1½ hours, stirring occasionally, until the beans are tender. If necessary, top up the stock with a splash of hot water halfway through cooking if the liquid no longer covers the beans. Fish out and discard the thyme sprigs and reheat before serving.

When you're ready to cook the fish, preheat the oven to 230°C/Gas Mark 8. Rub the cod fillets with olive oil and season with salt and pepper. Place the fish on a tray lined with baking parchment. Roast for 10–12 minutes, depending on the thickness of the fillets, until the fish is firm and just cooked through. Remove from the oven and serve immediately with the braised haricot beans.

SPICED POTTED RICE WITH COD

This is an easy one-pot meal, not unlike a kedgeree, which is perfect for a casual weeknight supper. It is a lovely warming dish that I like to serve to the family on a cold and dreary day with a little Indian chutney on the side. You could also serve it with a little natural yoghurt and my Smoked Tomato Chutney (see page 113) if you have any to hand.

SERVES 4

2 tablespoons olive oil
2 shallots, peeled and finely chopped
1 garlic clove, peeled and finely crushed
1 teaspoon grated ginger
½ tablespoon cumin seeds, lightly crushed
½ tablespoon coriander seeds, lightly crushed
1 teaspoon ground turmeric
250g basmati rice
500ml fish or Vegetable Stock (see page 219)
1 teaspoon sea salt, or to taste
400g skinless cod fillet, cut into 8–10cm chunks
½ lime, for squeezing
a small bunch of coriander, leaves only
freshly ground black pepper

Heat the oil in a heavy-based pan over medium–high heat. Add the shallots and stir frequently for 5 minutes, until they turn translucent and are beginning to soften. Add the garlic, ginger, cumin, coriander and turmeric, and stir well. Fry for another couple of minutes then add the rice. Stir and toast the rice for a minute or two before adding the stock. Season with salt and pepper. Bring the stock to the boil, then turn the heat down to low. Lightly season the fish pieces with salt and pepper, then place on top of the rice. Cover with a lid and simmer for 10 minutes until the rice and fish are just cooked through. Turn the heat off and leave the lid on for a further 5 minutes to allow the rice to absorb all the moisture.

Meanwhile, chop half the coriander leaves. When ready to serve, squeeze a little lime juice over the fish. Gently move the fish to a plate and fluff up the rice with a fork. Fold through the chopped coriander. Return the fish to the pan and scatter over the remaining coriander leaves. Serve piping hot.

Spiced Potted Rice with Cod, page 97

MAIN COURSES

SMOKED HADDOCK, MANCHEGO AND SPRING ONION TORTILLA

This is a vamped-up version of the classic Spanish tortilla, incorporating smoked haddock and spring onions to delicious effect. If you end up with leftovers, serve it up the next day with a green salad and a simple tomato and spring onion relish for a light lunch.

SERVES 4 OR 5

500ml whole milk
1 small onion, peeled and roughly chopped
1 bay leaf
2 cloves
a few sprigs of thyme
250g smoked haddock
25g butter
25g plain flour
100g Manchego cheese, grated, plus extra to finish
1 teaspoon Dijon mustard, or to taste
1–2 tablespoons olive oil, plus extra to drizzle
1 onion, peeled and finely sliced
100g potatoes, such as Desiree or Maris Piper, peeled and finely sliced (ideally using a mandolin)
5 large eggs
sea salt and freshly ground black pepper

For the spring onion salad
4 spring onions, trimmed and finely sliced
1 shallot, peeled and thinly sliced into rings
a handful (about 25g) of micro onion cress (or salad cress)
2 tablespoons Basic Vinaigrette (see page 222)

Pour the milk into a saucepan and add the onion, bay leaf, cloves and thyme. Bring to the boil then immediately turn off the heat and let the milk infuse for about 5 minutes. Strain the infused milk into another pan and discard the aromatics. Bring the milk to a simmer then lower in the smoked haddock and gently poach the fish for about 4–5 minutes. Remove the fish to a plate to cool, then strain the milk into a jug. When cool enough to handle, flake the fish, discarding the skin and any bones you come across.

Melt the butter in a heavy-based pan and stir in the flour. Cook the flour, stirring constantly, for a couple of minutes until the mixture has thickened. Take the pan off the heat and stir in a trickle of infused milk. Gradually add the rest of the milk until it is fully incorporated and the sauce is smooth. Return the pan to the heat and cook the sauce for 5–8 minutes, stirring frequently. Stir in the cheese and mustard and cook for another minute or two. Season well and taste. If you find the sauce lumpy, pass it through a fine sieve; if you like it a little thinner, add a splash more milk. Keep warm on the stove over a very low heat.

Heat the oil in a wide non-stick pan and add the onion and potatoes. Season with salt and pepper and add a little splash of water to the pan. Cover the pan with a lid (or a crumpled piece of greaseproof paper) and cook gently for 10 minutes until the onions and potatoes are tender and the water has cooked off. Leave to cool.

Crack the eggs into a large bowl, season with salt and pepper, then lightly beat them. Add the cooled potato and onion mixture and the flaked fish and gently stir to mix.

Preheat the oven grill on high. Heat a wide non-stick ovenproof pan (or four individual omelette pans) with a little oil. Ladle in the mixture and cook over a medium heat for 3–5 minutes, until the egg is just setting around the edge. Pour the white sauce evenly over the omelette. Place the pan under the grill for 2–3 minutes to finish cooking the top of the tortilla. Remove from the grill and finish with a grating of Manchego cheese.

For the salad, toss the spring onions, shallot and cress with the vinaigrette. Put into a serving bowl and serve alongside the tortilla.

SMOKED HADDOCK GRATIN WITH HARICOT BEANS AND GRUYÈRE HERB CRUST

This is a great comforting meal – savoury, rich and creamy with a gorgeous herb crust. It is a good dish to make ahead, as it freezes well. You could double or triple the recipe and portion it out in ovenproof casserole dishes or disposable foil containers. Seal well and pop them in the freezer, unbaked. The frozen gratin can go straight into the oven, but you may need to give it an extra 15–20 minutes of baking time to get the dish bubbling hot throughout.

SERVES 4

500g undyed smoked haddock
100ml Brown Fish Stock (see page 218)
500ml whipping cream
2 tablespoons dry sherry
1 teaspoon wholegrain mustard
1 x 400g can of haricot beans, drained
8 spring onions, chopped
200g Gruyère, grated
50g dried breadcrumbs
2 teaspoons chopped flat-leaf parsley
sea salt and freshly ground black pepper

Remove the skins from the smoked haddock then feel the fillets for any pin bones. Pick these out with a pair of kitchen tweezers. Cut the fish into 2cm cubes and set aside.

Put the fish stock, cream and sherry into a saucepan and bring to a simmer over a medium heat. Simmer for about 15 minutes until the mixture has reduced to the consistency of double cream. Stir in the mustard and season to taste with salt and pepper. Add the haricot beans and spring onions to the pan, then lower in the fish pieces. Give the mixture a gentle stir and simmer for about 4–6 minutes until all the ingredients have warmed through. Add a handful of grated Gruyère to the sauce. Taste and adjust the seasoning as necessary.

Preheat the grill to the highest setting and lightly grease a 1.2-litre ovenproof dish. Transfer the ingredients of the pan to the greased dish, levelling the mixture with a spatula. In a small bowl, mix together the breadcrumbs, chopped parsley and remaining cheese to make the topping. Scatter this over the smoked haddock mixture then pop it under the grill for 5–10 minutes, depending on the heat of your oven grill, until the topping is golden brown and crisp. Serve while still hot.

CURRIED MONKFISH WITH SAUTÉED CAULIFLOWER AND BULGUR WHEAT

I love the sweet taste and meaty texture of monkfish; however, it is on the vulnerable species list, so do check with your fishmonger to make sure that your fish comes from good sustainable fishing practices. I treat monkfish like a piece of good steak, roasting it in lots of foaming butter and leaving it slightly undercooked. I then leave it to rest and it will continue to cook in its residual heat. Lightly spiced, it is simply gorgeous with sautéed curried cauliflower and bulgur wheat.

SERVES 4

For the monkfish
4 skinless and boneless monkfish fillets, about 160g each
1 teaspoon mild curry powder
1 tablespoon olive oil
40g unsalted butter
sea salt and freshly ground black pepper

For the sautéed cauliflower and cauliflower purée
1 large cauliflower, stem trimmed
100g unsalted butter
2 shallots, peeled and chopped
1½ tablespoons mild curry powder
250ml Brown Fish or Chicken Stock (see page 218)
250ml double cream
a few sprigs of thyme
ground white pepper, to taste

For the bulgur wheat
20g unsalted butter
1 teaspoon caraway seeds
1 red chilli, deseeded and finely chopped
150g bulgur wheat
1 teaspoon ground turmeric
200ml Chicken Stock (see page 218)
3 tablespoons extra-virgin olive oil
1 tablespoon finely chopped flat-leaf parsley

First, prepare the cauliflower. Cut neat florets from the cauliflower then chop the core and stem into small pieces. Set aside half the florets for later. Cut the remaining florets into smaller pieces.

Make a cauliflower purée with the chopped stem and florets. Melt half the butter in a wide pan. Add the shallots and sweat for 6–8 minutes, stirring occasionally, until they begin to soften. Stir in the curry powder and fry for a minute. Tip in the chopped cauliflower, increase the heat and fry for a few minutes, stirring frequently. Pour in the stock and cream and bring to a simmer. Reduce the heat to low and cover the ingredients in the pan with a piece of damp baking parchment. Cook gently for 10–15 minutes, until the cauliflower is very soft.

Strain the cauliflower and shallots through a fine sieve set over another pan. Tip the cauliflower and shallots into a blender, adding some, but not all, of the creamy stock in the pan. Blend until smooth, adding more hot stock as necessary to get a thick purée. Season to taste with salt and white pepper and set aside.

For the bulgur wheat, melt the butter in a heavy-based pan and stir in the caraway seeds and chopped chilli. Fry for a few minutes until the spice is fragrant then add the bulgur wheat and stir to coat in the butter. Toast the bulgur wheat over a medium–high heat for a minute or two. Add the turmeric and chicken stock and bring to a simmer. Cover the pan with a lid and simmer for about 5 minutes. Turn off the heat and leave the bulgur wheat to continue steaming in the pan for another 10 minutes.

Meanwhile, melt the remaining butter for the cauliflower in a wide frying pan over a high heat. Add the thyme and reserved cauliflower florets. Season well and fry for 4–6 minutes until the florets are just tender and golden around the edges. Transfer to a plate lined with kitchen paper to drain off the excess butter. Keep warm.

To cook the monkfish, season the fillets with salt then roll in the curry powder until well coated. Heat the oil in a wide frying pan over a medium–high heat. Add the fish and butter and fry for 3–4 minutes on each side, depending on the thickness of the fish. Spoon the foaming butter over the monkfish as it cooks. The fish is ready when evenly golden brown and firm when lightly pressed. Transfer the fish to a warm plate, reserving the curried oil in the pan.

Rest the fish in a warm spot for a few minutes while you gently reheat the cauliflower purée and dress the bulgur wheat with the olive oil and parsley. Taste and adjust the seasoning. Spoon the purée into a piping bag.

To assemble, place the bulgur wheat in the middle of warmed serving plates. Spoon the sautéed cauliflower around the bulgur wheat and pipe spoonfuls of the cauliflower purée around the plate. Place a curried monkfish fillet on top of the bulgur wheat then drizzle with the reserved curried oil.

MAIN COURSES

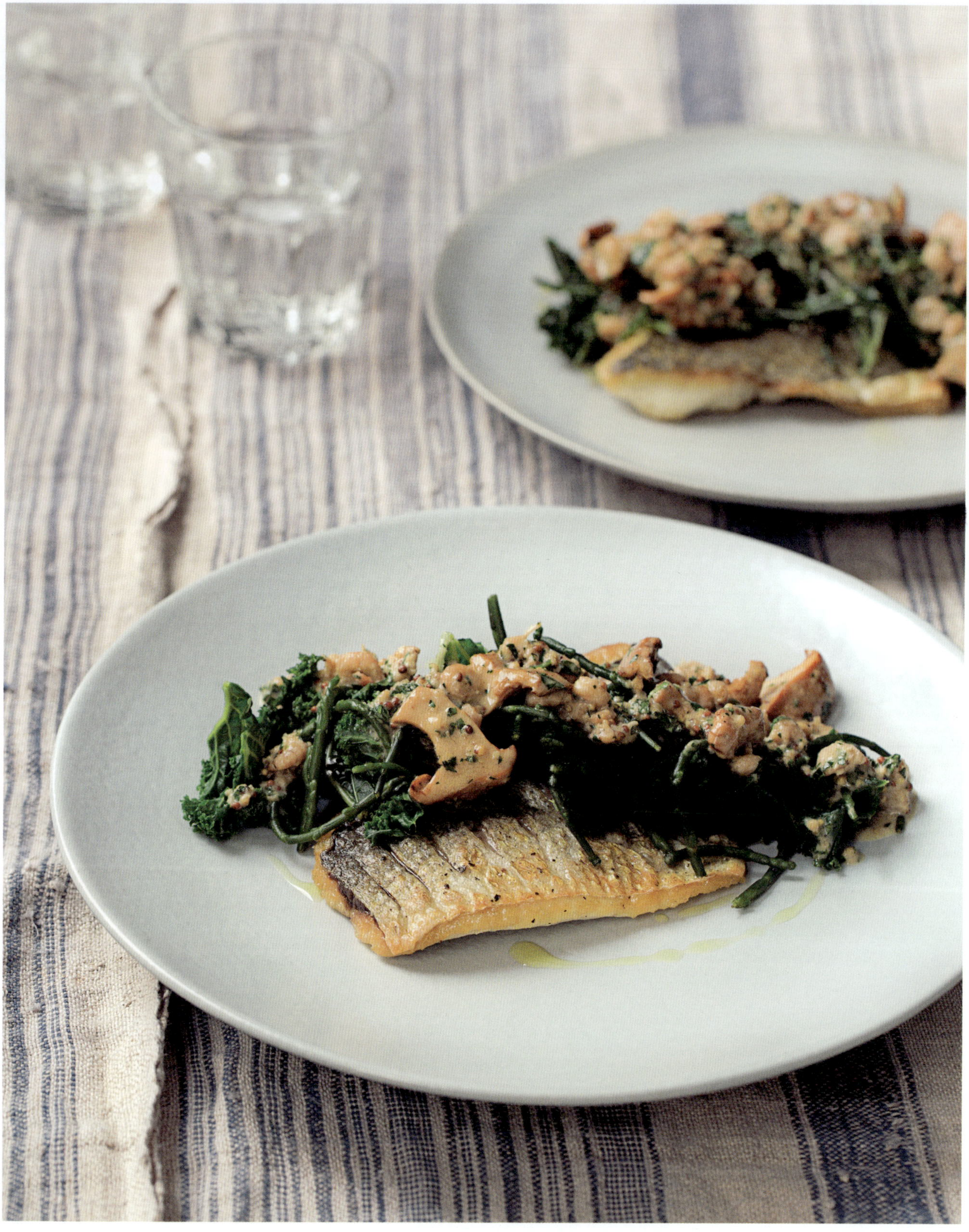

SEA BREAM WITH MORECAMBE BAY SHRIMPS, SAUTÉED KALE, SAMPHIRE AND MUSTARD VELOUTÉ

Tiny Morecambe Bay shrimps have such fantastic flavour that I treat them like a seasoning ingredient in my fish dishes. Here, I'm serving them with pan-fried sea bream, kale and a creamy mustard velouté. The dish looks impressive and sophisticated and would be ideal for a dinner party main course.

SERVES 4

4 boneless sea bream fillets, about 200g each
a squeeze of lemon juice
2 tablespoons olive oil
2 tablespoons butter
200g Morecambe Bay shrimps or brown shrimps
3 tablespoons chopped chives
sea salt and freshly ground black pepper

For the mustard velouté
2 tablespoons olive oil
3 shallots, peeled and finely sliced
4–5 garlic cloves, peeled and sliced
a handful of thyme
1 bay leaf
½ teaspoon white peppercorns, lightly crushed
a pinch of rock salt
375ml dry white wine
500ml Chicken Stock (see page 218)
250ml double cream
1 tablespoon wholegrain mustard

For the sautéed kale and samphire
250g marsh samphire, woody stems removed and soaked for an hour
1 tablespoon butter
1 teaspoon olive oil
2 shallots, peeled and thinly sliced
200g kale, thinly shredded
a squeeze of lemon juice

First, make the mustard velouté. Heat the oil in a deep pan over a medium–high heat. Tip in the shallots, garlic, herbs and peppercorns. Stir and sweat the vegetables for 4–6 minutes until the shallots begin to soften. Pour in the wine and bring to the boil. Let it boil until reduced by two-thirds. Now add the chicken stock and bring the liquid back to the boil. Cook until reduced again by half. Add the cream and mustard and bring to a simmer. Season with salt and pepper to taste. Strain the sauce through a fine sieve into a clean saucepan, ready to reheat before serving.

For the samphire and kale, bring a pot of water to the boil and have ready a bowl of iced water. Blanch the samphire for a minute, refresh in the iced water until cool, then drain again. Heat the butter and oil in a frying pan until very hot. Add the shallots and sauté for a minute. Add the kale and samphire and stir well. Sauté for 5–8 minutes, stirring occasionally, until the kale is tender. Season with salt, pepper and lemon juice to taste. Remove the pan from the heat. Keep warm or reheat just before serving.

Preheat the oven to 180°C/Gas Mark 4. Lightly score the skin of the sea bream fillets then rub them with salt, pepper and lemon juice. Heat the olive oil in a wide ovenproof frying pan until hot. Add the fillets, skin side down, and gently press them down with a spatula so the skins won't curl. Fry for 2–3 minutes until the skins are golden brown and crisp. Flip them over and cook the other sides for another 2–3 minutes or until the fish has cooked through. Remove the fish to a warmed platter and return the pan to the heat.

Add the butter and shrimps and sauté with a little salt, pepper and lemon juice for a minute. Stir in the chives and then remove the pan from the heat. Serve the sea bream fillets with the samphire and kale, buttered shrimps and mustard velouté.

BAKED JOHN DORY WITH RED ONIONS, TOMATOES AND ROSEMARY POTATOES

Where day-to-day eating is concerned, John Dory is a luxurious treat. I'd like to think of it as the king of the round fish. It is expensive but its cost is justified by its superlative flavour and texture. Here, I'm serving it in a Mediterranean style, based on a dish I once had in Sicily. Some spinach sautéed with garlic, lemon and olive oil would make a good accompaniment to the fish.

SERVES 4

4 x 150g John Dory fillets, pin bones removed, chilled until ready to cook
4 tablespoons olive oil
2 red onions, peeled and thinly sliced
3 garlic cloves, peeled and thinly sliced
a few sprigs of thyme
a few sprigs of rosemary
4 ripe plum tomatoes, cut into chunks
600g small potatoes (such as Charlotte), peeled and cut into 1–2cm dice
100g pitted black olives, chopped
100ml dry white wine
150ml Brown Fish Stock (see page 218)
juice of 1 lemon
sea salt and freshly ground black pepper

Preheat the oven to 200°C/Gas Mark 6.

Heat a large flameproof roasting pan with half the olive oil over a medium–high heat. Add the onion, garlic and herbs and toss in the olive oil with a pinch of salt and pepper. Fry for 6–8 minutes, stirring occasionally, until the onions are soft and translucent. Add the rest of the oil then tip in the tomato, potato and olives. Mix well then pour in the white wine and fish stock. Cover the pan with a large piece of foil then place in the oven. Bake for about 30–40 minutes, until the potatoes are tender.

When the vegetables are cooked, rub the John Dory fillets with lemon juice and salt. Place the fillets on top of the vegetables, skin side up, then cover again with foil and bake for another 10–12 minutes until the fish is cooked. Divide the fish and vegetables between warmed serving plates and drizzle over any pan juices before serving.

HERB-ROASTED SEA TROUT WITH PINK FIR APPLE POTATOES, SAMPHIRE AND ASPARAGUS SALAD

This salad is a true celebration of British ingredients and it makes a lovely, light lunch when warmer weather beckons. When the short British asparagus season is over, make the salad with green beans or even sliced runner beans.

SERVES 4

4 boneless and skinless sea trout fillets, about 180g each
a handful of chervil, finely chopped
a handful of dill, finely chopped
a handful of flat-leaf parsley (thick stalks removed), finely chopped
2 tablespoons extra-virgin olive oil
sea salt and freshly ground black pepper

For the pink fir apple potatoes

350g pink fir apple (or Anya) potatoes, washed well
90ml Mayonnaise (see page 224)
1 tablespoon wholegrain mustard

For the samphire and asparagus salad

16 green asparagus spears, stems peeled and woody ends trimmed
100g samphire, leaves picked
75g mixed salad
1 tablespoon red wine vinegar
2 tablespoons extra-virgin olive oil
a pinch of caster sugar

First, cook the potatoes. Bring a large pot of salted water to the boil. Add the potatoes and cook for about 15 minutes, until tender. There should be little resistance when you pierce the potatoes with the tip of a small knife. Drain the potatoes and return them to the hot pan. Keep warm.

Next, prepare the salad. Cut the asparagus on the diagonal into 4cm-long spears. Bring two pans of water to the boil: one salted, the other unsalted. Blanch the samphire in the unsalted water for 1 minute. Drain in a colander and pat dry with some kitchen paper. Set aside. Blanch the asparagus in the salted water for 3–5 minutes until tender. Drain well and refresh under cold running water (or in a bowl of iced water). Drain well and pat dry. Put the blanched asparagus, samphire and mixed salad into a large bowl.

Combine the vinegar, oil, sugar and a pinch each of salt and pepper in a bowl. Whisk until the dressing is well emulsified. Just before you are ready to serve, dress the asparagus salad with the dressing and toss to coat.

Cook the fish just before you are ready to serve. Season the fillets with salt and pepper on both sides. Put all the chopped herbs into a shallow bowl then coat the skinned side of the fish fillets with the herbs. Heat the olive oil in a wide frying pan until hot. Fry the fish fillets, herb side down for about 2 minutes; turn over and fry for 2 more minutes on the other side. Remove to a plate or tray and keep warm.

Crush the warm potatoes with a fork and mix with the mayonnaise and mustard. Season to taste with salt and pepper.

To plate, place a layer of crushed potatoes on warmed serving plates. Arrange the dressed salad on top of the potatoes. Gently break the fish fillets into bite-sized pieces and arrange these over the salad. Garnish with samphire leaves and serve at once.

SOCIAL SUPPERS

CHARGRILLED SOLE WITH SCOTTISH COCKLES

You can make this dish with any type of flat fish, from Dover or lemon sole to dab or plaice. Rather unusually for a fish dish, I'm marinating the sole with a brine mixture to infuse them with the flavours of garlic, Spanish ham and lemon salt. It really transforms the mild-flavoured fish and accentuates its natural sweetness. If you do not fancy skinning the sole yourself, your fishmonger should be able to do it for you in a flash. I serve this sole with Scottish cockles, an ingredient I've loved since I was a child, but you could simply substitute fresh clams or mussels if cockles are difficult to source.

SERVES 4

For the chargrilled sole
4 whole Dover or lemon sole, each about 350–450g, skinned, cleaned and gutted
60ml fresh lemon juice
2 garlic cloves, crushed
40g Serrano ham (or pancetta), cut into small dice
1 tablespoon fine sea salt
100ml water
extra-virgin olive oil, to brush

For the Scottish cockles
2 tomatoes
2 tablespoons extra-virgin olive oil
1 garlic clove, finely chopped
125ml fino sherry
a small bunch of flat-leaf parsley (thick stalks removed), finely chopped
300g cockles, washed

Wash the fish well, pat dry with kitchen paper and place them on a roasting tray. In a small bowl, combine the lemon juice, garlic, ham, salt and water. Give the mixture a stir, then coat the fish with the marinade, cover and chill for 20 minutes to let the flavours infuse.

Preheat the oven to 100°C/Gas Mark ¼.

Meanwhile, prepare the tomatoes. Bring a kettle of water to the boil. Lightly score the top and base of the tomatoes and place into a deep bowl. Pour over the boiling water and blanch the tomatoes for 50–60 seconds or until the skin starts to loosen from the scored ends. Drain the tomatoes and refresh in cold running water. Once cooled, peel off the skin and cut the tomatoes into quarters. Remove the seeds then finely dice the flesh. Place in a bowl and set aside.

Place a griddle pan over a medium heat. Season the sole with a little salt and brush the flesh generously with olive oil. Grill the fish for about 2–3 minutes on each side, drizzling a bit of the marinade over it. When cooked place the fish on to a baking tray and cover it with foil. Leave to rest for a few minutes in the oven.

To cook the cockles, heat the olive oil in a heavy-based pan over a medium–high heat. Add the garlic and stir. Before the garlic begins to colour, add the sherry. Boil the sherry for a couple of minutes, then add the parsley and diced tomato. Let the mixture simmer for about a minute. Tip the cockles into the pan, give the mixture a stir, then cover with a lid. Steam the cockles, shaking the pan a few times, for about 3 minutes until all the cockles have opened (discard any that haven't). Taste the sauce and adjust the seasoning as necessary. To serve, arrange the chargrilled sole on a big platter and spoon over the cockles and sauce.

CAULIFLOWER AND CRAYFISH RISOTTO

This is a risotto with a British twist featuring two fantastic local ingredients: cauliflower and crayfish. It is another Little Social recipe that our guests can't seem to get enough of. Here, a smooth cauliflower purée lightens the risotto and at the same time infuses it with a wonderful nutty flavour. The cauliflower acts as a base flavour for sweet, tender crayfish and creamy risotto rice. I think of this dish as a posh cousin of cauliflower cheese – comforting yet sophisticated.

SERVES 4

For the cauliflower purée:
1 head of cauliflower (about 300g), broken into florets
300ml double cream
300ml whole milk
sea salt and freshly ground black pepper

For the crayfish bisque
1kg live crayfish, washed and kept chilled
2 tablespoons olive oil
1 small onion, peeled and chopped
1 small carrot, peeled and chopped
2 garlic cloves, peeled and lightly crushed
1 lemongrass stalk, lightly bruised
3 white peppercorns
1 star anise
1 tablespoon tomato purée
80ml brandy
300ml dry white wine
600ml Chicken Stock (see page 218)
600ml Veal Stock (see page 219)
3 sprigs of tarragon
3 sprigs of coriander
a handful of basil

For the risotto
200g risotto rice (Arborio, carnaroli or vialone nano)
200ml Vegetable Stock (see page 219)
25g grated Parmesan
25g mascarpone
40g butter

For the sautéed girolles
a knob of butter
1–2 tablespoons olive oil
200g girolles, cleaned

For the sautéed cauliflower
50gm butter
100g cauliflower, cut into tiny florets

Put the crayfish into the freezer for about an hour to desensitise them and render them unconscious.

For the cauliflower purée, start by setting aside one large floret for garnish. Put the cream and milk in a saucepan and bring the mixture to the boil. Add the cauliflower and a generous pinch of salt. Simmer for 4–6 minutes until the cauliflower is soft. With a slotted spoon, transfer the cauliflower to a blender or food processor and blend to a smooth purée, adding a splash of the creamy milk if necessary (keep the leftover liquid in the pan to loosen the risotto if you need to). Pass the purée through a fine sieve into a saucepan. If making in advance, cover and chill once the purée has cooled.

For the crayfish bisque, bring a big pot of salted water to the boil. Have ready a large bowl of iced water. Parboil the crayfish in several batches, depending on the size of your pot. Keeping the water at a rolling boil, lower the crayfish into the pot and cook for 2 minutes. Remove the crayfish with a pair of tongs and immediately refresh them in the iced water. Once cool, extract the crayfish meat from the shells, keeping the shells to make the stock. Refrigerate the crayfish meat in a covered bowl until almost ready to serve.

To make the crayfish stock, heat the olive oil in a large pan placed over a medium–high heat. Tip in the onion, carrot, garlic, lemongrass, peppercorns and star anise. Sauté the vegetables, stirring frequently, until they are lightly browned. Add the tomato purée and stir over a high heat for a couple of minutes. Now add the crayfish shells, smash them with the base of a rolling pin to release more flavour and fry them for a minute. Add the brandy and white wine and boil until the liquid has reduced by half. Pour in the stocks and bring the liquid back to a simmer. Add the fresh herbs and simmer for about 35–40 minutes until the stock is flavourful. Pass the bisque through a fine sieve into a clean pan and return to the heat. Boil until reduced to a syrupy sauce consistency. Season to taste. Reheat the bisque before serving.

For the risotto, parboil the rice in a pan of salted water for 7 minutes. Drain well then spread the rice out on a tray to cool quickly. When you are about ready to serve, bring the vegetable stock to the boil in a saucepan. Add the parboiled rice to the stock and leave for another 2 minutes to finish cooking. Add the cauliflower purée, followed by the grated Parmesan and mascarpone. Stir well then taste and adjust the seasoning. Finally add the butter to the risotto and stir until the rice is well coated and glossy. Take the pan off the heat and leave the risotto to stand for a few minutes while you fry the girolles and crayfish.

Heat the butter and oil in a wide frying pan over a medium–high heat. Add the girolles with a pinch of salt and pepper and fry for 3–5 minutes until any moisture released has cooked off. Add the crayfish meat to the pan and fry for another 2–3 minutes until the crayfish is just cooked through. Taste and adjust the seasoning. Take the pan off the heat.

To sauté the cauliflower, heat the butter in a frying pan, add the small cauliflower florets and some seasoning and cook until the butter reaches a nutty brown and the cauliflower is cooked through.

Divide the risotto between 4 warmed shallow bowls. Spoon a little bisque over the risotto and then top with the girolle and crayfish mixture and the sautéed cauliflower. To garnish, very thinly slice the reserved cauliflower floret (ideally using a mandolin) and scatter over each dish. Serve immediately.

MAIN COURSES

SOCIAL SUPPERS

SQUID AND PRAWN BURGER WITH SMOKED TOMATO CHUTNEY

I am totally addicted to the prawn and scallop burgers at J. Sheekey's in London. Each time we visit this iconic restaurant, I keep telling myself to try other items on their menu, but inevitably, I always end up ordering the prawn burger. This recipe is my take on their dish, but with a slight twist. Here, squid takes the place of scallops and I'm substituting my favourite smoked tomato chutney for their delicious spiced mayonnaise.

SERVES 2

150g small squid tubes, cleaned and finely chopped
150g raw prawns, peeled, deveined and finely chopped
3 spring onions, trimmed and chopped
finely grated zest of 1 lemon
handful of flat-leaf parsley (thick stalks removed), finely chopped
1 tablespoon good-quality mayonnaise
50g fresh breadcrumbs
1 tablespoon butter
2 brioche burger buns
50g mixed salad leaves
2 tablespoons Basic Vinaigrette (see page 222)
sea salt and freshly ground black pepper

For the smoked tomato chutney
200g vine-ripened plum tomatoes
20ml olive oil
1 small red onion, finely chopped
2 small garlic cloves, crushed
1 teaspoon smoked paprika
1 lemongrass stalk, trimmed and finely chopped
2 teaspoons caster sugar, or to taste
1 teaspoon Cabernet Sauvignon vinegar or other red wine vinegar
2 teaspoons fish sauce
1 teaspoon lime juice

Preheat the oven to 180°C/Gas Mark 4.

Place the squid and prawns in a large bowl. Add the spring onions, lemon zest, parsley and mayonnaise. Mix well then fold in the breadcrumbs and season well with salt and pepper. To check the seasoning, fry off a little of the mixture and taste, adjusting the salt level as necessary. With wet hands, divide and shape the mixture into two patties. Place on a plate, cover with cling film and refrigerate for at least 30 minutes to allow them to firm up.

Meanwhile, make the chutney. Lightly score the top and base of each tomato then blanch them for 30 seconds in boiling water. Refresh in a bowl of iced water then drain well. Peel the skins from the tomatoes, then quarter and remove the seeds. Finely dice the tomato flesh and place in a bowl.

Heat the oil in saucepan and add the onion. Sweat the onion over a medium heat for 8–10 minutes, stirring occasionally, until soft and translucent. Add the garlic, paprika and lemongrass, and stir well. Gently cook for another 5 minutes, stirring every once in a while. Heat the sugar in another dry pan until it melts and begins to caramelise to a golden brown colour. Add the vinegar and fish sauce to the caramel. If the caramel hardens upon contact with the liquid, stir the mixture for a few minutes until it dissolves. Pour this over the onion mixture and add the lime juice. Cook for a minute then add the diced tomatoes and stir well. Cook for a further minute then remove the pan from the heat.

To cook the burgers, melt the butter in a non-stick frying pan. Add the patties and fry for 2–3 minutes on each side, depending on their thickness, until they are golden brown on each side. Place on a baking sheet in the oven to cook through for a further 5–7 minutes. As the patties are cooking, toast the burger buns in a frying pan or under a grill until golden around the edges. Mix the salad leaves with the dressing. Place the bun bases on warmed serving plates and the cooked patties on top. Spoon over a generous layer of tomato chutney, cover with the salad leaves and top with the brioche lids. Serve immediately.

CORNISH FISH STEW WITH GARLIC TOAST AND AÏOLI

This divine dish takes a little time to make, but it is absolutely worth the effort. I think it is a showstopper seafood recipe that is ideal for entertaining. Next time you have friends over, crack open a bottle of Chablis and serve this – it tastes as stunning as it looks!

SERVES 4

2–4 tablespoons olive oil
400g inexpensive fish steaks or trimmings, such as gurnard, hake, pollack, sardines or red mullet
100g small prawns, with shells
1 large fennel bulb, trimmed and chopped
2 banana shallots, peeled and chopped
1 carrot, peeled and chopped
1 celery stalk, trimmed and chopped
1 tablespoon tomato purée
250g plum tomatoes, chopped
1 star anise
a pinch of saffron threads
½ teaspoon cayenne pepper
300ml dry white wine
2 tablespoons Pernod
600ml Brown Fish Stock (see page 218)
600ml Chicken Stock (see page 218)
400g sea bass, cut into 4 pieces
400g cod, cut into 4 pieces
300g halibut, cut into 4 pieces
12 cockles
8 cooked tiger or king prawns, shell on
lemon juice, to taste
sea salt and freshly ground black pepper
½–1 quantity of Aïoli (see page 224), to serve

For the garlic toast
3 garlic cloves, peeled
200g softened butter
8–12 slices of baguette, cut on the diagonal

Heat 2 tablespoons of the oil in a wide, heavy-based pot. Lightly season the fish trimmings and small prawns and fry for 8–10 minutes until golden brown all over. Remove to a plate and set aside. If necessary, add a little more oil to the pan and fry the fennel, shallots, carrot and celery over a high heat. Stir occasionally for 8–10 minutes until they begin to brown. Add the tomato purée to the pan and stir for another minute or two. Add the chopped tomatoes, star anise, saffron and cayenne pepper and cook for another 3–4 minutes. Deglaze the pan with the white wine and Pernod, scraping the bottom of the pan with a wooden spoon to remove any residue and bring to the boil. Boil until the liquid has reduced to a syrupy glaze. Pour in the stocks and bring back to the boil. Continue to boil until the liquid has reduced by a third then stir in the fish and prawns.

To make the garlic bread, preheat the grill until hot. Blanch the garlic in boiling water for 20 seconds. Drain then crush it to a fine paste. Mix with the softened butter then spread this over the baguette slices. Arrange the slices on a baking sheet and grill for 1–2 minutes until lightly toasted.

Carefully blend the liquid in batches, taking care to cover and hold down the lid of the blender with a cloth to avoid scalding yourself. Pass the mixture through a fine sieve into a clean pan, then start to reheat it over a medium heat.

Meanwhile, season the fish pieces on both sides with salt and pepper. Heat a tablespoon of olive oil in a large frying pan and cook the fish pieces in batches until golden on both sides.

Add the cockles to the hot liquid and when they open add the prawns to heat through. Season to taste with lemon juice, salt and pepper.

To serve, divide between 4 bowls and add fish pieces to each. Serve with the garlic toast and aïoli.

MAIN COURSES

PULLED PORK SANDWICHES WITH PICKLED KOHLRABI AND COLESLAW

When we opened Berners Tavern, we decided to have a sandwich section on the menu. My head chef, Phil Carmichael, came up with a great pulled pork sandwich recipe – inspired by his travels in America – which he serves with pickled cucumber, coleslaw and chips. Any leftover pulled pork freezes beautifully and you can add it to burgers, stews, hearty soups and chilli.

SERVES 6–8

½ teaspoon black peppercorns
1 teaspoon fennel seeds
½ teaspoon cumin seeds
½ teaspoon coriander seeds
3½ teaspoons smoked paprika
1 teaspoon garlic powder
20g caster sugar
40g soft dark brown sugar
40g fine sea salt
2.5kg pork shoulder
100ml hot Chicken Stock (see page 218)
6–8 brioche burger buns, halved, to serve

For the pickled kohlrabi
1 kohlrabi
65g caster sugar
65g sea salt
5 cloves
7g yellow mustard seeds
1 star anise
½ cinnamon stick
175ml cider vinegar
125ml water

For the barbecue sauce
4 banana shallots, peeled and chopped
1 head of garlic, cut in half horizontally
1–2 tablespoons olive oil
½ teaspoon black peppercorns
1 tablespoon brown mustard seeds
2 star anise
1 bay leaf
½ tablespoon mixed spice
½ tablespoon smoked sweet paprika
110ml white wine vinegar
115ml pure maple syrup
150ml clear honey

To serve
Coleslaw (see page 225)

First, prepare the pork shoulder. Preheat the oven to 140°C/Gas Mark 1. Toast the peppercorns, fennel, cumin and coriander seeds in a small, dry pan for about a minute or until they begin to release their oils and fragrance. Tip into a small bowl and leave to cool, then blend to a fine powder using a spice (or coffee) blender. Sift the blended spice into a large bowl then add the smoked paprika, garlic powder, sugars and salt.

Evenly coat the pork shoulder with the spice blend, rubbing it well into the meat. Place the pork on a lightly oiled baking tray, pour in the chicken stock, then cover the tray with kitchen foil. Roast slowly for 7–8 hours until the pork is very tender and you can pull it apart effortlessly with a fork. Remove from the oven and leave to cool a little. Pull the pork into shreds with two forks then moisten the meat with the juices in the pan. Taste and adjust the seasoning, as necessary.

For the pickled kohlrabi, peel the kohlrabi and slice thinly, using a mandolin if you have one. Put the kohlrabi slices into a large colander and sprinkle with the sugar and salt. Leave it for an hour, then rinse well under cold running water for about 3–4 minutes. Drain and pat dry with a clean kitchen towel, then place in a large bowl. Meanwhile put all the remaining ingredients into a small saucepan and bring up to the boil. As soon as it boils, remove the pan from the heat and leave to cool and infuse for 20 minutes. Strain the pickling liquid through a fine sieve over the kohrabi slices and toss until evenly coated. Set aside.

To make the barbecue sauce, sweat the shallots and garlic with the olive oil for 6–8 minutes, stirring occasionally, until the shallots are tender. Add the rest of the ingredients and bring to a simmer. Simmer for about 20 minutes, giving the mixture a stir every once in a while, as the sugars may catch and burn at the base of the pan. Pass the sauce through a fine sieve into a saucepan, ready to reheat before serving.

When you are about ready to serve, toast the brioche buns then place the bottom halves on warmed serving plates. Add a layer of pickled kohlrabi, followed by a generous layer of pulled pork, then spoon over some barbecue sauce. Sandwich with the top halves of the buns and serve with the coleslaw on the side.

B.B.L.T. (BELLY, BRIOCHE, LETTUCE AND TOMATO)

Professionally, my name has been synonymous with the B.L.T. ever since I invented my deconstructed bacon, lettuce and tomato dish for Maze, and subsequently featured it on The Great British Menu. *That dish contained all the elements of a good B.L.T. sandwich, minus the bread, and it was served elegantly in layers in a martini glass. This time, however, I wanted to make a proper B.L.T. sandwich in its traditional form but using brioche and pork belly. I think it is the best B.L.T. sandwich you can make.*

SERVES 4

For the pork belly
1–1.5kg pork belly
1 head of garlic, halved horizontally
1 Spanish onion, peeled and halved
½ head of celery, roughly chopped
20 peppercorns
2 bay leaves
a small bunch of thyme

For the bacon soy mayonnaise
250ml vegetable oil
125g smoked streaky bacon, coarsely chopped
1 large egg yolk
½ teaspoon rice wine vinegar
½ teaspoon Dijon mustard
1 tablespoon lemon juice
2 tablespoons light soy sauce

To serve
olive oil
4 brioche burger buns, halved
4 tablespoons Smoked Tomato Chutney (see page 113)
4 crisp Little Gem lettuce leaves

Place all the ingredients for the pork belly in a large pan and pour in enough water to cover the pork by 3–4cm. Bring the liquid to a simmer and skim off any froth or scum that rises to the surface. Once the water is reasonably clear, place a crumpled piece of baking parchment, cut to the diameter of the pan, on top of the pork belly. This will help keep the moisture in the pan during cooking.

Gently simmer the pork belly for 2 hours until it is very tender. There should be no resistance when you pierce it with a knife. Let the belly cool completely in the cooking liquid. Lift it out of the pan and place on a baking tray. Cover with cling film and refrigerate for at least an hour until it has firmed up, which will make it easier to slice. Once firm, remove the pork belly from the refrigerator and cut into individual portions.

While the pork is cooking, make the bacon soy mayonnaise. Heat the oil in a small pan over a low heat. Add the bacon and gently fry until it has rendered all of its fat. Strain the bacon through a fine sieve and reserve the bacon-flavoured oil. Let the oil come to room temperature before you begin to make the mayonnaise or it may split.

Whisk the egg yolk, vinegar and mustard together in a large bowl. Whisking continuously, drizzle the cooled bacon oil slowly into the bowl in a steady stream to create an emulsion. Once all the oil has been incorporated, add the lemon juice and soy sauce, which will thin down the mayonnaise. Taste and adjust the seasoning to taste. Cover the bowl and refrigerate until ready to use.

When you are about ready to serve, remove the thick rind from the pork belly. Heat a thin layer of olive oil in a frying pan. Add the pork belly pieces and fry for about 2 minutes on each side until golden brown and warmed through. Toast the brioche buns and spread some bacon soy mayo on the bottom halves. Arrange a few lettuce leaves on each brioche base, then place pork belly pieces and a generous spoonful of smoked tomato chutney on top. Cover with the brioche lids and serve at once.

BRAISED PORK CHEEKS WITH HONEY, SOY AND CRISP SHALLOTS

Pork cheeks are really good value and I use them quite a lot at my restaurants. They do take a bit of time and effort to trim down, but you can always ask your butcher to do this for you. For this recipe, I'm combining European and Chinese flavours to create a stunning dish full of deep, sweet and savoury notes.

SERVES 4

1kg pork cheeks, trimmed of sinew
2 tablespoons olive oil
1 small onion, peeled and chopped
1 small carrot, peeled and chopped
2 small garlic cloves, peeled and chopped
4 teaspoons sherry vinegar
1 teaspoon tomato purée
1 tablespoon clear honey
2 tablespoons dark soy sauce
400ml Veal Stock (see page 219)
400ml Chicken Stock (see page 218)
1 star anise
a few white peppercorns
sea salt and freshly ground black pepper

For the crisp shallots
2 banana shallots, sliced into rings
40g cornflour
vegetable or groundnut oil, for deep-frying

To serve
1 quantity of Creamy Mashed Potatoes (see page 228)
6 sprigs of thyme

Season the pork cheeks well with salt and pepper. Heat a little of the oil in a wide heavy-based pan and then fry the pork cheeks over a medium–high heat for 2 minutes on each side, until golden brown. Remove the pork cheeks to a plate and set aside.

Add the remaining oil to the pan and tip in the onion, carrot and garlic. Fry, stirring frequently, for 6–8 minutes until they begin to soften. Add the vinegar and stir well. Once the vinegar has cooked off, stir in the tomato purée, honey and soy sauce. Keep stirring, frequently, for a couple of minutes. Pour in the stocks and add the star anise and peppercorns. Return the pork cheeks to the pan and give the mixture another stir. If the stock does not cover all the ingredients, top up with a little water. Partially cover the pan with a lid and turn the heat down low. Slowly simmer for 2½–3 hours, until the meat is tender.

Meanwhile, make the crisp shallots. Heat the oil in a deep saucepan (or deep-fat fryer) until it reaches 160°C. You can also check it's hot enough by throwing in a piece of shallot – it should sizzle but shouldn't burn. Coat the shallot rings with the cornflour. Shake off any excess and fry the shallot rings in batches until evenly golden brown, turning them halfway. Make sure you don't crowd the pan, otherwise you'll reduce the temperature of the oil and the shallots won't crisp. Remove from the oil with a slotted spoon and drain on a tray lined with kitchen paper. Sprinkle with a little salt and continue to fry the rest of the shallots. Keep warm in a low oven until you are ready to serve. Using the same oil, drop the thyme sprigs into the oil for 5 seconds, remove and drain on kitchen paper.

Remove the pork cheeks from the pan and leave to cool. Strain the sauce through a fine sieve into a clean saucepan, pressing down on the vegetables to extract all the juice. Boil the sauce until it has reduced to a syrupy glaze. Reheat the pork cheeks in the sauce before serving with the crisp shallots, thyme and creamy mashed potatoes.

MAIN COURSES

PORK CHEEKS WITH SOFT POLENTA AND APPLE

This is a dish I invented for the lunch menu at Pollen Street Social. Cheek is a really flavoursome cut of meat. Get your butcher to trim the fat away and you'll end up with an excellent cut of pork. At the restaurant, we serve the braised cheek with soft polenta spiked with small pieces of raw chopped apple. The apple provides a surprise element – as you wouldn't expect to find a tangy crunch in the midst of the creamy polenta – but it is wonderful with the braised pork.

SERVES 4

1kg pork cheeks, trimmed of any sinew
1–2 tablespoons olive oil
1 small onion, peeled and chopped
1 small carrot, peeled and chopped
3 garlic cloves, peeled and chopped
3 tablespoons tomato purée
1 tablespoon clear honey
50ml sherry vinegar
1 star anise
½ teaspoon white peppercorns
500ml Veal Stock (see page 219)
500ml Chicken Stock (see page 218)

For the polenta
500ml whole milk
500ml Chicken Stock (see page 218)
a few sprigs of thyme, leaves only
175g polenta
50g unsalted butter
50g grated Parmesan
1 Granny Smith apple
sea salt and freshly ground black pepper

For the cabbage
25g unsalted butter
1 Hispi or pointed spring cabbage, tough outer leaves removed (use these to make Cabbage and Mint Pesto, see page 152, if you wish), quartered, cored and thinly sliced

Rub the pork all over with a little salt and pepper. Heat a little of the olive oil in a wide, heavy-based pan over a medium–high heat. Fry the pork for 2 minutes on each side until evenly golden brown all over. Remove from the pan and set aside.

Add a little more oil to the pan, if necessary, then add the onion, carrot and garlic. Stir well and sauté for 6–8 minutes until the vegetables begin to soften. Add the tomato purée and honey and stir-fry for another 1–2 minutes until the vegetables are golden brown. Tip in the sherry vinegar and let the liquid boil and reduce by half. Add the star anise, peppercorns and stocks. Bring the liquid to a simmer and skim off any froth and scum that rise to the surface. Return the pork to the pan, making sure the meat is submerged in the stock. If not, top up with a little boiling water. Partially cover the pan with a lid and gently simmer for 3 hours until the pork is tender. Leave the pork to cool in the stock.

To finish off the pork, once cool remove the meat from the pan and set aside. Strain the braising stock through a fine sieve into a clean heavy-based saucepan, pushing down on the vegetables to extract all the liquid. Boil the strained stock until reduced to a syrupy sauce consistency. Taste and adjust the seasoning. Warm the pork in the sauce before serving.

For the polenta, put the milk and stock in a heavy-based saucepan and bring to a simmer. Add the thyme leaves and gradually whisk in the polenta. Slowly simmer the polenta, stirring frequently, for 15–20 minutes until it is soft and creamy. Stir in the butter and Parmesan and season well with salt and pepper, to taste. Cover the pan and turn off the heat. Peel, core and finely dice the apple then stir this into the creamy polenta. Keep warm until ready to serve.

For the cabbage, melt the butter in a large heavy-based pan over a medium–high heat. As the butter begins to foam, stir in the cabbage, some seasoning and a small splash of water. Cover the pan with a lid and let the cabbage steam for a few minutes. Take off the lid and stir the cabbage over a high heat for a couple of minutes until the cabbage is just tender. Serve the braised pork with the soft polenta and cabbage while still hot.

BRAISED PORK BELLY WITH CHORIZO AND PEPPER PURÉE AND SPICED ONIONS

This is another dish inspired by my time in Spain. Here I'm pairing pork belly with the typical Spanish ingredients of chorizo, peppers and onions. The braised belly is delicious on its own, but it is excellent with the spiced purée.

SERVES 6–8

For the braised pork
2kg boneless pork belly, with skin, unscored
1–2 tablespoons olive oil
2 onions, chopped
2 celery stalks, trimmed and sliced
2 carrots, peeled and chopped
1 head of garlic, cut in half horizontally
1 leek, trimmed and sliced
2 bay leaves
a handful of thyme
a handful of rosemary
3 star anise
125ml soy sauce
375ml dry white wine
500ml Chicken Stock (see page 218)
500ml Veal Stock (see page 219)
10 black peppercorns, crushed
a pinch of rock salt
sea salt and freshly ground black pepper

For the pepper and chorizo purée
1½ tablespoons olive oil
2 small shallots, peeled and chopped
1 garlic clove, peeled and chopped
1 cooking chorizo sausage, sliced
a few sprigs of thyme
2 x 300ml jar roasted piquillo peppers, drained

For the spiced onions
60g unsalted butter
60ml olive oil
6 onions, sliced
1 teaspoon finely chopped garlic
1 teaspoon thyme leaves
½ teaspoon cayenne pepper
½ teaspoon sea salt
½ teaspoon freshly ground black pepper

Preheat the oven to 140°C/Gas Mark 1. Rub the flesh of the pork belly with a little salt and pepper. Heat 1 tablespoon of oil in a wide ovenproof pan until hot. Fry the pork belly for about 3–5 minutes on each side until golden brown all over. Remove to a plate and set aside.

Add a little more oil to the pan and tip in the vegetables, herbs and star anise. Stir well and fry the vegetables over a medium–high heat for about 6–8 minutes, until they begin to colour. Add the soy sauce and let it boil until reduced by half. Pour in the white wine and bring back to the boil. As with the soy sauce, boil the wine until it has reduced by half. Return the pork belly to the pan and add the chicken and veal stocks. If the stocks do not cover the pork belly, top up the liquid level with boiling water. Simmer the stocks for a few minutes and skim off any froth or scum that rise to the surface. Add the peppercorns and a pinch of rock salt then cover the pork belly with a dampened piece of baking parchment. Place the pan in the oven and let the pork braise for about 2–2½ hours until the meat is tender.

To make the pepper and chorizo purée, heat a heavy-based pan with the olive oil. Add the shallots, garlic and a pinch each of salt and pepper, and stir well. Sweat them over a low–medium heat for 6–8 minutes until the shallots begin to soften. Add the chorizo and increase the heat slightly. Sauté for 4–5 minutes, stirring occasionally, then add the thyme and piquillo peppers.

Give the mixture a stir and cook for another 4–6 minutes until all the vegetables are soft. Carefully transfer the mixture to a food processor or blender and blend until smooth. If you wish, pass the sauce through a fine sieve into a clean saucepan, ready to reheat before serving.

For the spiced onions, heat the butter and oil in a heavy-based pan. Add the onions and the rest of the ingredients and stir well. Sweat the onions over a low–medium heat for 10–12 minutes, stirring frequently, until they are soft and translucent, then turn off the heat. Warm the onions through gently when you are ready to serve.

When the pork is ready, remove the pan from the oven and discard the baking parchment. Lift out the pork belly, reserving the stock, and place it on a large baking tray. Put a smaller baking tray on top and weigh it down with a can of baked beans or a bag of rice. Press and chill the belly in the refrigerator for about 2 hours. Strain the stock into a clean saucepan and boil it until reduced to a syrupy sauce consistency. Taste and adjust the seasoning, if necessary.

To finish the pork belly, cut it into individual portions and pat dry with kitchen paper. Heat a little oil in a wide frying pan over a medium–high heat and sear the pork belly pieces, skin side down, for about 2–3 minutes, until golden brown and crisp. Turn over to brown the other side. Finally, add the sauce to the pan to reheat, making sure the flesh of the pork belly is coated with the syrupy sauce. Serve immediately with the warm pepper and chorizo purée and spiced onions.

SOCIAL SUPPERS

SLOW-ROASTED PORK BELLY WITH BLACK PUDDING, CRUSHED POTATOES AND GREEN BEANS

The belly is one of my favourite cuts of pork because I love the alternating layers of fat and meat. During slow roasting, the flavoursome fat melts and bastes the meat, leaving you with a really tender and succulent piece of pork. This dish, with all its components, is a great option for a Sunday roast.

SERVES 4–6

For the pork belly
1kg boneless pork belly, with rind
sea salt and freshly ground black pepper

For the crushed new potatoes
500g new potatoes, scrubbed
5 pitted black olives, diced
2 ripe plum tomatoes, peeled, deseeded and diced
50ml olive oil
½ tablespoon chopped basil
½ tablespoon chopped chervil
½ tablespoon chopped chives

For the green beans and black pudding
300g green beans, topped and tailed
100g smoked streaky bacon, diced
100g black pudding, cut into 5mm dice
1 tablespoon wholegrain mustard
50g unsalted butter, diced

Preheat the oven to 160°C/Gas Mark 3 and place a wire rack on to a roasting tray. If the pork belly is tied, unroll it on to a chopping board with the boned side upwards. Rub the meat with a pinch of salt and pepper. Turn the pork belly over and place it on the wire rack, rind side up. Pat the rind with kitchen paper, then pop the roasting tray into the oven. Roast for about 3 hours until the meat is tender and the rind has become golden and crisp. If the skin isn't completely crisp everywhere, place under a hot grill for 5 minutes or until all the skin is evenly crisp. Remove and leave to rest in a warm spot.

Cook the potatoes 20 minutes before the pork is ready. Place the potatoes in a deep pan and cover with cold water. Add a generous pinch of salt and bring the water to the boil. Cook for 10–15 minutes until the potatoes are tender. There should be little resistance when you pierce them with a small knife. Drain the potatoes and tip them into a large bowl. While they are still hot, roughly crush the potatoes with a fork or a potato masher. Season to taste with salt and pepper then add the olives, tomatoes, olive oil and chopped herbs. Toss to mix. Keep warm or reheat gently just before serving.

Bring a pan of salted water to the boil and have ready a bowl of iced water. Add the beans and boil them for 3–5 minutes until they are just tender but still green and vibrant. Drain and immediately refresh in the iced water to stop the cooking process. Drain again once the beans have cooled and place in a bowl.

Fry the bacon in a hot, non-stick frying pan for 5–8 minutes until evenly golden brown and crisp. Tip the crisp bacon on to a plate lined with kitchen paper to absorb the excess fat. Carefully wipe the pan clean with kitchen paper then return to the heat. Add a little oil if necessary and fry the black pudding for about 2 minutes on each side until crisp around the edges. Remove from the heat.

Put the mustard into a small saucepan with 3 tablespoons of boiling water. Heat until the mixture starts to simmer then gradually whisk in the diced butter. You should get a shiny sauce flecked with mustard seeds. Season to taste. Just before you are ready to serve, put the blanched beans and a third of the bacon into the pan and toss with the mustard sauce to reheat.

Slice the pork belly and divide between warmed plates. Serve on top of the crushed potatoes, with the green beans, bacon and black pudding. If there is any leftover sauce (or pan juices), spoon this over the pork and serve immediately.

TAMARIND-GLAZED PORK BELLY WITH BRAISED RED CABBAGE AND SAUTÉED MUSHROOMS

This is a lovely autumnal dish, especially if you serve the braised pork belly with wild mushrooms. After spending a lot of time in Asia, I've been using a lot more tamarind in my cooking. I love the natural sourness it provides, which is perfect for countering the richness of pork belly.

SERVES 4–6

2 tablespoons coarse sea salt
½ teaspoon garlic powder
a few sprigs of thyme, leaves only
1–1.5kg boneless and rindless pork belly
3 garlic cloves, peeled and chopped
2 teaspoons ground ginger
2 tablespoons coriander seeds

For the braised red cabbage

1 red cabbage (700–800g), cored and finely shredded
25g unsalted butter
100ml Cabernet Sauvignon vinegar (or other red wine vinegar)
300ml red wine
175ml port
60–75g caster sugar, to taste

For the tamarind glaze

30g tamarind pulp, soaked in 140ml warm water for 20 minutes
1½ teaspoon coriander seeds
50g palm sugar, grated if hard (or soft brown sugar)
2 tablespoons light soy sauce
2½ tablespoons oyster sauce
½ teaspoon ground white pepper
½ teaspoon ground black pepper

For the sautéed mushrooms

250g chestnut or wild mushrooms, cleaned and sliced
20g unsalted butter
2 tablespoons Cabernet Sauvignon vinegar (or red wine vinegar)
a splash of double cream

For the pork belly, mix the salt, garlic powder and thyme together in a bowl then rub this all over the pork belly. Put the pork on a baking tray, cover with foil and leave to cure in the refrigerator for a couple of hours.

Preheat the oven to 180°C/Gas Mark 4. Wash the salt cure off the pork belly and pat dry with kitchen paper. Place on a clean, lightly oiled baking tray. Grind the garlic, ginger and coriander together using a pestle and mortar then rub this paste all over the pork belly. Add a splash of water to the baking tray then cover it with foil and put it into the oven. Roast the pork for about 3 hours or until tender.

Remove the pork from the oven and leave to cool slightly. While it is still warm, place a small tray on top of the pork and weigh it down with a few heavy cans to flatten it. Cool completely, then chill for 4 hours (or overnight) in the refrigerator to set its shape.

For the red cabbage, melt the butter in a heavy-based pan then add the shredded cabbage and the rest of the ingredients. Cover the pan and gently simmer over the lowest heat for 1–1½ hours, stirring occasionally until the cabbage is tender. Season well to taste.

To prepare the tamarind glaze, rub the tamarind and its soaking water through a sieve set over a bowl to remove any seeds. Toast the coriander seeds in a dry frying pan over a medium–high heat for 1–2 minutes, until golden brown and aromatic. Tip them into a mortar and crush to a powder with the pestle then add to the tamarind. Mix in all of the remaining marinade ingredients.

For the mushrooms, melt the butter in a wide frying pan then tip in the sliced mushrooms. Add a little seasoning and fry over a high heat, tossing occasionally, until the mushrooms are golden brown and any moisture from the mushrooms has cooked off. Add the vinegar and a splash of cream and let the liquid boil until reduced by half. Taste and adjust the seasoning. Remove to a plate and keep warm.

To finish cooking the pork belly, preheat the grill to a medium–high setting. Remove the weights from the pork then cut the meat into neat portions. Put the pork belly pieces on a lightly oiled baking tray or a casserole dish and then spoon the tamarind glaze over each piece. If necessary, turn the pieces of pork in the glaze so they are evenly coated all over. Grill for about 10 minutes, basting every couple of minutes, until the pork belly pieces are nicely glazed and heated through. Remove from the heat.

To serve, place neat piles of braised cabbage on warmed serving plates then rest the glazed pork belly pieces alongside. Add the sautéed mushrooms and, if you wish, drizzle over any remaining tamarind glaze from the tray. Serve immediately.

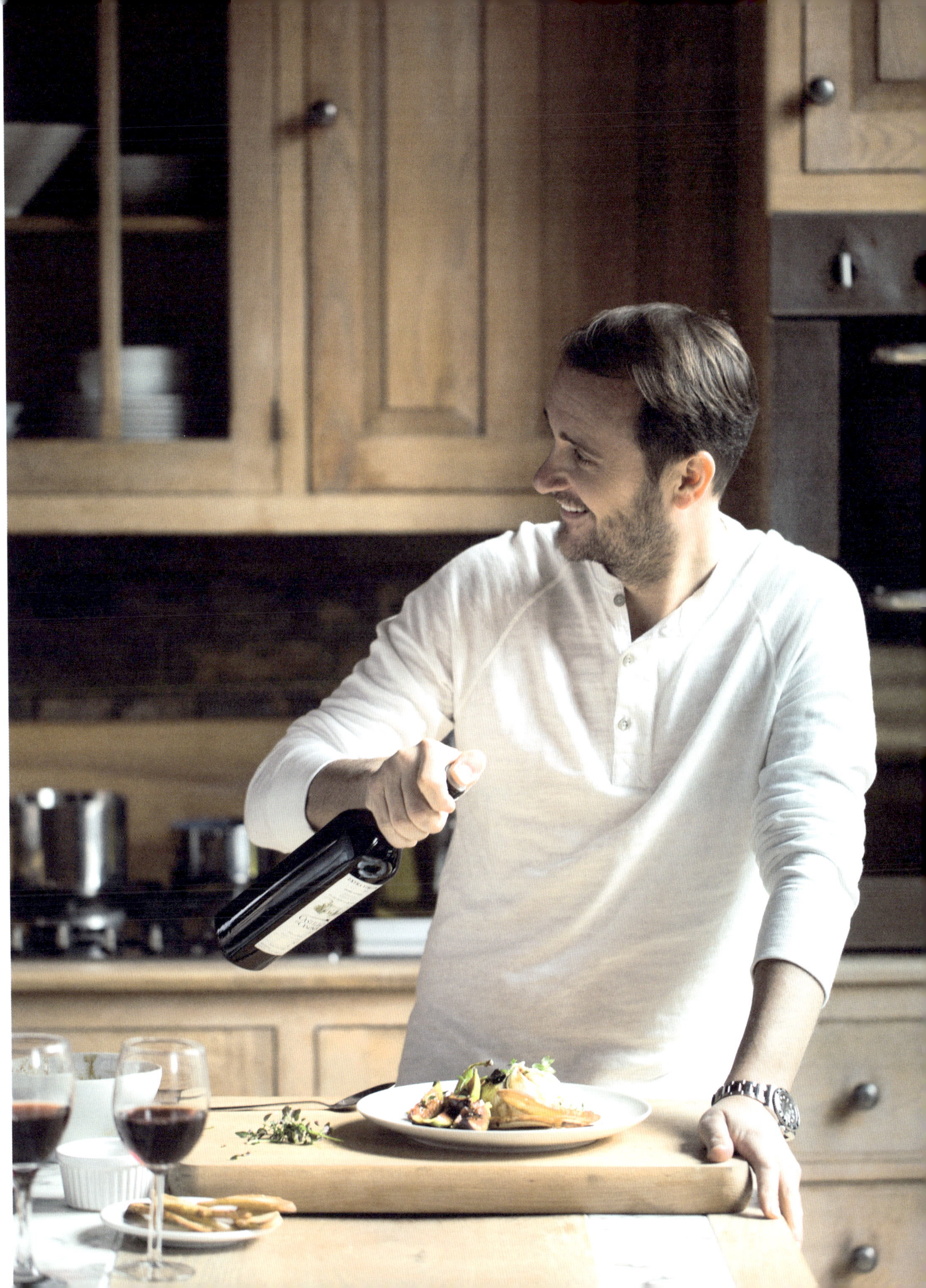

HONEY-ROAST HAM HOCK WITH CRISP PIG'S EARS, BLACK PUDDING AND PICCALILLI

I really support the concept of nose-to-tail eating and this recipe shows that you can take a traditional dish such as roast ham and give it a modern twist by using ham hocks and pig's ears. In a way, the hock is better for making ham because the meat is cooked on the bone, keeping it flavourful and succulent.

SERVES 6

2 small ham hocks, about 2kg in total
1 large onion, roughly chopped
1 large carrot, peeled and roughly chopped
1 leek, trimmed and roughly chopped
1 celery stalk, trimmed and roughly chopped
4 garlic cloves, peeled
a sprig of thyme
6 white peppercorns

For the ham glaze

40g English mustard
40g Dijon mustard
1 tablespoon clear honey
100g demerara sugar
10 cloves
10 rosemary needles

For the crisp pig ears

8 pig's ears
2 tablespoons olive oil, plus extra for frying
1 carrot, chopped into large chunks
1 leek, chopped into large chunks
1 onion, cut into quarters
1 head of garlic, halved lengthways
a small bunch of thyme
a small bunch of rosemary
2 bay leaves
10 black peppercorns
10 Szechuan peppercorns
250ml dry white wine
250ml sherry vinegar
125ml soy sauce
750ml Veal Stock (see page 219)
500ml Chicken Stock (see page 218)
plain flour, for frying
olive oil, for frying

To serve

1–2 tablespoons olive oil
4–6 slices of black pudding
300g Piccalilli (see page 227)

Start by preparing the pig's ears. Use a blowtorch to singe any hairs from the ears. Set aside. Heat the olive oil in a wide heavy-based pan over medium–high heat. Add the carrot, leek, onion and garlic to the pan and fry for 8–10 minutes, stirring occasionally, until the vegetables are golden brown. Add the herbs and spices and pour in the wine. Boil the wine until it has reduced down and the pan is almost dry. Add the vinegar and bring back to the boil. Again, boil the vinegar until it has cooked off and the pan is virtually dry. Pour in the soy sauce and stocks. Add the pig's ears to the pan and top up with water if the liquid does not cover the ears. Gently simmer for 1–2 hours until the pig's ears are tender. Remove the pan from the heat and leave to cool completely.

Lift the pig's ears out of the pan. Pick out the large pieces of the cartilage from the base of each ear, trying to keep the ear as whole as possible. Put the ears in a single layer in one or two resealable bags, then sandwich them between two baking trays. Place a heavy pan or a few cans on top of the tray to press and weigh it down. Place the trays and weights in the refrigerator and chill for at least 8 hours, preferably overnight.

Rinse the ham hocks well under cold running water then place them in a pot. Add the chopped vegetables, garlic, thyme and peppercorns then pour in enough water to cover the meat. Bring to the boil, then skim off any froth or scum from the surface of the liquid. Simmer, partially covered, for 3–5 hours until the ham hocks are very tender and the meat slides away from the bone easily.

When the ham hocks are ready, preheat the oven to 190°C/Gas Mark 5. Leave the hocks to cool slightly in the liquid until they are cool enough to handle. Peel off and discard the skins, leaving a thin, even covering of fat on each hock. (Save the stock to make pea and ham soup, if you wish.) Mix together the mustards, honey and demerara sugar for the glaze. Place the ham hocks on a roasting tray then spread each one with the glaze. Stud the glazed hocks with the cloves and rosemary needles. Roast in the hot oven for 15–20 minutes, basting frequently with the glaze, until the ham hocks are golden brown. Remove from the oven and leave to rest for about 5 minutes.

While the ham is roasting, cook the pig's ears and the black pudding. Remove the pig's ears from their bag and finely slice them into long matchsticks. Dip the pig's ear strips in the flour, coat them well and shake off any excess flour. Heat a little olive oil in a large frying pan and fry the strips in batches for 5–8 minutes until they are golden brown and crisp. Drain on kitchen paper while you fry the remaining batches (it will be about 8–10 batches).

For the black pudding, heat the oil in a frying pan over a medium heat. Add the black pudding slices and fry for 6–10 minutes, turning halfway, until the slices are golden brown and crisp. Serve with the glazed ham hocks, crisp pig's ears and piccalilli.

MAIN COURSES

SOCIAL SUPPERS

PORK SHANKS WITH HARICOT BEANS

I love the shank of any animal, be it beef, pork or lamb. This pork shank osso bucco is an ideal dish to serve a crowd or a family gathering. It looks really impressive if you bring the shanks and haricot beans to the table spread out on a large platter (as shown). Encourage your guests to have a bit of fun, tucking into the meal medieval-style.

SERVES 4

1 tablespoon vegetable oil
4 pork shanks, about 2kg in total
1 large onion, peeled and quartered
1 large carrot, peeled and chopped
1 celery stalk, trimmed and chopped
½ small fennel bulb, trimmed and chopped
1 head of garlic, cut in half horizontally
2 bay leaves
2 sprigs of rosemary
2 litres Veal Stock (see page 219)
2 tablespoons unsalted butter
sea salt and freshly ground black pepper

For the haricot beans

125g dried haricot beans (or butter beans), soaked overnight in plenty of cold water
6 sprigs of rosemary
6 sprigs of thyme
7 baby turnips, peeled
170g baby carrots, scrubbed and trimmed
12 pearl onions, peeled

Preheat the oven to 150°C/Gas Mark 2. Tie each shank with butcher's string in order that they hold their shape while cooking. Heat the oil in a wide heavy-based pan over a medium–high heat. Generously season the pork shanks all over, then place in the pan and sear the sides for 8–10 minutes until golden brown all over. Remove the meat from the pan and set aside.

Add the onion, carrot, celery and fennel to the hot pan with a generous pinch of salt. Sweat the vegetables for 8–10 minutes, stirring occasionally, until they are tender. Return the shanks to the pan and add the garlic, bay leaves and rosemary. Now add the veal stock to cover the meat. Cover the pan with a lid then place it into the oven and braise for 3–3 ½ hours until the pork is tender. Remove the pan from the oven and let the pork shanks cool in their braising stock.

Cook the beans while the pork shanks are in the oven. Drain the beans and place them in a large pan or pot. Add half the rosemary and thyme sprigs and cover the beans with cold water. Bring to a simmer and gently cook for around 45 minutes until the beans are soft. You may need to top up the water level halfway through cooking. When ready, drain the beans and discard the herb sprigs. Put the beans into a clean pan and season with salt and pepper.

Once cooled, transfer the pork shanks to a plate and then strain the braising stock through a fine sieve into a clean saucepan, pressing down on the vegetables to extract all the juices. Boil over a high heat until the stock has thickened slightly and reduced by half. Season to taste with salt and pepper. Divide the stock between two pans. Reduce the stock in one pan until it is a very thick and syrupy glaze and keep warm.

To the other pan, add the remaining sprigs of rosemary and thyme along with the baby turnips, carrots and pearl onions. Gently cook the vegetables for about 10 minutes until just tender. Return the beans to the pan to warm them through.

Melt the butter in a large pan, add the shanks and toss to coat, then leave until heated through and golden all over. Add 2 tablespoons of the syrupy stock to glaze the shanks.

To serve, place the beans and braised vegetables in a large serving dish. Place the pork shanks on top and then spoon over the glaze. Serve while still hot.

PORK CHOPS WITH HARICOT BEANS AND SPICY TOMATO SAUCE

As a boy I used to hate pork chops because my mother would overcook them and they ended up dry and tasteless. Worst of all, I used to get stringy bits stuck in my teeth. I now have a fantastic method to keep the chops moist and succulent. To start, ask your butcher for good-quality pork chops, preferably from happy, free-range pigs, then brine the chops for four hours. The brining process not only tenderises the pork but also reduces the strong porky smell that may put some people off. It is also important to rest the chops after cooking to allow the juices to redistribute throughout the meat.

SERVES 4

4 pork chops (about 180g each)
olive oil
200ml Spicy Tomato Sauce (see page 226)

For the aromatic brine
80g clear honey
12 bay leaves
3 sprigs of rosemary
small handful of thyme
small bunch of flat-leaf parsley
2 heads of garlic, halved horizontally
2 tablespoons crushed black peppercorns
140g sea salt
1.2 litres water

For the haricot beans
250g dried haricot beans, soaked overnight
½ leek, trimmed and chopped
3 sprigs of thyme
3 garlic cloves, finely chopped
1 celery stalk, trimmed and chopped
1 small carrot, peeled and chopped
1 small onion, peeled and chopped
sea salt and freshly ground black pepper

First, marinate the pork chops. Put all the ingredients for the brine into a stockpot and bring to the boil, stirring initially to dissolve the salt. Boil for a few minutes, then turn off the heat and leave to cool slightly, then strain the brine through a fine sieve and discard the aromatics. Put the pork chops into a large container (or bowl) and pour over enough brine to cover. Cover the container and refrigerate for 4 hours.

Drain the haricot beans and put them into a saucepan along with the rest of the ingredients. Pour in enough water to cover the ingredients by 5–6cm then bring to a simmer. Don't salt the water at this stage; otherwise the beans can become tough. Gently simmer for 30 minutes–1 hour, until the beans are soft. Season well with salt and pepper and leave the beans to cool in their liquid.

When ready to serve, preheat the oven grill or a griddle pan until hot. Pat the pork chops dry with kitchen paper, then brush with a little olive oil. Cook them under the grill or griddle them for 2–3 minutes on each side until cooked through. Rest the meat for a few minutes. Meanwhile drain the beans, place in a pan with the spicy tomato sauce and heat through. Serve with the pork chops.

'SPANISH-STYLE' ROAST SUCKLING PIG WITH CANDIED PINEAPPLE AND ROAST PEPPERS

Suckling pig is a celebratory dish that is very popular in Spain and many Spanish-speaking countries. Generally in the UK, we're warming up to the idea of eating suckling pig, thanks to the efforts of chefs such as Fergus Henderson. When you have guests over, I can't think of anything more impressive than bringing a beautifully burnished suckling pig to the table. In the UK, the piglets are generally more mature (and subsequently bigger) than the suckling pigs sold on the Continent. When you order one, do check that it will fit comfortably in your oven. You may need to carve it in half if it is too large. I'm serving my piglet with roast peppers and candied pineapples, which is a step up from the usual apple sauce.

SERVES 8–10

1 oven-ready whole suckling pig, about 5–7kg (make sure it fits in your oven)
olive oil, to drizzle
fine sea salt

For the pork jus
a knob of butter
375g pork trimmings (ask your butcher for these)
2 banana shallots, peeled and chopped
½ head of garlic, cloves halved
a small bunch of thyme
2 bay leaves
½ teaspoon white peppercorns
½ teaspoon rock salt
a splash of Armagnac
375ml Marsala
375ml dry white wine
1 litre Chicken Stock (see page 218)
1 litre Veal Stock (see page 219)

For the roast peppers and candied pineapple
180g caster sugar
30ml cold water
4 piquillo peppers, deseeded and split in half
15 thin slices of fresh ginger
2 cinnamon sticks
5 allspice berries, lightly crushed
4 fresh baby pineapples
4 vanilla pods
a large knob of butter

First, prepare the peppers. Put the sugar into a clean heavy-based pan and place over a high heat. Without stirring, let the sugar melt into a caramel. As it melts around the edges, swirl the pan slightly to even out the caramel. When the caramel has turned a deep amber colour, pour in the cold water to stop the caramelisation. Some of the caramel may harden upon contact with the cold water. Stir over a medium heat until it dissolves again. Add the peppers to the caramel along with the ginger, cinnamon and allspice berries. Leave to cool then pour the caramel and spices into a jar, seal and chill overnight to allow the flavours plenty of time to infuse.

Remove the suckling pig from the refrigerator 1–2 hours before cooking to allow it to come to room temperature. Preheat the oven to 140°C/Gas Mark 1. Place the pig on a large baking tray so that it is lying upright. Drizzle with olive oil and generously cover it with fine salt. Rub in the salt thoroughly. Leave the pig for a few minutes as the salt will gradually draw out moisture from the skin.

Dab away the moisture with kitchen paper, then cover the delicate ears and tail with a double layer of kitchen foil. Pop the tray on to the middle shelf of the oven and leave for 4½–5½ hours until the meat is very tender.

To make the pork jus, melt the butter in a heavy-based pan and add the pork trimmings and a pinch of salt. Fry the trimmings for 4–6 minutes, turning over halfway, until they are evenly golden brown. Transfer to a plate and set aside. Add the shallots, garlic, herbs, peppercorns and rock salt to the pan and fry, stirring occasionally, until the shallots are golden brown. Deglaze the pan with the Armagnac and Marsala, scraping the base of the pan with a wooden spoon to loosen any browned bits. Boil the liquid until reduced to a syrupy consistency. Pour in the white wine and boil until the combined liquid has once again reduced to a syrupy texture. Add the stocks and bring to a simmer. Skim off any scum and froth that rise to the surface then simmer for about 45 minutes. Taste and adjust the seasoning with salt then strain the jus through a fine sieve into a clean saucepan. If you find the jus too thin, boil it until reduced to a syrupy sauce consistency. Reheat just before serving.

Cut the skins off the pineapples and trim off any remaining brown eyes. Cut the vanilla pods in half lengthways. Using a metal skewer, pierce a hole through the width of each pineapple – wide enough for the vanilla pods to fit in the hole. Melt the butter in a heavy-based pan. Add the pineapples and fry on each side for about 2 minutes until evenly golden brown all over. Remove the pineapples from the pan and set them aside.

When the suckling pig is tender, remove from the oven and cover it loosely with foil.

(continued on page 133)

SOCIAL SUPPERS

(continued from page 131)

Increase the oven temperature to 230°C/Gas Mark 8. Lay the pineapples sideways in a large ovenproof dish then pour the caramel sauce over them, adding the piquillo peppers around the pineapples. Roast the pineapples on the lower oven shelf for about 1 hour, turning them regularly to baste and evenly glaze with the caramel. As you baste the pineapples, add a splash of hot water to the caramel if necessary, as you do not want it to dry out and burn. (If you've added too much water to the caramel and it becomes too thin, it can be boiled down until reduced to a syrupy consistency once the pineapples are ready.)

After the suckling pig has rested for about 15–20 minutes, remove the foil and rub off the salt from the skin with kitchen paper. Place the pig on a clean tray and on the top or middle shelf of the hot oven to crisp up the skin. This should take about 15–20 minutes. Cut the pineapples in half or into quarters, removing the vanilla pod. Carve the roast pig and arrange it on a warmed platter or bring it whole to the table and serve with the pork jus, candied pineapples and roast piquillo peppers.

MAIN COURSES

CHARGRILLED RIB-EYE STEAKS WITH CHIMICHURRI SAUCE

I just love the honesty of a simple grilled steak, served with a no-fuss Argentinian chimichurri sauce. The success of this dish lies in the quality of the meat, so be sure to get a really good rib-eye steak from your butcher and don't forget to let the meat rest after grilling. Serve with chunky chips or a watercress and tomato salad.

SERVES 4

4 x thick rib-eye steaks (about 250g each)
250ml olive oil
2–3 garlic cloves, peeled and finely chopped
1 green chilli, trimmed and finely sliced
sea salt and freshly ground black pepper
1 quantity of Chunky Chips (see page 228), to serve

For the chimichurri sauce
125g shallots (about 6), peeled and finely chopped
5 garlic cloves, peeled and finely chopped
2 tablespoons sherry vinegar
1 tablespoon Tabasco sauce, or to taste
½ tablespoon wasabi paste, or to taste
a pinch of caster sugar, to taste
2 jalapeño peppers, finely chopped
60g flat-leaf parsley, leaves only, finely chopped
small bunch of chives, finely chopped
small handful of thyme, leaves only

Put the steaks into a wide, non-metallic bowl, and marinate with the olive oil, garlic and chilli. Cover the bowl with cling film and chill for at least 30 minutes, preferably overnight. Remove the steaks from the refrigerator at least 15 minutes before cooking so that they can come to room temperature.

Make the chimichurri sauce shortly before serving, as the herbs will discolour with time. Place the shallot in a sieve and rinse with cold running water (this will help to remove the harsh flavour). Drain and pat dry with kitchen paper. Transfer to a bowl and mix with all the remaining ingredients. Season to taste with salt and pepper.

Preheat a charcoal grill; or, if cooking indoors, heat a griddle pan until hot. Scrape off the excess oil, garlic and chilli from the steaks and season with salt and pepper on both sides. Sear the steaks for 2–3 minutes on each side, depending on thickness, until browned and medium-rare (they will continue cooking as they rest). If your griddle pan is not wide enough, cook the steaks in batches to avoid overcrowding the pan. Leave the steaks to rest in a warm place for 8–10 minutes. Slice the steaks on the diagonal and serve on warm plates with the chimichurri sauce and chips.

MAIN COURSES

SOCIAL SUPPERS

GARLIC HERB BEEF WITH KOHLRABI REMOULADE AND WATERCRESS

Flank steak is very popular in America where you can find it on every steakhouse menu. My kohlrabi remoulade is a scrumptious take on the classic version using celeriac. Kohlrabi may look like something out of a Star Trek movie, but flavourwise it has attributes similar to those of celeriac and turnip. I think it is underrated and I try to incorporate it in my cooking as much as possible.

SERVES 4

4 x 200g bavette or flank steaks
4 garlic cloves, peeled and finely chopped
a few sprigs of thyme, leaves only, chopped
a few sprigs of rosemary, leaves only, chopped
a few sprigs of oregano, leaves only, chopped
2 tablespoons coarsely ground black pepper
sea salt
a drizzle of olive oil

For the beef jus vinaigrette
2 tablespoons olive oil
a knob of butter
175g beef trimmings (ask your butcher for these)
1 banana shallot (or 2 or 3 regular shallots), peeled and chopped
4 garlic cloves, lightly crushed
a few sprigs of thyme
2 bay leaves
¼ teaspoon white peppercorns
185ml port
500ml red wine
500ml Chicken Stock (see page 218)
500ml Veal Stock (see page 219)

For the kohlrabi remoulade
1 medium kohlrabi
juice of ½ lemon, plus a little extra to soak the kohlrabi
3 tablespoons good-quality mayonnaise
1 teaspoon Dijon mustard
1 garlic clove, peeled and crushed

For the watercress salad
75g watercress, leaves only
50ml Basic Vinaigrette (see page 222)

Put the steaks in a wide, shallow dish. Mix together the garlic, herbs, pepper and a pinch of salt. Rub this mixture all over the steaks, cover the dish with cling film and leave to marinate in the refrigerator for at least an hour, preferably overnight. Remove from the refrigerator and let the steaks come to room temperature half an hour before cooking.

For the beef jus vinaigrette, heat the oil and butter in a heavy-based pan over a medium high heat. Season the beef trimmings with salt and pepper then add to the hot pan. Fry for 4–5 minutes, turning over halfway, until the trimmings are golden brown (do this in 2 batches if your pan is not very wide to avoid overcrowding the pan and stewing the beef). Transfer to a plate and set aside.

Add the shallot, garlic, herbs and peppercorns to the pan. Stir and fry for another 4–6 minutes until the shallots are lightly golden, stirring every once in a while. Return the beef trimmings to the pan and pour in the port and red wine. Bring to a boil and let the liquid bubble until reduced by half. Add the chicken and veal stocks and return to a simmer. Reduce the heat slightly and simmer the sauce for 30 minutes until reduced by half. As the sauce is simmering, skim off any froth and scum that rise to the surface of the liquid. Strain the sauce through a fine sieve into a clean saucepan, pressing down on the vegetables to extract as much juice as possible. Boil the sauce until reduced to a syrupy consistency. Taste and adjust the seasoning with salt and pepper. Reheat just before serving.

Peel the kohlrabi, cut into thin slices, then cut the slices into fine matchsticks. Place in a bowl of cold water with a little lemon juice to prevent the kohlrabi from browning. In a small bowl, whisk together the mayonnaise, mustard, garlic and lemon juice, adding salt and pepper to taste. Drain the kohlrabi well then toss with the dressing.

When you are about ready to serve, heat a wide frying pan until hot. Scrape the marinade off the steaks and then rub each steak with a little olive oil. Add them to the pan and fry for 2–3 minutes on each side for medium–rare depending on their thickness. The steaks should feel slightly springy when lightly pressed. (Cook them for a minute longer if you prefer them well done.) Transfer to a warm plate and leave to rest in a warm spot for 5 minutes.

Meanwhile, place the watercress leaves in a bowl. In a separate bowl, mix together the vinaigrette and a few tablespoons of beef jus to taste. Add this to the watercress and toss until the leaves are nicely coated.

To serve, put a steak on each warmed serving plate and add any juices released when the meat was resting to the sauce. Neatly place some kohlrabi and watercress salad on top of the steaks, then spoon the sauce over the meat. Serve immediately.

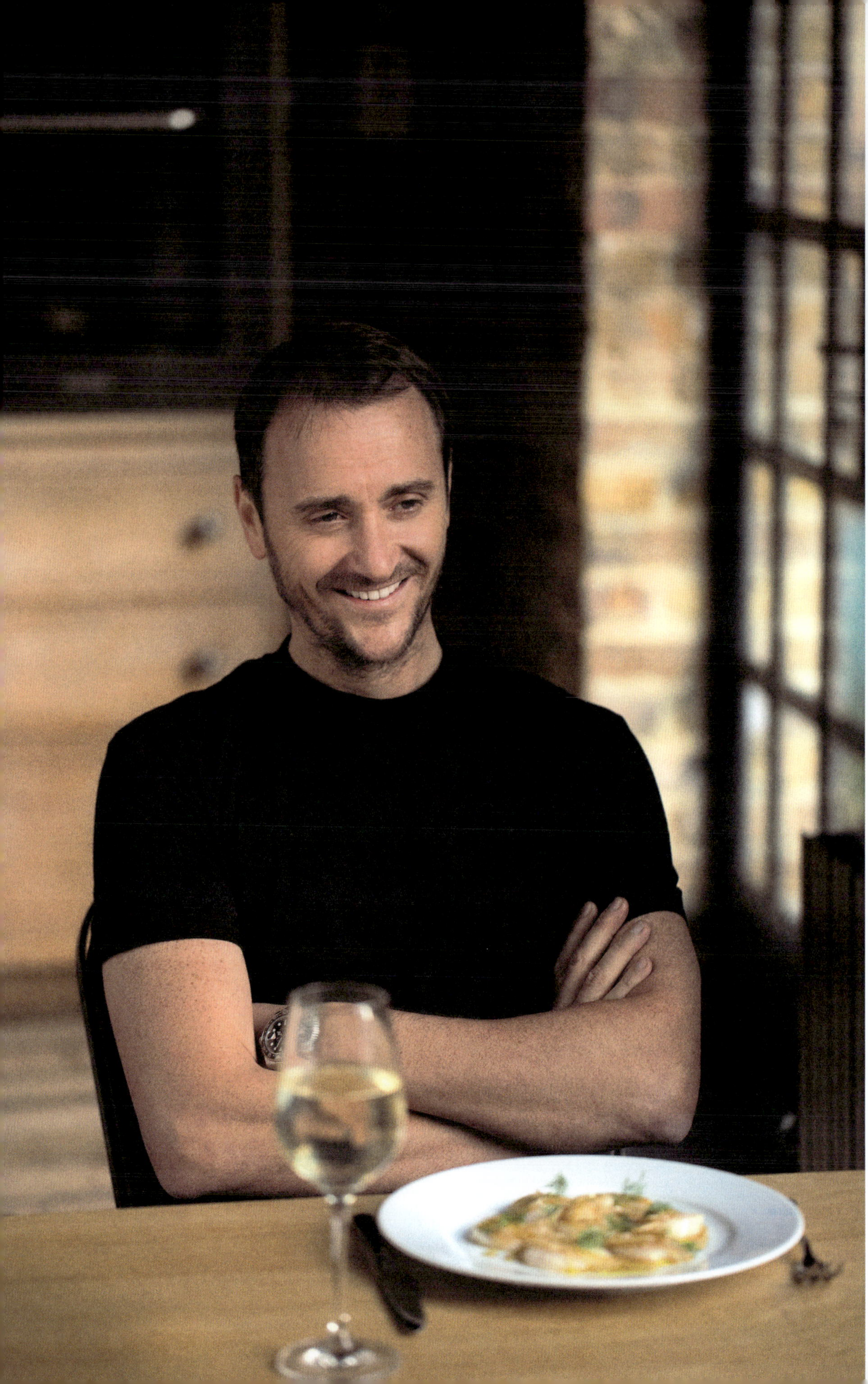

BRAISED OXTAIL WITH PASTA

At Pollen Street Social, we serve our braised oxtail with a silky, buttery mash. It is the ultimate comfort food! I love cooking with oxtail because the bones provide so much flavour and the high gelatine content means that at the end of the braise, you are left with an unctuous sauce with a wonderful depth of flavour. For this dish, I'm using the braising sauce as a 'ragu' to coat golden nuggets of gnocchi, but you could use any type of pasta.

SERVES 6–8

50ml olive oil
1.5kg oxtail
50g unsalted butter
1 small onion, chopped
1 small carrot, peeled and chopped
1 celery stalk, trimmed and chopped
handful of thyme
2 bay leaves
½ teaspoon white peppercorns
1 plum tomato, quartered
500ml red wine
200ml Beef Stock (see page 219)
750g shop-bought gnocchi
70g Parmesan, shaved
sea salt and freshly ground white pepper

For the parsley breadcrumbs
4 thick slices of sourdough, crusts removed
50g unsalted butter
2–3 tablespoons finely chopped flat-leaf parsley

Heat a thin layer of oil in a wide heavy-based pan over a high heat. Season the oxtail pieces and add them to the pan. Fry for about 2 minutes on each side until golden brown. Once the oxtail pieces are evenly browned, transfer to a plate and set aside.

Add the butter, onion, carrot and celery to the pan and stir frequently for 6–8 minutes until the vegetables begin to brown. When they are golden brown, return the oxtail to the pan and add the thyme, bay leaves, peppercorns and tomato. Pour in the red wine and bring it to the boil. Reduce the heat and let it simmer for 3½–4 hours until the meat is very tender and comes off the bone easily. Remove the pan from the heat and leave the oxtail to cool in its sauce.

Once the oxtail is cool enough to handle, remove the meat from the bone and place in a bowl. Cover the bowl with cling film and chill. Strain the sauce through a fine sieve into a clean saucepan. Put a lid on the saucepan and place in the refrigerator for about 1 hour until the fat layer on top has solidified. Scrape off and remove the fat, then boil the sauce until it has reduced by half.

For the parsley breadcrumbs, pulse the sourdough to coarse crumbs in a food processor. Melt the butter in a frying pan until it begins to foam. Add the breadcrumbs and fry for 3–5 minutes until golden brown and crisp. Stir through the chopped parsley and then tip on to a plate lined with kitchen paper to drain off any excess butter.

When you are ready to cook the gnocchi, bring a large pot of salted water to the boil. Add the gnocchi and cook for about 2–4 minutes or according to the packet instructions. While the gnocchi are cooking, return the oxtail meat to the sauce. Gently reheat the mixture over a medium heat until it is hot. Drain the gnocchi and divide between warmed bowls. Spoon the oxtail mixture over the gnocchi and garnish with Parmesan and parsley breadcrumbs.

MAIN COURSES

BRAISED OX CHEEKS, CARROTS, BONE MARROW, SOURDOUGH CRUMBS AND HORSERADISH POMME PURÉE

This is an adaptation of my signature dish called Tongue and Cheek, which appears in many of my restaurants in some shape or form. It's just a great British dish showcasing the sumptuousness of the less popular off cuts. I've left out the beef tongue in this recipe, allowing the cheeks to be the main star alongside the carrots, bone marrow and horseradish mash.

SERVES 6

4 ox cheeks, trimmed of any sinew
2 small onions, peeled and roughly chopped
2 celery stalks, trimmed and roughly chopped
2 carrots, peeled and roughly chopped
1 head of garlic, cloves separated and smashed with skin on
small handful of thyme
1 teaspoon black peppercorns, lightly crushed
3 bay leaves
750ml red wine
200ml port
sea salt and freshly ground black pepper

For the horseradish pomme purée
150g creamed horseradish sauce
1kg Ratte potatoes
300ml whole milk
100g unsalted butter

For the breadcrumbs
¼ loaf of sourdough, crusts removed
50g unsalted butter
a few sprigs of thyme, leaves only

For the roasted carrots
250ml Chicken Stock (see page 218)
100g unsalted butter
4 young carrots, trimmed but left whole

For the bone marrow
6 x 7–8cm veal marrowbones

Note: you will need a meat thermometer for this recipe.

Put the ox cheeks in a large bowl or pot along with all the remaining ingredients. Cover and chill overnight (or for 24 hours).

The next day, put everything into a pan with a pinch of salt and pepper. Bring to a simmer over a medium heat. Skim off any impurities which rise to the surface of the liquid. Lower the heat, place a circle of greaseproof paper (a cartouche) over the ox cheeks and gently simmer for 2½–3 hours, until the cheeks are tender. Leave to cool in the cooking liquid.

Once cooled, remove the ox cheeks from the pan and strain the sauce through a fine sieve into a saucepan, pressing down on the vegetables to extract all the juices. Bring the sauce to a simmer and cook for 10–15 minutes, until reduced to a syrupy consistency. Reheat the ox cheeks in the sauce before serving.

To make the horseradish pomme purée, blend the horseradish cream in a food processor for 5 minutes, then pass through a fine sieve. Set aside. Put the potatoes into a large pan of cold salted water. Bring the water to the boil then turn down the heat to a simmer. Gently simmer for 20–30 minutes until the potatoes are tender. There should be no resistance when you pierce the middle of a potato with a sharp knife. Once the potatoes are ready, remove the pan from the heat. Peel 3 or 4 potatoes at a time then immediately push them through a potato ricer. Continue until all the potatoes have been peeled and mashed. For a very fine mash, push the mashed potatoes through a fine sieve. Put the milk and butter into a saucepan and gently heat until the butter has melted. Slowly add the milk mixture to the potatoes, stirring well. Add the horseradish cream, to taste, along with a little more salt and pepper. Serve while still warm.

For the breadcrumbs, blitz the bread to coarse crumbs in a food processor. Melt the butter in a frying pan until it begins to foam. Add the breadcrumbs and fry for 3–5 minutes until golden brown and crisp. Stir through the thyme leaves then tip on to a plate lined with kitchen paper to drain any excess butter.

For the roasted carrots, put the chicken stock and 75g of the butter in a saucepan and bring to the boil. Add some seasoning and whisk to combine. Tip in the carrots and parboil them for 6–8 minutes, until they begin to soften. Remove the carrots and set aside until you are ready to serve. (The cooking stock can be saved to cook other vegetables.) To reheat the carrots before serving, toss them with the remaining butter in a hot pan and cook for another 5–7 minutes until tender and nicely glazed.

For the roasted bone marrow, preheat the oven to 180°C/Gas Mark 4. Place the marrowbones on a baking tray, season with a pinch of salt and pepper, then roast for about 15–20 minutes or until the marrow reaches a core temperature of 70°C. The marrow should be wobbly but not melting away. Remove from the oven and set aside.

To serve, spoon the horseradish pomme purée into shallow serving bowls. Divide the ox cheeks between them, then place the carrots and veal bones next to them. Drizzle over the remaining sauce and sprinkle the breadcrumbs on top. Serve immediately.

MAIN COURSES

SOCIAL SUPPERS

CÔTE DE BOEUF WITH HERB SALSA, COURGETTE FRITES AND CEPS

Seven years ago, I went to Tuscany for the first time with my older brother, Dean. We were recommended to go to a restaurant where they serve only one dish for a starter, one dish for the main, and if the chef can be bothered, there'll be a simple dessert on offer. That night, we had a plate of super fresh crudités with a Tuscan dipping sauce to start, followed by beef Florentine for the main. The beef came with a beautiful red wine sauce and these amazing fried courgettes and ceps. It turned out to be one of the most unforgettable dinners I've ever had. This dish is my way of recreating that truly memorable meal.

SERVES 4

1 x côte de boeuf (bone-in rib steak), about 900g–1kg
1 tablespoon olive oil
125g unsalted butter
½ head of garlic
4 sprigs of thyme
sea salt and freshly ground black pepper

For the herb salsa
1 garlic clove, peeled
small bunch of flat-leaf parsley, roughly chopped
small bunch of coriander, roughly chopped
small bunch of basil, leaves only
pinch of dried chilli flakes
2 teaspoons Chardonnay vinegar or other white wine vinegar
120ml extra-virgin olive oil

For the courgette frites
1 large courgette, trimmed and cut into matchsticks
100ml whole milk
50g plain flour
vegetable oil, for deep-frying

For the ceps
1 tablespoon olive oil
250g ceps, cleaned and sliced
60g unsalted butter

Note: you will need a meat thermometer for this recipe.

Take the beef out of the refrigerator at least 1 hour before cooking and allow it to come to room temperature.

To make the herb salsa, put all the ingredients into a food processor and blend to a coarse paste, stopping to scrape down the sides of the blender once or twice. Taste and adjust the seasoning. Transfer to a bowl and set aside.

For the courgette frites, heat the oil in a deep saucepan (or deep-fat fryer) until it reaches 180°C. Test it by throwing in a courgette matchstick – it should sizzle but not burn. Dip the courgettes in the milk, then coat them in the flour. Deep-fry the courgettes in batches for 3–4 minutes, until golden. Remove with a slotted spoon and drain on a tray lined with kitchen paper. Sprinkle with a little salt and pepper and keep warm in a low oven.

For the ceps, heat the olive oil in a heavy-based frying pan over a medium–high heat. Add the ceps and fry for 3–4 minutes, until lightly golden and any moisture released has cooked off. Season to taste with salt and pepper then add the butter and leave to melt. You may need to adjust the heat so that the butter foams rather than burns.

Toss the mushrooms to coat them in the foaming butter and cook for another 3–4 minutes until the ceps are golden brown. Keep warm in the low oven.

To cook the steak, heat the oil in a wide, heavy-based frying pan until it begins to smoke. Season the meat liberally with salt and pepper on both sides then put in the hot pan and let it fry for about 2 minutes until a dark brown crust has developed on the underside. Flip it over and fry the other side, until browned. Lower the heat and add the butter, garlic and thyme. Spoon the foaming butter over the steak to baste and fry until the beef is cooked to your liking. For medium rare, the steak should feel slightly springy when pressed. A more accurate way to tell when the meat is cooked is to use a meat thermometer: the beef should reach an internal temperature of 54°C for rare and 58°C for medium-rare once rested. (The steaks will continue to cook once they have been removed from the heat, so you remove the beef 7°C below the required temperature.)

Remove the steak from the pan and rest for 10–15 minutes on a resting rack. Serve the beef with the herb salsa, courgette frites and ceps.

MEATBALLS WITH TOMATO SAUCE

I believe everyone should be able to make a great meatball dish and this is something I'll often cook with the kids at home. The key is to use good-quality mince with a decent amount of fat and make sure you season well. Another tip: keep the meatballs loose as you shape them – squashed meatballs will end up hard and dense. I also try to make a big batch each time so that we can freeze a portion for another meal.

SERVES 4
(MAKES 16–18 BALLS)

For the meatballs
250g minced beef
250g minced pork
½ onion, peeled and finely chopped
2 garlic cloves, peeled and finely chopped
50g fresh breadcrumbs
½ teaspoon ground cumin
½ teaspoon smoked paprika
1 teaspoon dried oregano
1 large egg
2 tablespoons whole milk
3–4 tablespoons plain flour
2–4 tablespoons olive oil, for frying
sea salt and freshly ground black pepper
1 tablespoon chopped flat-leaf parsley, to serve
grated Parmesan, to serve
1 quantity of Creamy Mashed Potatoes
    (see page 228), to serve

For the tomato sauce
2 tablespoons olive oil
½ onion, peeled and finely chopped
½ red chilli, deseeded and finely chopped
1 tablespoon balsamic vinegar
800g plum tomatoes, finely chopped

In a large mixing bowl, combine the minced beef and pork, onion, garlic, breadcrumbs, cumin, paprika and oregano. Beat the egg and milk together in a separate bowl then add to the mince mixture. Mix until well incorporated then season well with salt and pepper. To check the seasoning, fry off a little of the mixture and taste it, adding more salt and pepper to your liking. Shape the mixture into small golfball-sized meatballs with damp hands. Put the flour in a shallow bowl then lightly coat the meatballs in it.

Heat a little of the olive oil in a wide pan until hot. Cook the meatballs in small batches, taking care not to overcrowd the pan, otherwise you would end up stewing the meatballs. Fry the meatballs for 2 minutes on each side until golden brown. Transfer to a tray lined with kitchen paper. Add more oil to the pan as necessary then continue to fry the rest of the meatballs in small batches.

Use the same pan in which you browned the meatballs to make the tomato sauce. Place the oil in the pan and tip in the onion and some seasoning. Fry over a medium heat for about 8–10 minutes, stirring occasionally, until the onion is soft and lightly golden. Add the chilli, balsamic vinegar and tomatoes. Add a little more salt and pepper to the pan, then bring the sauce to a simmer. Return the meatballs to the pan and simmer for around 10 minutes until they are cooked through.

Transfer the meatballs and sauce to a warm serving platter and sprinkle with the chopped parsley and Parmesan. Serve hot with the mashed potatoes.

MAIN COURSES

SOCIAL SUPPERS

LITTLE SOCIAL BURGER WITH SMOKY BACON AND BALSAMIC ONION CHUTNEY

I am very proud of our Little Social burger, not only because it's delicious but also because it has amassed numerous accolades and has been named London's best burger several times. My head chef at Little Social, Cary Docherty, came up with the recipe when we opened the bistro and it is now used in all my casual restaurants.

SERVES 4

600g good-quality beef mince (ask your butcher for aged beef mince, if possible)
1–2 tablespoons olive oil
sea salt and freshly ground black pepper

For the balsamic onion chutney
1–2 tablespoons olive oil
4 Spanish onions (about 500g), peeled and sliced
100ml balsamic vinegar

To serve
8 thin rashers of smoked streaky bacon
4 slices of mild Cheddar cheese
4 brioche burger buns
2 large gherkins, thinly sliced
1 quantity of Chunky Chips (see page 228)

Divide the beef mince into four 150g portions, then press each portion into a 10cm wide pastry ring to form neat patties. Arrange the patties in a single layer on a plate, cover with cling film and chill for at least 30 minutes to allow them to firm up.

Next, make the balsamic onion chutney. Heat a heavy-based pan with the oil until hot. Add the onions and a generous pinch of salt and cook over a medium–high heat for 10–12 minutes, stirring occasionally, until the onions begin to soften and colour. Once they are golden, turn the heat down and continue to cook for another 15–20 minutes until they darken further and become soft and sticky. Do remember to stir frequently to prevent the onions from burning. Tip in the balsamic vinegar and cook until the vinegar has reduced to a sticky glaze. Leave to cool.

When ready to cook, preheat the oven grill to the highest setting. Arrange the bacon rashers on a baking sheet in a single layer. Grill for 5–6 minutes until they are golden brown and crisp. Remove and leave to cool slightly. Set the oven to 200°C/Gas Mark 6.

Heat a wide ovenproof frying pan over high heat with a little of the olive oil. Season both sides of the burger patties. Fry them for 2 minutes on each side until golden brown. Place 2 crisp bacon rashers and a slice of Cheddar on top of each patty then transfer the pan to the hot oven to finish the cooking. For medium burgers, remove them from the oven after 3 minutes, by which time the cheese should be oozing over the patties. If you prefer the burgers well done, leave them in the oven for 8 minutes.

Meanwhile, halve and toast the burger buns. Put the bottom halves on warmed serving plates, then spread over an even layer of onion chutney. Arrange 3 slices of gherkin on top of the chutney, followed by the burgers. Top with the lids of the buns and serve immediately with piping hot chips.

SIMPLE ROAST LEG OF LAMB WITH ROSEMARY RUB AND POTATO DAUPHINOIS

This is an impressive way to present a Sunday roast, particularly if you are offering a generous leg of lamb. It is an honest dish with little pretension – just lovely spring lamb served with broccoli, beans and potatoes. Whether at home or in the restaurants, we never waste the broccoli stalks. Trim off the hard woody skins around the base and you'll end up with a lovely, sweet and crunchy core. For the picture, I've chilled, sliced, reheated and presented the potato dauphinois in a fun and modern way, but you could simply bring it to the table in its gratin dish.

SERVES 6–8

1 leg of lamb, bone in, about 2 kg
3 garlic cloves, peeled
1 tablespoon sea salt
4 sprigs of rosemary, leaves only, finely chopped
olive oil, to drizzle
6 carrots, peeled
1 head of broccoli, broken into florets, stalk reserved
1 tablespoon olive oil
2 tablespoons butter
sea salt and freshly ground black pepper

For the potato dauphinois
1.2kg baking potatoes
3 garlic cloves, peeled and finely crushed
a pinch of grated nutmeg
about 500ml double cream

For the potato dauphinois, preheat the oven to 160°C/Gas Mark 3. Peel the potatoes and put them into a bowl of water to prevent them from getting brown. Thinly slice the potatoes using a mandolin or very sharp knife and place in another large bowl. Add the crushed garlic and season well with grated nutmeg, salt and pepper. Pour two-thirds of the cream over the potatoes and mix well. Layer the potatoes into a gratin dish and pour over the rest of the cream. Press down the potatoes with a fork or spatula, so the cream reaches the top layer of potatoes. If necessary, top up with more cream. Bake the potatoes for 1 hour, until tender and golden brown on top. Remove from the oven and set aside, lightly covered with foil.

Increase the oven temperature to 200°C/Gas Mark 6. Place the leg of lamb on a large baking tray. Use a pestle and mortar to crush the garlic cloves and salt to a fine paste. Stir in the chopped rosemary and a splash of olive oil then rub the paste all over the lamb. Pop the tray into the oven and roast for about 1 hour for medium-rare meat. (Roast for another 15 minutes if you prefer the lamb well done.) Remove the lamb from the oven, loosely cover with foil and leave to rest for 15–20 minutes.

Lower the oven temperature to 180°C/Gas Mark 4. While the lamb is resting, pop the potato dauphinois into the oven for 10–15 minutes to reheat. Place the carrots in a pan of boiling salted water and boil until tender, about 15 minutes. Remove with a slotted spoon and transfer to a bowl of iced water to cool, then drain on kitchen paper. Add the broccoli stalk to the water and blanch for 1 minute, then add the florets and blanch for a further minute. Cool in iced water and drain. Heat the olive oil and butter in a pan, then add the carrots and broccoli stalk and cook for 3–4 minutes or until everything begins to brown all over, then add the florets to the pan, and cook for a further 2 minutes. Season well to taste. Carve the lamb at the table and serve with the vegetables and potato dauphinois.

MAIN COURSES

SOCIAL SUPPERS

BRAISED LAMB NECK, PEAS, BROAD BEANS, ASPARAGUS AND CREAMED WILD GARLIC

To me, this dish has the essence of spring. It is a fantastic dish to cook after a cold and dreary winter as the availability of British asparagus, fresh peas, broad beans and wild garlic signifies that warmer weather is upon us. Lamb neck is an affordable cut of meat and it has much more flavour than the more expensive loin or fillet.

SERVES 4

4 tablespoons olive oil
1kg trimmed lamb neck
2 onions, peeled and chopped
2 garlic cloves, peeled and finely sliced
4 celery stalks, trimmed and cut into 2cm pieces
2 carrots, peeled and cut into 2cm pieces
1 small leek, trimmed and sliced
1 bouquet garni (2 bay leaves, 6 sprigs of thyme and 1 sprig of rosemary tied together with kitchen string)
5 white peppercorns
150ml dry white wine
300ml Brown Chicken Stock (see page 218)
300ml Veal Stock (see page 219)
sea salt and freshly ground black pepper

For the broad beans, peas and asparagus
125g broad beans, thawed if frozen
1 bunch of green asparagus, trimmed, woody ends removed
125g fresh peas, thawed if frozen
50g unsalted butter
1 sprig of thyme
1 bay leaf

For the creamed wild garlic
150ml double cream
175g wild garlic, finely chopped

Heat half the oil in a large heavy-based pan over a medium–high heat. Season the lamb neck with salt and pepper and fry for about 2 minutes on each side until evenly brown all over. Transfer to a plate and set aside.

Add the remaining oil to the pan and tip in the onion and some seasoning. Fry for 6–8 minutes, stirring occasionally, until the onion begins to soften. Add the garlic, celery, carrot, leek, bouquet garni and peppercorns. Stir and fry for another 6–8 minutes until the vegetables are lightly golden brown. Deglaze the pan with the white wine, scraping the base of the pan with a wooden spoon to release any browned bits. Let the wine boil until reduced by half then add both stocks. Bring the stocks to a simmer then return the lamb to the pan. Season with salt and pepper to taste. Cover the ingredients with a damp piece of baking parchment, then partially cover the pan with a lid. Gently simmer for 1½–2 hours, until the lamb is tender.

Next start to prepare the vegetables. Bring a large pot of water to the boil and have ready two bowls of iced water. Blanch the broad beans for 2 minutes, then drain and refresh in the first bowl of iced water. Drain again then squeeze out the broad beans and discard their pale skins. Set aside until ready to serve. Blanch the asparagus spears for 2–3 minutes, until tender, then scoop them out with a slotted spoon (or use a pair of kitchen tongs) and refresh them in a bowl of iced water. Drain and set aside.

To make the creamed wild garlic, put the double cream into a saucepan and place over a medium heat. Bring to a simmer then add the wild garlic and some seasoning to taste. Simmer for a few minutes until the cream has reduced by a third. Reheat gently before serving.

When the lamb is ready, transfer it to a plate and leave to rest for about 10 minutes. Strain the sauce through a fine sieve into a saucepan. Bring to a simmer then add the peas and cook for 2–3 minutes, until tender. Add the skinned broad beans and return the lamb to the sauce to reheat. Take the pan off the heat.

To finish off the asparagus, melt the butter in a frying pan then add the thyme and bay leaf. Add the blanched asparagus and pan-fry it for 1–2 minutes, tossing the spears repeatedly in the melted butter. Season well and remove them from the heat once they are lightly golden brown all over.

Serve the lamb with the broad beans, peas, sauce, roasted asparagus and creamed wild garlic.

SLOW-ROASTED LAMB SHOULDER WITH AUTUMN VEGETABLES AND CABBAGE AND MINT PESTO

I invented my cabbage and mint pesto about four years ago for a television programme called The Great British Food Revival. *Participating chefs were given British ingredients to champion and I was unlucky enough to be assigned the humble cabbage. I saw it as a challenge to make a sexy cabbage dish. After some research, I had the idea of transforming cabbage into a dressing and my mint and cabbage pesto was born! It is a very versatile sauce and goes wonderfully with roast lamb, duck, salmon and root vegetables.*

SERVES 4

a few sprigs of rosemary, leaves only, roughly chopped
1½ tablespoons sea salt
1.5–2kg shoulder of lamb, bone-in
1 head of garlic, cut in half horizontally
1 onion, peeled and quartered
1 carrot, peeled and cut into large chunks
2 celery stalks, trimmed and cut into large chunks
rapeseed or olive oil, to drizzle
300ml Madeira
500ml Beef Stock (see page 219)
freshly ground black pepper

For the mashed swede
1kg swede, peeled and cut into 1cm dice
50g butter
2.5cm knob of ginger, peeled and finely grated

For the roast carrots and parsnips
4 carrots, peeled
4 small parsnips, peeled (or, if medium, also halved lengthways)

For the pan-fried cabbage
1 spring cabbage, 3 outer green leaves removed, washed and reserved for the pesto
a large knob of butter

For the cabbage and mint pesto
3 outer green leaves from a spring cabbage
50g pine nuts, toasted
30g grated Parmesan
60–100ml rapeseed oil
a large bunch of mint (about 100g), leaves only, chopped

Preheat the oven to 100°C/Gas Mark ¼. Put the chopped rosemary into a small bowl and stir in the salt. Rub the rosemary salt all over the lamb.

Put the garlic, onion, carrot and celery into a large roasting tray and rest the lamb on top. Drizzle the lamb and vegetables with a little oil and sprinkle with a little more seasoning. Cover the tray with foil then slow-roast for 7 hours, turning over once or twice.

To make the mashed swede, put the swede into a pan of salted water, bring to the boil and cook for about 10–15 minutes until tender. Drain well and press it through a potato ricer. Stir through the butter and grated ginger and season to taste. Reheat before serving.

For the cabbage pesto, blanch the cabbage leaves in salted boiling water for 45–60 seconds then refresh in iced water. Drain well then put into a food processor along with the pine nuts and Parmesan. Blend for a few seconds, then, with the motor running, slowly drizzle in the oil until you get a wet, coarse pesto. Add the mint leaves and some salt and pepper and blend again. Transfer to a clean jar and chill until ready to use.

Toss the carrots and parsnips with a little olive oil, salt and pepper. When the lamb has been cooking for 7 hours remove the tray from the oven and increase the temperature to 180°C/Gas Mark 4. Add the carrots and parsnips to the roasting tray, scattering them around the lamb. Return the tray to the oven and roast for another 40 minutes until the lamb is golden brown and the carrots and parsnips are just tender when pierced with a knife.

Transfer the lamb and vegetables to a platter and lightly cover with a piece of foil. Leave to rest for 30 minutes. While the lamb is resting, prepare the sauce and pan-fried cabbage.

To make the sauce, put the baking tray on the hob over a medium–high heat. Pour in the Madeira, scraping the base of the pan to loosen the sediment and browned bits. Boil the Madeira until reduced by half, then add the stock and return to the boil. Cook until reduced by a third or until thickened to a sauce consistency. Strain the sauce through a fine sieve into a sauceboat and keep warm.

For the pan-fried cabbage, first blanch the cabbage heart in salted water for 7 minutes, then immediately place into iced water. Once cool, heat the butter in a frying pan until foaming. Drain and dry the cabbage thoroughly, cut into quarters and fry in the butter until golden brown.

Serve the lamb with the roasted vegetables, mashed swede, cabbage quarters and pesto.

MAIN COURSES

SOCIAL SUPPERS

ROAST RACK OF LAMB WITH SPICED OLIVE JUS AND CREAMY MASHED POTATOES

I love the spices of North Africa. Instead of making a tagine, however, I am serving my herb-crusted lamb with a sauce rich with Moroccan spices and flavourings. To avoid too many conflicting flavours, I'm serving the dish with simple, creamy mashed potatoes. It makes a superb supper for entertaining.

SERVES 4

2 x 6-bone rack of lamb
75g blanched or flaked almonds
4 slices of stale bread, crusts removed and torn into large pieces
a handful of mint, leaves only, roughly chopped
a few sprigs of rosemary, leaves only, roughly chopped
a handful of marjoram, leaves only, roughly chopped
a handful of flat-leaf parsley, (thick stalks removed), roughly chopped
2 tablespoons Dijon mustard, to brush
olive oil, to drizzle
sea salt and freshly ground black pepper
a few thyme sprigs, leaves only, to garnish

For the spiced olive jus
1–2 tablespoons olive oil
500g lamb breast, cut into 2.5cm pieces
a knob of butter
1 onion, peeled and chopped
1 large garlic clove, peeled and finely chopped
2 teaspoons harissa paste
½ teaspoon ras el hanout (Moroccan mixed spice)
70ml dry white wine
3 tablespoons sherry vinegar
250ml Chicken Stock (see page 218)
250ml Veal Stock (see page 219)
1 star anise
2 teaspoons clear honey
2 shallots, peeled and sliced into rings
6 black pitted olives, thinly sliced
125g cherry tomatoes, halved
a sprig of coriander
a sprig of flat-leaf parsley
a sprig of rosemary

To serve
1 quantity of Creamy Mashed Potatoes (see page 228)

First, make the spiced olive jus. Heat some oil in a large heavy-based pan until hot. Season the lamb breast with salt and pepper, then fry in batches for 2 minutes on each side until golden brown. Transfer to a plate and set aside. Add the butter, onion and garlic to the pan and stir well. Fry for 6–8 minutes, stirring frequently, until the onion is tender. Stir in the harissa and ras el hanout and cook for another minute. Pour in the wine and sherry vinegar and let the liquid boil until reduced by a third. Add the chicken and veal stock, star anise, honey and browned lamb pieces to the pan. Return to a simmer and skim off any scum that arises to the surface of the liquid. Simmer for about 20 minutes until the sauce is flavourful and the liquid has reduced by one-half.

Meanwhile, sweat the shallots with a little oil in a saucepan until they are tender. When the sauce is ready, strain it through a fine sieve into a large jug, pressing down on the solids to extract all the flavourful juices. If you have time, cool the stock and spoon off as much fat from the surface as you can. Tip the sauce into the saucepan containing the shallots then add the olives, tomatoes and herb sprigs. Simmer for another 5–10 minutes. Taste and adjust the seasoning with salt and pepper. If you would prefer the sauce a little thicker, boil it for a few minutes until reduced to a desired consistency. Reheat just before serving.

Preheat the oven to 200°C/Gas Mark 6. Remove most of the fat from around the lamb racks then lightly score the thin layer of fat left and set aside. Put the almonds, bread and chopped herbs into a food processor and blitz to coarse crumbs. Add a pinch each of salt and pepper then pulse to combine. Tip into a shallow bowl.

Heat a frying pan over a medium heat. Rub the lamb racks all over with a little salt and pepper then place into the hot pan, skin side down and leave for 1–2 minutes until the meat is golden brown and some of it has rendered. Transfer to a baking tray then brush the mustard over the fat. Coat with the herb breadcrumbs then drizzle over a little olive oil and roast in the hot oven for 12–15 minutes until the lamb is cooked to medium-rare. The meat should feel slightly springy when pressed. Roast for another 5–10 minutes if you prefer the lamb well done. The meat will feel firm when lightly pressed. Remove from the oven and let the lamb rest for 10 minutes in a warm spot.

Slice the lamb racks and serve on warm plates with the creamy mashed potatoes and spiced olive jus, garnished with the thyme leaves.

LOIN OF VENISON WITH BEETROOT AND VENISON SAUCE AND BRAISED CABBAGE

Venison and beetroot pair wonderfully well. Here, the beetroot plays a supporting role by lending its vivid red colour to my richly-flavoured venison sauce. The star of the dish is a gorgeously tender saddle (loin) of venison. At my restaurants, wild venison comes from Muntjac deer, which has a delicious but lean meat with a close-grained texture.

SERVES 4

800g venison loin
2 tablespoons light olive oil, plus extra for cooking
8–10 juniper berries
4 garlic cloves, peeled and sliced
a few sprigs of thyme
a few sprigs of rosemary

For the beetroot and venison sauce

2 beetroot, peeled and diced
100g venison trimmings, cut into small pieces (ask your butcher for these when ordering your venison loin)
1–2 tablespoons olive oil
2 banana shallots, peeled and chopped
5 garlic cloves, peeled and chopped
a few sprigs of thyme
2 bay leaves
½ teaspoon white peppercorns
a pinch of rock salt
100ml gin
2 tablespoons sherry vinegar
600ml red wine
400ml Chicken Stock (see page 218)
400ml Veal Stock (see page 219)
sea salt and freshly ground black pepper

For the braised cabbage

25g unsalted butter
75g pancetta, cut into 5mm dice
1 garlic clove
1 sprig of thyme, chopped
1 small carrot, peeled and cut into 5mm dice
100g celeriac, cut into 5mm dice
1 pointed or Savoy cabbage (light leaves only), finely shredded
150ml Chicken Stock (see page 218)

Trim any sinew off the venison, then cut into four 200g portions. Put the venison into a large bowl (or a large, resealable bag) and add the olive oil, juniper berries, garlic, thyme and rosemary. Cover the bowl and refrigerate overnight to allow the flavours to infuse.

To make the venison sauce, put the beetroot into a saucepan and pour in enough water to cover. Bring the water to the boil over a medium–high heat and simmer for about 15 minutes until the beetroot is soft. Tip the beetroot and poaching liquid into a blender and blitz until the mixture is smooth. Pass the mixture through a fine sieve into a heavy-based saucepan, pressing down on the pulp to extract all the juices. Boil the beetroot juice until it has reduced to a thick syrup. Set aside.

Season the venison trimmings and fry them in a hot pan with the olive oil. When the trimmings are golden brown, stir in the shallots, garlic, thyme, bay leaf, peppercorns and salt. Fry over a medium–high heat, stirring occasionally, until the vegetables are golden brown. Deglaze the pan with the gin, scraping the base of the pan with a wooden spoon to dislodge the flavourful browned bits, then boil until the gin has reduced to a syrupy glaze. Add the sherry vinegar and red wine and boil again until reduced to a glaze. Now add the stocks and bring to a simmer. Turn down the heat and leave to simmer for 30 minutes. Pass the sauce through a fine sieve lined with a piece of muslin into a clean saucepan. Add the beetroot juice to the strained sauce and boil until the combined liquid is reduced to a syrupy sauce consistency. If you wish, strain it again through a fine sieve to remove any froth or sediment. Season with a little salt and pepper to taste. Gently warm up the sauce before serving.

Preheat the oven to 200°C/Gas Mark 6.

For the braised cabbage, heat a large, heavy-based pan and melt the butter until it starts to foam. Add the pancetta and fry in the foaming butter over a medium–high heat. When the pancetta is golden brown, add the garlic, thyme, carrots and celeriac and stir well. Sweat the vegetables for 3 minutes, stirring frequently. Add the cabbage, stock and some seasoning and stir well. Cover the mixture with a damp piece of baking parchment, to keep in the moisture. Gently braise the vegetables for 10 minutes until just tender.

Cook the venison loin while the cabbage is braising. Heat a wide ovenproof frying pan over a medium–high heat until hot. Drain the venison from its marinade, season with salt and pepper then add to the pan. Fry for 2 minutes on each side until golden brown. When evenly browned all over, place the pan in the hot oven to finish the cooking. Roast for 4–5 minutes until the venison is medium-rare. The meat should feel slightly springy when pressed. Remove the pan from the oven and keep in a warm spot. Rest the meat for 5 minutes, lightly covered with a piece of foil.

To serve, slice the venison thickly. Put a neat pile of braised cabbage on each warmed serving plate then top with the venison slices. Drizzle over the beetroot and venison sauce and serve immediately.

ROAST VENISON AND BEETROOT WITH POACHED PEARS

In the autumn, we always have this venison and beetroot dish on the menu at Pollen Street Social. Gamey venison has a natural affinity with sweet fruit, such as apples and pears, and it is wonderful with earthy beetroot, so I make no apologies for pairing these ingredients together again!

SERVES 6

6 x 100g boned loin of venison (ask your butcher for any trimmings for the sauce, if available)
25g unsalted butter
sea salt and freshly ground black pepper

For the red wine sauce
1 tablespoon olive oil
1 shallot, sliced
1 garlic clove, chopped
1 sprig of thyme
¼ teaspoon white peppercorns
1 bay leaf
1 tablespoon sherry vinegar
325ml red wine
400ml Veal Stock (see page 219)

For the roast beetroot
600g beetroot (a mixture of baby and normal-sized)
4 tablespoons caster sugar
4 sprigs of thyme
4 garlic clove, peeled
4 teaspoons sea salt
a few dashes of sherry vinegar

For the spiced honey sauce
½ teaspoon lavender
½ teaspoon coriander seeds
½ teaspoon cumin seeds
¼ teaspoon Szechuan peppercorns
60ml sherry vinegar
25g unsalted butter
½ teaspoon sea salt
200ml clear honey
squeeze of lemon juice

For the spiced poached pears
1 litre water
375g caster sugar
1 tablespoon lemon juice
4–5 star anise, lightly crushed
4 cinnamon sticks
6 pears, peeled and cut into wedges

First, prepare the beetroot. Wash the beetroot and trim off the stalks. Place the baby and normal-sized roots into separate saucepans and cover with cold water. Add half the sugar, thyme, garlic, salt and a dash of vinegar to each pan. Simmer for about 40–45 minutes until the beetroot are tender. Drain and leave to cool. When cool enough to handle, peel the beetroot and cut each one into 2.5cm cubes. Set aside.

For the spiced honey sauce, toast the lavender for a few seconds in a dry hot pan. Tip in the coriander seeds, cumin seeds and Szechuan peppercorns, and toast for a few more seconds until the spices release their oils and fragrance. Pour in the sherry vinegar and boil until it has reduced to a sticky glaze. Add the butter, salt and honey and bring back to a simmer. Continue to simmer until the sauce has reduced by two-thirds to a syrupy consistency. Strain it through a fine sieve and discard the spices. Season to taste with a little squeeze of lemon juice. Set aside until ready to serve.

Next, make the red wine sauce. Heat the oil in a heavy-based pan until hot. If you have them, add the venison trimmings and fry them over a medium–high heat until golden brown on each side. Stir in the shallot and garlic and fry for a few minutes until they are lightly golden then add the thyme, peppercorns and bay leaf. Deglaze the pan with the sherry vinegar and red wine, scraping the base of the pan with a wooden spoon to release any browned sediment. Boil the liquid until reduced by three-quarters. Add the stock and bring to the boil. Reduce the heat slightly and simmer for 20 minutes until the sauce is flavourful. Pass the sauce through a very fine sieve (or one lined with muslin) into a clean pan and boil steadily until reduced to a syrupy consistency. Reheat the sauce before serving.

For the poached pears, put the water, sugar, lemon juice and spices into a wide pan. Stir to dissolve the sugar then bring the syrup to the boil. Gently lower the pears into the syrup. Cover the pears with a dampened piece of baking parchment roughly cut to the diameter of the pan. Simmer gently for about 8–10 minutes until the pears are tender. Gently reheat before serving.

To cook the venison, heat the butter over a medium heat in a heavy-based pan. Add the venison pieces and sear until golden brown all over, keeping the meat medium-rare. This should take 5–8 minutes, depending on their thickness. Remove the venison to a warm tray and let the meat rest for a few minutes, while you reheat the pears, sauces and beetroot.

Place the beetroot pieces in a frying pan with 3 tablespoons of the spiced honey sauce and toss to coat. Heat for a couple of minutes, stirring frequently, until warmed through. Thickly slice the venison and divide between warmed plates. Serve with the spiced beetroot, poached pears and red wine sauce.

ROAST ANJOU SQUAB WITH YAKITORI OF INNARDS, BRUSSELS SPROUTS AND BRAISED RED CABBAGE

Squabs are young domesticated pigeons and the ones from Anjou are considered to be the best in the world. They have a beautiful slightly gamey flavour and I think that they are such a treat. In a bid to use every edible bit of the bird, I'm using their hearts and livers to make yakitori skewers, inspired by my travels in Japan. I make my own yakitori sauce, which has a richer depth of flavour than the shop-bought versions. If you make it, you'll have more than you need for the dish. Any extra will keep well in clean bottles in the refrigerator. It is delicious on salmon, chicken or pork.

SERVES 4

4 Anjou squabs or young pigeons with hearts and livers intact
1 litre milk
a few sprigs of thyme
3 garlic cloves, peeled and finely crushed
250g duck fat, melted
4 Brussels sprouts
3–4 tablespoons olive oil
a few knobs of butter
4 cep or oyster mushrooms, halved lengthways
sea salt and freshly ground black pepper

For the yakitori sauce
250g chicken bones or carcass (ask your butcher for this)
1 tablespoon vegetable oil
1 tablespoon sesame oil
1 bunch of spring onion tops
4 baby leeks, white part only
625ml light soy sauce
125ml sake
375ml mirin
375g caster sugar

To serve
Braised Red Cabbage (see page 124)

Remove the heart and liver from the birds, trim off any sinew or veins and then place them in a bowl of milk to remove any bitterness and excess blood. Leave to soak in the milk for 1 hour, changing the milk twice. Cut out the wings from the squabs, then carve out the legs and cut along the joint to separate the thighs from the drumsticks. Finally, carve out the breasts from the main carcass.

Next, confit the squab thighs. Put the thighs into a large bowl (or a plastic container) and sprinkle liberally with sea salt. Add the thyme sprigs and garlic, then cover the bowl with cling film and refrigerate for about 30 minutes. Preheat the oven to 120°C/Gas Mark ½. Remove the squab thighs from the refrigerator and rinse off the salt. Place the thighs in an ovenproof pan into which they fit snugly, then pour in enough duck fat to cover. Cover the pan and place it in the low oven. Gently cook for 1½ hours or until the meat is tender. There should be no resistance when you pierce the thighs with a small knife. Remove from the oven and leave to cool completely then carefully remove the meat from the bones and reserve for the yakitori skewers.

For the yakitori sauce, preheat the oven to 200°C/Gas Mark 6. Place the chicken bones and the squab wings and drumsticks in a baking tray and roast in the hot oven for 40 minutes until they are golden brown.

Heat the vegetable and sesame oils in a heavy-based pot until hot. Add the spring onions and leeks and fry them for 4–6 minutes until they begin to soften. Add the rest of the ingredients, plus the roasted chicken bones and squab wings and drumsticks and bring to a simmer. Gently simmer for about 1¼ hours until thickened and slightly syrupy. Take the pan off the heat and allow to cool. Spoon a tablespoon or two of fat off the top, then strain the sauce through a fine sieve. Store in clean jars and refrigerate if not using immediately.

Next, prepare the yakitori ingredients. Bring a small saucepan of salted water to the boil. Blanch the sprouts for 2–3 minutes until they are just tender. Drain and refresh under cold running water, then cut the sprouts in half lengthways. Heat a frying pan with a little oil and a knob of butter over a medium–high heat. Fry the sprouts and mushrooms, cut side down, for about 1–2 minutes on each side until they are golden brown. Remove to a plate and set aside.

Add a little more oil to the pan. Season the squab breasts and add to the pan, skin side down. Fry for 2–3 minutes until the skin is golden brown and crisp. Add a knob of butter and flip the breasts over. Spoon the foaming butter over the breasts and cook for another 1–2 minutes, just until the breasts are medium-rare and slightly springy when pressed. Remove from the pan and leave to rest.

Drain and dry the soaked squab hearts and livers with kitchen paper. If necessary, add a more oil to the frying pan. Lightly season the hearts and livers with salt and pepper and add to the pan. Fry for about 2 minutes on each side until the hearts and livers are golden brown outside but still rare in the middle. Remove from the pan and set aside.

Preheat the grill to the highest setting. Thread the Brussels sprout halves, squab hearts, livers and confit thigh meat and the mushrooms on to four metal (or soaked wooden) skewers and place them on a baking sheet. Brush them generously with the yakitori sauce and place under the grill for 1–2 minutes until the livers and hearts are cooked to medium-rare. They should be slightly springy when pressed.

To serve, spoon a little yakitori sauce on to 4 warmed plates. Place the pan-roasted squab breasts on top. Add a spoonful of braised red cabbage alongside then top with the yakitori skewers. Serve immediately.

ROAST DUCK BREAST WITH MINI ROAST POTATOES, TURNIPS, BEETROOT AND CARROT PURÉE

This is a lovely autumnal dish featuring a mixture of humble but delicious root vegetables, all of which have a nutty, earthy sweetness that goes beautifully with the duck breasts.

SERVES 4

4 duck breasts
sea salt and freshly ground black pepper

For the potatoes and vegetables

3 tablespoons duck or goose fat
2 small garlic cloves, peeled and finely crushed
4 sprigs of thyme, leaves only
1 teaspoon sea salt
¼ teaspoon freshly ground black pepper
12–16 mini potatoes, rinsed
4 small golden beetroot
4 carrots, peeled and thinly sliced
8 baby turnips
200ml Duck Jus (page 220)
2 tablespoons olive oil

First, roast the potatoes. Preheat the oven to 200°C/Gas Mark 6. Melt the duck fat in a saucepan, then add the garlic, thyme, salt and pepper. Take the pan off the heat. Place the potatoes in a roasting tray, pour over the duck fat mixture and toss to coat. Roast the potatoes in the hot oven for about 45–60 minutes, until they are golden brown and cooked through.

Roast the golden beetroot on a baking tray in the same oven, for around 25 minutes or until soft. Remove and allow to cool before removing the skin. Cut each beetroot into 4 or 5 pieces and set aside.

Next, make a carrot purée. Put the carrots into a pan and pour in enough cold water to cover. Add a generous pinch of salt to the pan then bring the water to the boil. Reduce the heat and simmer the carrots for about 15–20 minutes until they are soft. Drain the carrots, reserving a little of the cooking water, and tip them into a food processor. Blend to a smooth purée, adding a tiny splash of cooking water if necessary. Pass the purée through a fine sieve into a bowl. Cover with cling film and refrigerate if making in advance.

Wash the turnips well and place in boiling salted water for 10 minutes or until soft. Drain and set aside until needed.

Lower the oven temperature to 190°C/Gas Mark 5. Score the skin of the duck breasts then season well with salt and pepper. Put the breasts, skin side down, in a cold ovenproof pan then place the pan over a very low heat. Gently cook the breasts for about 8 minutes until the fat beneath the skins has been rendered and the skins are golden brown and crisp. Flip the duck breasts over to cook the flesh side for about 2 minutes until golden brown. Place the pan into the hot oven to finish off cooking. Roast for about 3–4 minutes until the breasts are cooked to medium-rare. They should feel slightly springy when pressed. Remove the pan from the oven and rest the breasts for 4–5 minutes.

Heat the duck jus in a small pan. Reheat both the turnips and the beetroot in separate pans with a little olive oil. Gently reheat the carrot purée in a small pan.

Slice the duck breasts. Place spoonfuls of carrot purée on plates and top with duck slices. Arrange the roast potatoes, beetroot and turnips around them and spoon over the duck jus.

MAIN COURSES

SOCIAL SUPPERS

SPICED ROAST PHEASANT WITH PUMPKIN, BREAD SAUCE AND HOME-MADE GRANOLA

As with most game birds, pheasant is very lean and hence very likely to dry out during cooking. Since my days of working with Marco Pierre White, I've always part-poached the birds before roasting. This method ensures that they stay succulent and tender. For this autumnal feast, I'm serving the roast pheasant with roast pumpkin, bread sauce and home-made granola to add a little texture and crunch. I make this bread sauce really thick, but you can thin it down with a little milk if you prefer.

SERVES 4

4 young oven-ready pheasants
2 tablespoons ground ginger
2 tablespoons ground coriander
2 tablespoons ground white peppercorns
4 tablespoons olive oil
a few knobs of butter
12–16 thin slices of pancetta
800g pumpkin, peeled, deseeded and sliced into wedges
sea salt and freshly ground black pepper

For the gravy
4 tablespoons olive oil
1 shallot, peeled and finely chopped
2 garlic cloves, lightly crushed
a few sprigs of thyme
1 bay leaf
½ leek, cut into 2cm pieces
1 celery stalk, cut into 2cm pieces
165ml dry white wine
165ml Madeira
500ml Chicken Stock (see page 218)
500ml Veal Stock (see page 219)

For the bread sauce
50g butter
1 shallot, peeled and sliced
2 garlic cloves, peeled
200ml whole milk
400ml double cream
75g sourdough (3–4 slices), crusts removed and diced
75g white bread (3–4 slices), crusts removed and diced

To serve (optional)
4–6 tablespoons Home-made Granola (see page 230)

First, prepare the pheasants. If necessary, run a blowtorch over the skins of the birds to singe any fine hairs or feathers that remain. Cut the legs from the crown and set aside. Mix the ground ginger, coriander, peppercorns and a generous pinch of sea salt together in a small bowl. Rub each pheasant crown with the spice mixture all over then set aside while you cook the legs and make the gravy.

For the gravy, heat the oil in a heavy-based pan placed over a medium–high heat. Cut the pheasant legs into small pieces, season with salt and pepper and add to the pan. Tip in the shallot, garlic, thyme, bay leaf, leek and celery. Fry over a high heat for 4–6 minutes, stirring occasionally, until the vegetables begin to colour. Deglaze the pan with the white wine, scraping the base of the pan with a wooden spoon to release the browned sediment. Boil the wine until it has reduced by half, then add the Madeira and return to the boil. Reduce again by half. Finally add the stocks. Bring the combined liquid to the boil and let it simmer for about 20 minutes. Strain the gravy through a fine sieve into a saucepan and boil until reduced to a syrupy consistency. Season well to taste. When the legs are cool enough to handle, trim the skin from the bones to neaten the legs. Reheat them in the sauce before serving.

To make the bread sauce, melt the butter in a pan then add the shallot and a bit of salt and pepper. Sweat the shallot for about 6–8 minutes, stirring often, until soft. Add the garlic, milk and cream. Bring the liquid to a simmer and cook for 5 minutes. Add the diced bread and simmer for a few more minutes until the bread is soft. Transfer the sauce to a food processor and blitz until smooth, then season to taste with salt and pepper.

Preheat the oven to 220°C/Gas Mark 7. Heat 2 tablespoons of the oil in a wide heavy-based pan until hot. Brown the pheasant crowns in 2 batches if your pan is not wide enough to accommodate all 4. Fry for 2 minutes on each side until golden brown all over. Halfway through frying, add the butter and spoon over the pheasant to baste. Transfer to a roasting tin and cover the breasts with the strips of pancetta. Place the tin in the oven and roast for 10–12 minutes until just cooked through.

Meanwhile, heat the remaining oil in an ovenproof pan over a medium heat. Season the pumpkin wedges and fry for about 4–6 minutes until golden brown on both sides. Place the pan into the oven, on the lower shelf, and roast for 10–15 minutes until the pumpkin is just tender.

When the pheasant is ready, remove the roasting tin from the oven and leave to rest for 10–15 minutes in a warm spot. Carve out the breasts and serve on warmed plates with the roast pumpkin, crisp pancetta, gravy, bread sauce and home-made granola, if you wish.

DESSERTS

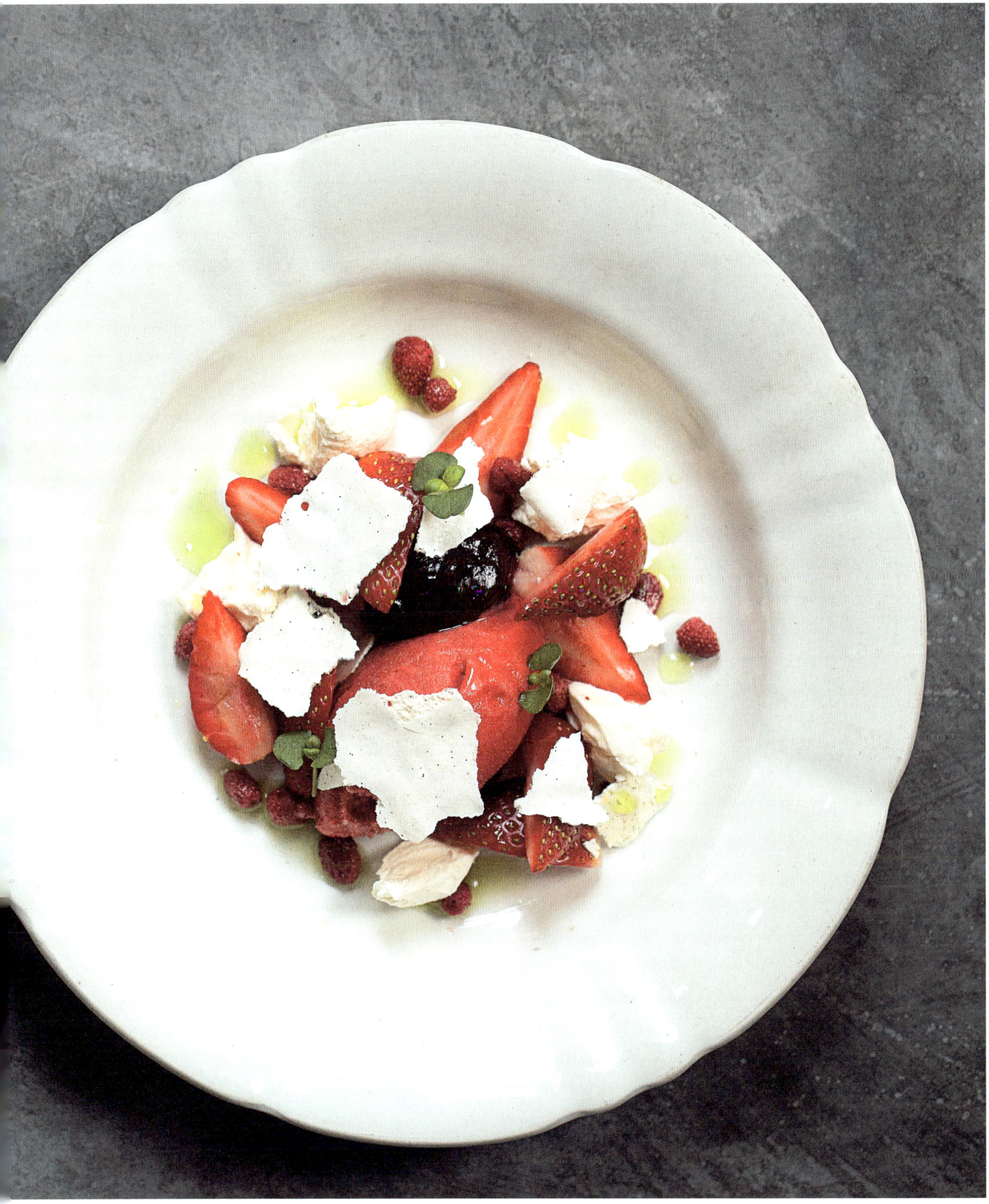

DESSERTS

170/ GRILLED BRIOCHE WITH LEMON CURD AND YOGHURT SORBET
173/ GARIGUETTE STRAWBERRY ETON MESS **174/** BROWN SUGAR TART WITH BLACK SESAME CRUMBLE AND CRÈME FRAÎCHE SORBET **176/** PISTACHIO AND OLIVE OIL CAKE WITH GARIGUETTE STRAWBERRIES AND CRÈME CHANTILLY **177/** CARROT CAKE WITH CREAM CHEESE SORBET **179/** LONDON HONEY AND ALMOND CAKE WITH HONEY JELLY **180/** GOAT'S CHEESE ICE CREAM WITH HONEYCOMB AND MILK BISCUIT **183/** THAI RUM ICE CREAM WITH COCONUT WAFERS **184/** PASSION FRUIT ICE CREAM WITH MILK MOUSSE AND CONFETTI FRUIT **185/** CHOCOLATE GANACHE WITH SPANISH OLIVE OIL AND SUGARED BREAD **186/** CHOCOLATE MOUSSE, BLOOD ORANGE JELLY AND CHOCOLATE CRUMBS **188/** SPICED CHOCOLATE CREAM WITH CARAMEL RICE CRISPIES **189/** CREAMED RICOTTA AND STRAWBERRY PEPPER COMPOTE ON THYME SOURDOUGH TOASTS

191/ BLOOD ORANGE GRANITA WITH CRÈME CHANTILLY AND CANDIED LIME
192/ APPLE AND BLACKBERRY CRUMBLE **195/** RICE PUDDING WITH OAT CRUMBLE BISCUIT
196/ MASCARPONE MOUSSE TARTS WITH POACHED RHUBARB AND RHUBARB SORBET
199/ TARTE TATIN WITH CLOTTED CREAM ICE CREAM **200/** ALMOND, PRUNE AND RUM
TART **201/** SPICED MELON SOUP WITH GINGER SORBET AND BASIL
202/ SUMMER FRUIT COOKED IN LIQUORICE WITH FROMAGE BLANC SORBET
205/ SLOE GIN AND ORANGE CURD ICE CREAM WITH SOFT BLACKBERRIES AND
SHORTBREAD **206/** ELDERFLOWER AND VANILLA PANNA COTTA WITH PEACH, RASPBERRY
AND THYME **208/** ROASTED PINEAPPLE WITH LONG PEPPERCORNS, MANGO AND LYCHEE
SORBET **209/** SMOKED BACON AND PEACH CORNBREAD WITH CANDIED PECAN AND
MAPLE CREAM **211/** BAKED VANILLA CHEESECAKE WITH PRUNES IN ARMAGNAC

GRILLED BRIOCHE WITH LEMON CURD AND YOGHURT SORBET

I don't know a single person who does not like lemon curd and it features in quite a few of my desserts. Of course, you can buy a good jar of lemon curd easily, but it is such a simple and rewarding jam to make yourself, plus I think the results are superior to shop-bought ones. You can use any type of bread for this dessert, but I prefer sweet and enriched breads like brioche or panettone.
The yoghurt sorbet transforms what could be breakfast toast with lemon curd into a fun dessert.

SERVES 4
(WITH EXTRA SORBET)

4 thick slices of brioche
icing sugar, to dust
Confit Lemon Strips, to serve (see page 230)

For the lemon curd (makes 500ml)
175g caster sugar
135ml fresh lemon juice (about 3–4 large lemons)
137g unsalted butter
2 large eggs

For the yoghurt sorbet
200ml water
150g caster sugar
25g liquid glucose
400g full-fat natural yoghurt

First, make the sorbet. Put the water, sugar and liquid glucose into a saucepan and stir over a medium–high heat until the sugar has dissolved. Boil the syrup for a few minutes until the temperature reaches 119°C on a sugar thermometer (soft ball stage), then take the pan off the heat and leave to cool completely.

Put the yoghurt into a large bowl and whisk to loosen it slightly. Pour in the cooled syrup and whisk again to mix. Strain the combined mixture through a fine sieve to get rid of any lumps. Pour the sieved mixture into the bowl of an ice-cream machine and churn until softly set. Transfer the sorbet to a clean container and freeze for at least 4 hours or overnight. (If you don't have an ice-cream machine, freeze the sorbet in a suitable container for a couple of hours then stir the ice crystals with a fork to break them down. Freeze again and repeat the process 2 or 3 more times.)

To make the lemon curd, put the sugar, lemon juice and butter into a large heatproof bowl. Place the bowl over a pan of gently simmering water, making sure the bottom of the bowl does not touch the water. Stir the mixture every once in a while until the butter has melted. Lightly beat the eggs then add them to the butter mixture. Whisk until all of the ingredients are well combined, then leave to cook for 15–20 minutes, stirring every now and again, until the mixture is creamy and thick enough to coat the back of a spoon. While still hot, spoon the lemon curd into sterilised jars and seal (keep chilled and use within 2–3 weeks).

Just before you are ready to serve grill the brioche. Preheat the grill to the highest setting. Arrange the brioche slices in a single layer on a baking tray. Evenly dust the slices with icing sugar then grill for 1–2 minutes until golden brown. Turn them over, dust with a little more icing sugar and grill for another minute.

Cut each brioche slice in half then top with a generous spoonful of lemon curd and a few lemon confit strips. Serve immediately with a scoop of yoghurt sorbet on the side.

DESSERTS

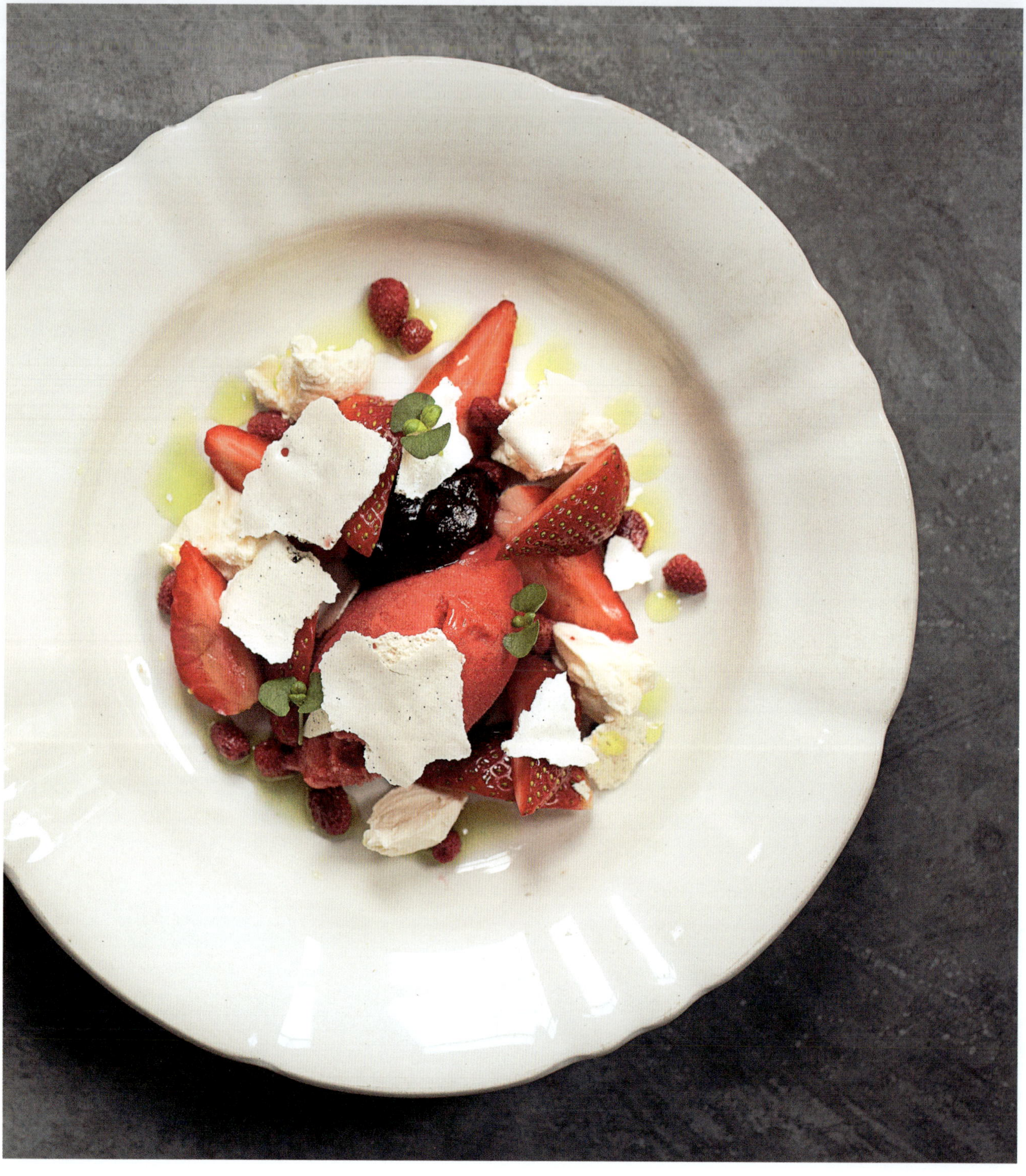

GARIGUETTE STRAWBERRY ETON MESS

I love Eton Mess and always have it on my menus in the summer when strawberries are in their prime. There is nothing better than ruby red strawberries nestled in bowl of cool meringue and cream. In the early summer, do try to get sweet and fragrant Gariguette strawberries, a Provençal variety which is gaining popularity amongst British farmers. This variety is quite soft and does not travel well so it is best to get locally grown ones or grow them yourself.

SERVES 4
(WITH EXTRA SORBET)

For the strawberry sorbet
750g strawberries, hulled and sliced
100g liquid glucose
50g icing sugar
1 tablespoon lemon juice

For the meringue
3 medium egg whites
1 vanilla pod, split in half, seeds scraped out with a knife
100g caster sugar

For the spiced strawberry purée
250g strawberries, hulled and sliced
4 tablespoons balsamic vinegar
½ teaspoon mixed peppercorns
2 star anise

To serve
150ml double cream
50g icing sugar
200g wild or Gariguette strawberries, hulled, to garnish
small basil leaves

Start by making the strawberry sorbet. Put the strawberries into a blender and blend until smooth. Pass the purée through a fine sieve, pressing the pulp with the back of a wooden spoon or a ladle to extract as much juice as possible.

Pour the purée into a saucepan and warm over a low heat but do not allow it to get too hot. Add the liquid glucose and icing sugar, and stir until dissolved. Remove from the heat and add the lemon juice. Taste and add more icing sugar or lemon juice, as you like. Pour into a bowl, cover and cool in the refrigerator.

Once cold, pour the mixture into an ice-cream maker and churn until almost firm. Transfer to a freezerproof container and freeze until ready to serve. (If you don't have an ice-cream maker, transfer the strawberry mixture to a container and freeze for 4–5 hours, whisking with a fork every hour or so to break down the ice crystals to give a smoother texture.)

For the meringue, preheat the oven to 100°C/Gas Mark ¼ and line a baking sheet with silicone or baking parchment. Put the egg whites and vanilla seeds into the bowl of an electric mixer then beat until soft peaks form. Gradually whisk in the sugar, a little at a time, until all the sugar is incorporated and the meringue holds soft peaks. Spread the meringue thinly on to the prepared baking tray and bake for about 2 hours, or until the meringue is dry and sounds crisp when tapped underneath. Leave to cool on the tray or a cooling rack, then break into shards and store in an airtight container if making ahead.

For the spiced strawberry purée, blend the strawberries to a purée in a blender. Pass the purée through a fine sieve into a saucepan. Add the balsamic vinegar and bring to a simmer. Wrap the spices in a small piece of muslin and add to the pan. Increase the heat slightly and boil the purée for about 5 minutes or until reduced by one-third. Turn off the heat and allow to cool and infuse for at least 30 minutes. Remove and discard the spice bag, then chill the purée.

When you're ready to serve, whip the double cream and icing sugar to soft peaks. Place a few dollops of cream on individual plates. Drop small spoonfuls of strawberry purée around each plate and top them with the fresh and wild strawberries. Add neat scoops of strawberry sorbet to each plate then top with meringue shards and basil leaves. Serve at once.

BROWN SUGAR TART WITH BLACK SESAME CRUMBLE AND CRÈME FRAÎCHE SORBET

My Canadian head chef at Little Social, Cary Docherty, created this dish for the restaurant and it became an instant hit. The tart takes little effort to make but looks enticing and tastes divine. Believe me, one bite and you'll be hooked! The black sesame crumble adds a nutty crunch alongside the smooth tart and sorbet.

SERVES 8–10

750ml double cream
150g caster sugar
7 large egg yolks
50g light muscovado sugar

For the sweet pastry
200g plain flour
40g icing sugar
100g cold unsalted butter, diced
finely grated zest of ½ lemon
1 medium egg, lightly beaten, plus another beaten egg for glazing

For the sesame crumble (optional)
100g white chocolate
40ml sesame oil
75g black sesame seeds, toasted
75g crisped rice
20g tahini or sesame paste

For the crème fraîche sorbet
150g caster sugar
150ml water
45g liquid glucose
1 vanilla pod, split in half, seeds scraped out with a knife
2 tablespoons lemon juice
500g crème fraîche

Start by making the sorbet. Put the sugar, water, liquid glucose and vanilla seeds and pod into a saucepan and stir over a medium heat. Once the sugar has dissolved, take the pan off the heat and stir in the lemon juice and crème fraîche. Cool completely then pour into the bowl of an ice-cream machine and churn until softly set. Transfer to a freezerproof container and freeze until needed. (If you don't have an ice-cream machine, freeze the ice cream in a suitable container for about 90 minutes until it starts to freeze around the edges. Stir well then repeat the process twice more until the mixture is smooth and frozen. Freeze until needed.)

To make the pastry, put the flour, icing sugar, butter and lemon zest into a food processor and blitz until the mixture resembles fine crumbs. Add the egg and pulse until the mixture is just combined into a dough. Scrape the dough out on to a lightly floured surface and knead lightly until smooth, taking care not to overwork the pastry or it will become tough. Cover the pastry with cling film and leave to rest in the refrigerator for at least 20 minutes.

Roll out the pastry to a rough circle the thickness of a £1 coin. Use a 20cm loose-bottomed tart tin (at least 5cm deep) as a template to cut out a neat circle and lift it gently into the tin to line the base. Lightly press the pastry around the sides so that it reaches the sides of the tin and completely covers the base without any gaps. Chill again for at least 30 minutes to allow the pastry to firm up.

Preheat the oven to 170°C/Gas Mark 3. To blind-bake the pastry, line the pastry base with baking parchment and baking beans then place it on a baking sheet. Bake for 15–18 minutes, until the pastry is just set around the edges, then remove the beans and parchment. Brush the base with the beaten egg, then return to the oven for another 5 minutes until the pastry is lightly golden around the edges and there are no grey patches left. Remove and leave to cool slightly.

While the pastry is in the oven, make the filling. Heat half the cream in a saucepan over a medium heat. Put 100g of the caster sugar in a heavy-based pan and place over a high heat. As the sugar begins to melt around the edges, swirl the pan to dissolve the rest of the sugar evenly. Heat the caramel until it becomes a deep golden brown, but do not let it burn. Pour in the warm cream and stand back, as the caramel may spit and splatter. Stir over a medium heat to mix until any hardened caramel has melted and the sauce is smooth. Remove from the heat and stir in the remaining cream. Beat the egg yolks with the remaining 50g of caster sugar and the muscovado sugar then slowly stir in the caramel sauce. Strain the combined mixture through a fine sieve into a large jug.

Lower the oven temperature to 140°C/Gas Mark 1. Put the baking sheet with the pastry tin on the middle shelf of the oven and pull it out halfway, making sure that it is level. Carefully pour in the caramel and brown sugar filling until it almost reaches the top of the tin. Bake for about 1 hour until the edges are just about set and the top is lightly golden brown. The tart will be quite wobbly in the middle when you gently shake the tin, but it will firm up and set as it cools. Remove from the oven and leave to cool for a few minutes. If you find that the caramel has hardened, place the pan over a medium heat for a couple of minutes. Leave to cool completely, then let it continue to firm up for a few hours in the refrigerator.

To make the sesame crumble, melt the white chocolate in a bowl set over a pan of gently simmering water, making sure the base of the bowl does not touch the water. Take the bowl off the heat, add the rest of the ingredients and mix well. Spread the mixture out on a baking sheet lined with a silicone liner (or baking parchment) and bake at 140°C/Gas Mark 1 for 25 minutes, until golden and crisp. Remove from the oven and cool. Store in an airtight container if not using all at once.

To serve, unmould the tart then cut into neat slices with a thin knife warmed slightly in a jug of hot water. Place a slice on each plate. Add mounds of the crumble next to each slice and top with a scoop of sorbet. Serve at once.

DESSERTS

PISTACHIO AND OLIVE OIL CAKE WITH GARIGUETTE STRAWBERRIES AND CRÈME CHANTILLY

This green pistachio cake reminds me of the polenta cakes I enjoyed in Italy, but it is lighter and superbly moist thanks to the ground nuts and olive oil. The cake is delicious on its own, but it is amazing eaten with fresh strawberries and cream.

SERVES 6–8

For the cake
3 large eggs
200g caster sugar
100g unsalted butter, melted and cooled
125ml olive oil
juice and zest of ½ lemon
juice and zest of ½ orange
50g fine polenta
50g plain flour
1 teaspoon baking powder
200g ground pistachio nuts (you can grind whole nuts yourself in a food processor but pulse them very, very slowly so they don't become oily and turn to a paste)

For the Gariguette strawberry purée
100ml red wine
100ml water
30g caster sugar
600g Gariguette strawberries (or whichever type is available to you)
juice of 1 lemon

For the crème Chantilly
250ml double cream
½ vanilla pod, split in half, seeds scraped out with a knife
25g icing sugar

First make the cake. Preheat the oven to 150°C/Gas Mark 2. (For this cake, it really is best to use a conventional setting and not a fan oven.) Grease and line a 20cm round cake tin.

Put the eggs and sugar into the bowl of an electric mixer and beat on a high speed for a few minutes, until light and frothy. In another bowl, mix the melted butter, olive oil, and orange and lemon juices together. Fold this into the egg mixture. Sift the polenta, flour and baking powder together then fold in the ground pistachios. Fold the dry mixture into the wet mixture, taking care not to overwork the cake batter. Pour the batter into the prepared cake tin and bake for 35–40 minutes until a cake skewer inserted into the middle of the cake comes out clean.

For the strawberry purée, place all ingredients into a saucepan and bring to the boil. Strain the liquid from the strawberries and blend the mixture to a fine purée in a food processor or blender. Leave to cool, cover and chill, if making ahead.

For the crème Chantilly, whip the cream, vanilla seeds and icing sugar to soft peaks. Cut the cake into slices and serve each portion with a dollop of crème Chantilly and a drizzle of the strawberry purée.

CARROT CAKE WITH CREAM CHEESE SORBET

At our dessert bar at Pollen Street Social, we once offered a double carrot cake pudding. It was, essentially, a carrot cake hidden inside a carrot cake sorbet. It looked great and tasted sensational, and the surprise element blew people away. That dessert was complicated and time-consuming to make, so I'm sharing a simpler but equally delicious carrot cake recipe here.

SERVES 8–10

250g unsalted butter, melted and cooled
350g soft light brown sugar
4 large eggs, lightly beaten
350g self-raising flour
3 teaspoons baking powder
2 teaspoons ground cinnamon
1 teaspoon ground nutmeg
1 teaspoon fine sea salt
400g grated carrots
100g chopped walnuts
200g raisins

For the cream cheese sorbet
260ml water
300g caster sugar
80ml fresh lemon juice
35g liquid glucose
800g softened cream cheese, whipped until smooth

First, make the sorbet. Combine the water, sugar, lemon juice and liquid glucose in a saucepan and stir over a medium heat to encourage the sugar to dissolve. Increase the heat and bring to the boil. Once all the sugar crystals have dissolved, take the pan off the heat and leave the syrup to cool completely. To speed up the cooling process, pour the syrup into a bowl then sit the bowl in a larger bowl of iced water. Give the mixture a stir every once in a while as it cools.

Once the syrup has cooled, whisk in the cream cheese. Use an electric whisk in order to avoid any lumps – the mixture will be quite thick. Transfer the mixture to the bowl of an ice-cream machine and churn until almost set. Scrape the ice cream into a freezerproof container, cover and freeze for a few hours or overnight. (If you don't have an ice-cream machine, put the mixture into the container and freeze for about 90 minutes. Take it out and beat the ice crystals with a fork to break them up. Repeat this every 90 minutes 2 or 3 more times until the sorbet is smooth and set.)

To make the cake, preheat the oven to 180°C/Gas Mark 4. Butter and line a 23cm springform cake tin, making sure you line it with paper that rises at least 2.5cm higher than the rim, as the cake will rise. Beat the butter and sugar until light and fluffy. Gradually beat in the eggs, adding a bit of flour if the batter looks like it is about to split. Sift the flour, baking powder, cinnamon, nutmeg and salt over the bowl then fold the dry mixture into the wet. Finally fold through the carrots, walnuts and raisins. Place the cake batter in the cake tin, levelling the top, then bake for 1 hour 40 minutes, until the cake is golden brown and springy and a skewer inserted into the centre comes out clean.

Remove the cake from the oven and leave to cool slightly, then unmould from the tin and place on a wire rack to cool. Once cooled, transfer to a cake plate or stand. Slice and serve with the cream cheese sorbet.

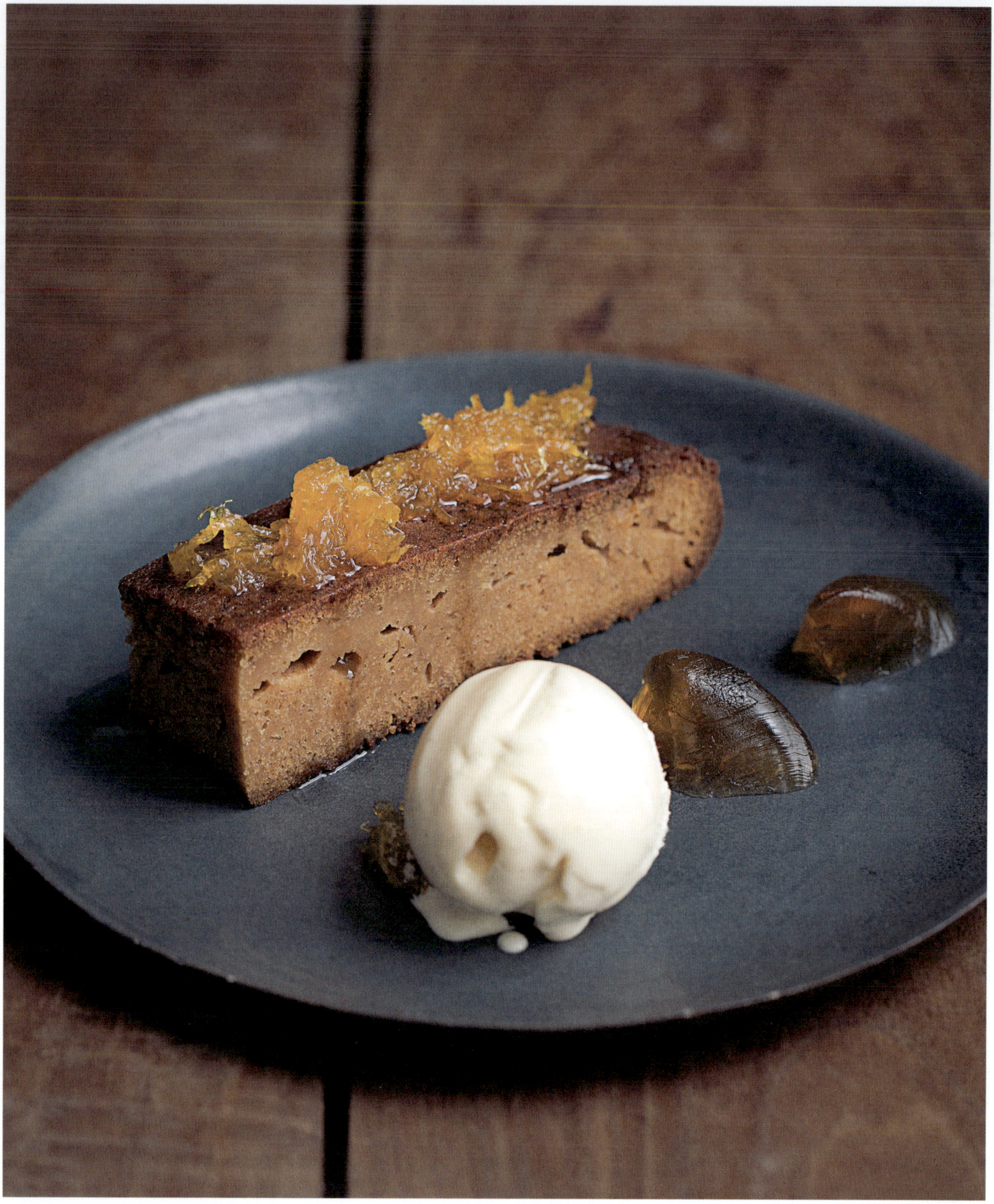

LONDON HONEY AND ALMOND CAKE WITH HONEY JELLY

This fragrant and dense cake is one of our main desserts at Social Eating House. My head chef there, Paul Hood, and I worked on this recipe with the aim of inventing a cake to showcase the amazing flavours of our local honey. In our case, the honey literally came from the rooftops of Islington, supplied by the London Honey Company. If you bake the cake, don't leave out the jelly accompaniment – it really gives the dessert another dimension.

SERVES 8–10

200g unsalted butter
150g clear honey, plus extra to glaze
150g caster sugar
200g ground almonds
40g plain flour
8 medium egg whites, at room temperature
crème fraîche or Vanilla Ice Cream (see page 231), to serve

For the honey jelly
3 small gelatine leaves
150g clear honey
3.5ml moscatel or sherry vinegar
150ml hot water

Orange marmalade (optional)
4 Seville oranges, about 500g, well scrubbed, quartered
500ml water
700g granulated sugar

To make the honey jelly, soak the gelatine leaves in a bowl of cold water. Heat the honey in a heavy-based saucepan until it begins to colour. As soon as it turns a caramel colour, add the vinegar and water. Stir well to combine. If the honey hardens upon contact with the liquid, continue to heat and stir until it melts. Squeeze the excess water from the gelatine leaves and add these to the pan. Stir to dissolve. Pour the honey mixture into a small sealable container and leave to cool completely. Cover the container and chill the jelly for a few hours until set.

For the marmalade, cut out the segments from the orange quarters. Thinly slice the orange skins using a sharp knife and set aside. Put the segments into a heavy-based pan and add the water and sugar. Bring to the boil then reduce the heat to the lowest setting and gently simmer for about an hour. Strain the mixture through a fine sieve into a clean pan, pressing down on the pulp to extract all the juice. Add the sliced orange skins and bring to a simmer. Gently simmer for another hour until the skins are tender and you have a loose marmalade consistency. To test if the marmalade has reached setting point, remove the pan from the heat then spoon a little on to a cold plate. Leave to cool for a few minutes. If the marmalade thickens and forms a skin, it's ready. If not, return the pan to the heat and cook for a few more minutes and test again.

Preheat the oven to 180°C/Gas Mark 4. Grease and lightly flour a 20cm loose-bottomed square cake tin. Melt the butter in a saucepan over a medium heat. Let it cook until it turns golden brown and releases a nutty fragrance, then remove the pan from the heat and stir in the honey. Leave to cool.

Meanwhile, mix the sugar, almonds and flour in a large mixing bowl. Make a well in the centre of the dry mixture then pour in the butter and honey. Fold the mixture until combined. Lightly beat the egg whites with a fork in another bowl, then add this to the batter. Fold through until the mixture is smooth and well combined. Pour the mixture into the prepared cake tin. Bake for 30–40 minutes, until the top is golden brown and a skewer inserted into the centre of the cake comes out clean. Remove from the oven and leave to cool on a cooling rack. While the cake is still warm, brush a little honey on the top to glaze it.

Run a thin knife around the cake tin before unmoulding the cake. Cut into slices or squares and serve with the honey jelly, orange marmalade, if using, and crème fraîche or vanilla ice cream, as you prefer.

GOAT'S CHEESE ICE CREAM WITH HONEYCOMB AND MILK BISCUIT

Goat's cheese is not normally a flavour you'd associate with ice cream, but it really works! It doesn't happen often, but once every few years I come across a dish that makes me stop and think about what I'm eating. The last time this happened I was dining at a three-Michelin-starred restaurant in Tokyo called Quintessence, where they served a toasted Japanese rice and marshmallow ice cream. It was unfamiliar but mesmerising and I was completely sold on the dessert. I'd like to think that this goat's cheese ice cream delivers a similar effect.

SERVES 6

For the goat's cheese ice cream
150g caster sugar
350ml water
500g creamy goat's cheese
100g crème fraîche
lemon juice, to taste

For the honeycomb
130g granulated sugar
3–4 tablespoons water
20g clear honey
1 teaspoon bicarbonate of soda

For the milk biscuit (optional)
450ml whole milk
150g liquid glucose

Note: you will need to make the milk biscuits the day before you want to serve the dessert.

If you're making the milk biscuit, preheat the oven to its lowest setting. Put the milk and liquid glucose into a deep saucepan and scald over a medium–high heat. Before the liquid begins to bubble up the sides of the pan, remove the pan from the heat. Using a hand-held stick blender, carefully blend until the syrupy milk is light and foamy. Scoop up the foam and spoon on to a baking sheet lined with a silicone mat or baking parchment. Once you've removed all the foam, repeat the process 3 or 4 times or until you have enough foam to cover the tray. Put the baking sheet in the oven and leave the foam to dry out and crisp overnight. Break into pieces and store in an airtight container until ready to serve.

To make the ice cream, put the sugar and water in a saucepan and stir over a medium heat to dissolve the sugar. Take the pan off the heat and whisk in the goat's cheese, crème fraîche and lemon juice. Strain the mixture through a fine sieve into the bowl of an ice-cream machine, then chill until the mixture is cold. Put the bowl into the ice-cream machine and churn until softly set. Transfer the ice cream to a freezerproof container, cover and freeze for at least 4 hours until set. (If you do not have an ice-cream machine, freeze the mixture in a suitable container for 90 minutes then stir the ice crystals that are beginning to form. Return to the freezer and repeat this process 2 or 3 times.)

For the honeycomb, line a baking sheet with silicone or baking parchment. Put the sugar, water and honey into a heavy-based saucepan and heat the mixture gently, stirring initially to dissolve the sugar and honey. Once the sugar has dissolved, increase the heat to high and let the syrup boil until it turns golden brown and begins to caramelise. Stir in the bicarbonate of soda. The mixture will immediately bubble up into a foaming mass. Pour it on to the lined baking sheet. Tip the sheet from side to side to spread out the mixture. Leave to cool completely, by which time the honeycomb will harden and become crisp and brittle. Break the honeycomb into small pieces and store in an airtight container until ready to use.

To serve, scoop the ice cream into shallow bowls and scatter over the honeycomb and milk biscuit pieces.

DESSERTS

SOCIAL SUPPERS

THAI RUM ICE CREAM WITH COCONUT WAFERS

This is a Stephen Terry recipe and I remember making it for the time at Coast restaurant. It is one of my favourite ice creams because it is surprising yet delicious. It is a good dessert for entertaining, as it provides a fun end to the meal. Bring it out to the table and let everyone guess the flavour of the ice cream. The coconut wafers are lovely with the ice cream, but do try to spread the wafers thinly before you bake them, as they can be tough if they're too thick.

SERVES 8

For the rum ice cream
150ml Malibu
250ml coconut milk
250ml double cream
1 lemongrass stalk, roughly chopped
3 Kaffir lime leaves, roughly chopped
1 red chilli, deseeded and roughly chopped
1 teaspoon chopped ginger
1 teaspoon chopped galangal
5 large egg yolks
100g caster sugar

For the coconut wafers
150g desiccated coconut
150g icing sugar
50g plain flour
4 large egg whites
100g unsalted butter, melted and cooled

To make the ice cream, put the Malibu into a saucepan and boil it over a high heat until reduced by half. Pour into a bowl and leave to cool completely.

Pour the coconut milk and cream into the same saucepan and add the lemongrass, lime leaves, chilli, ginger and galangal. Slowly bring the liquid to a simmer. Meanwhile, whisk the egg yolks and sugar together in a large bowl.

Strain the coconut cream mixture through a fine sieve and discard the aromatics. Gradually whisk it into the sugary eggs, whisking the whole time to prevent the eggs from scrambling. Pour the mixture back into the saucepan and stir over a medium heat until the mixture begins to thicken to a custard that lightly coats the back of a spoon. Take the pan off the heat and stir in the reduced Malibu.

To cool the custard quickly, transfer it to a tall bowl and then set the bowl into a larger basin half-filled with iced water. Stir every once in a while to prevent a skin from forming on top of the custard. Once cooled, pour the mixture into the bowl of an ice-cream machine and churn until almost set. Scrape the ice cream into a freezerproof container and freeze for at least 4 hours until set. (If you don't have an ice-cream machine, freeze the custard in a suitable container for 90 minutes then stir the ice crystals with a fork to break them down. Freeze again and repeat the process 2 or 3 more times.)

Next, make the wafers. Preheat the oven to 180°C/Gas Mark 4. Line a baking tray with baking parchment or a silicone mat. Put the coconut, icing sugar and flour into the bowl of a stand-alone mixer. Add the egg whites and beat on a low speed until the ingredients are well incorporated. Beat in the melted butter. The mixture should be smooth and shiny at this point.

Put teaspoons of the mixture on to the silicone sheet and spread with the back of the spoon to a thin circle, about 5–6cm wide. Repeat until the silicone sheet is filled, leaving space between the circles. Cook the wafers for about 7 minutes until the edges are golden brown. Remove from the oven and use a palette knife to carefully transfer the wafers to a wire rack to cool (Alternatively you can leave them to dry over a rolling pin to give them a little curve.) Repeat until all the wafer mixture is used up.

Put the ice cream into the refrigerator about 15–20 minutes before serving so that it softens a little. Place neat scoops into chilled bowls and serve with the coconut wafers.

PASSION FRUIT ICE CREAM WITH MILK MOUSSE AND CONFETTI FRUIT

This is a dessert that I've been making since I opened Maze in 2005. We're basically offering the flavours of a passion fruit ice cream in two parts: a tart passion fruit sorbet and a smooth and creamy milk mousse. The confetti fruit is just a fun way to garnish the dessert with fresh tropical fruit. For best results, do make sure that the fruits are firm but ripe so that you can chop them finely. It also helps to freeze the fruit briefly before doing this.

SERVES 6

For the passion fruit ice cream
250g double cream
250g whole milk
4 large egg yolks
100g caster sugar
juice from 12–14 passion fruits (120ml in total)

For the milk mousse
2 gelatine leaves
300ml evaporated milk
70g caster sugar

For the confetti fruit
350g finely diced mixed tropical fruit (such as mango, papaya, kiwi, pineapple and guava)

First, make the ice cream. Pour the double cream and milk into a heavy-based saucepan. Gradually bring the liquid to the boil. Beat the egg yolks and sugar together in a mixing bowl. As soon as the creamy milk begins to bubble up the sides of the pan, take it off the heat and slowly trickle it into the sugary eggs, whisking the whole time. When fully incorporated, pour the mixture into a clean saucepan and stir with a wooden spoon over a medium–low heat until the mixture thickens to a light custard that thinly coats the back of the spoon.

Pass the custard through a fine sieve into a wide bowl. Stir in the passion fruit juice. Leave to cool, stirring every once in a while to prevent a skin from forming. Once cooled, pour the custard into the bowl of an ice-cream machine and churn until thick and almost set. Transfer to a freezerproof container, seal and freeze for at least a couple of hours until firm. (If you don't have an ice-cream machine, freeze the ice cream in a suitable container for about 90 minutes until it starts to freeze around the edges. Stir well then repeat the process twice more until the mixture is smooth and frozen. Freeze until needed.)

For the milk mousse, soak the gelatine leaves in a bowl of cold water for a few minutes. Meanwhile, bring the milk and sugar to the boil in a small saucepan, stirring to dissolve the sugar. Once the sugar has dissolved, take the pan off the heat. Drain and squeeze out the excess water from the softened gelatine leaves and add to the pan. Stir until the gelatine has dissolved. Strain the mixture through a fine sieve into a freezerproof container. Leave to cool then cover and freeze the mixture for a few hours until it is frozen. Transfer the frozen mixture to a mixing bowl and use a hand-held electric whisk to beat it until it is light and airy. Return to the freezerproof container, cover and freeze until ready to serve.

To serve, spoon the confetti fruit into chilled bowls and spoon over a layer of milk mousse. Top each bowl with a scoop of passion fruit ice cream and serve at once.

CHOCOLATE GANACHE WITH SPANISH OLIVE OIL AND SUGARED BREAD

Many of the tapas bars in Spain have a version of this modest dessert on their menu. It is simplicity at its best – just some really good chocolate ganache spread on lightly sweetened caramelised bread. A drizzle of good extra-virgin olive oil and a tiny sprinkle of sea salt really bring the flavours alive.

SERVES 4

100g dark chocolate (65–70 per cent cocoa solids), roughly chopped
120ml double cream
a pinch of sea salt
extra-virgin olive oil, preferably Spanish, to drizzle

For the sugared bread
4 slices of sourdough
softened butter, for spreading
icing sugar, for dusting

Place the chocolate in a bowl. Pour the double cream into a small saucepan and bring to the boil. As soon as it begins to bubble, tip it over the chocolate. Let it rest for 2 minutes then whisk until the chocolate has melted and the sauce is smooth. Transfer the chocolate ganache to a clean jar or bowl and leave to cool.

Preheat the oven to 200°C/Gas Mark 6. Spread some butter onto both sides of the sourdough slices and dust each side with icing sugar. Arrange them in a single layer on a baking tray lined with baking parchment and toast in the oven for 8–10 minutes, turning once, until golden brown and crisp on both sides. Divide the sugared bread between individual serving plates then spread each one with the chocolate ganache. Drizzle with a little olive oil, add a sprinkle of sea salt and serve immediately.

CHOCOLATE MOUSSE, BLOOD ORANGE JELLY AND CHOCOLATE CRUMBS

This is one for chocoholics and it is my way of adding the flavour of a hot chocolate drink to a mousse. Together with the blood orange jelly and crunchy chocolate crumbs, it is a truly satisfying way to end a meal.

SERVES 4

200g dark chocolate (at least 65 per cent cocoa solids), roughly chopped
150ml double cream
5 large egg whites

For the chocolate crumbs
50g caster sugar
60g ground almonds
40g plain flour
25g cocoa powder
¼ teaspoon sea salt
30g softened unsalted butter

For the blood orange jelly
250ml blood orange juice
2 sheets of leaf gelatine

Place the dark chocolate in a large bowl. Heat the cream in a small saucepan until it begins to scald. Take the pan off the heat and pour the hot cream over the chopped chocolate. Stir until the chocolate has completely melted and the mixture is smooth. Set aside to cool.

Whisk the egg whites to medium peaks (the whites will be fairly stiff but the tops of the peaks will be curling over), then fold this through the cooled chocolate mixture. Spoon into individual serving glasses then chill the glasses until ready to serve.

To make the blood orange jelly, gently heat the blood orange juice in a small saucepan until it is almost simmering. Meanwhile, soak the gelatine leaves in cold water for a few minutes to soften. Drain the gelatine and squeeze out the excess water. Add to the orange juice and take the pan off the heat. Stir to dissolve then strain the juice through a sieve into a small rigid plastic container. Leave to cool completely then cover and refrigerate until set.

For the chocolate crumbs, preheat the oven to 200°C/Gas Mark 6. Place all the ingredients into a food processor and blitz until you have a coarse crumble texture. Line a baking tray with baking parchment and spread the crumble evenly over the tray. Bake for 10–12 minutes, stirring once or twice until the mixture is dry and crisp. Allow to cool completely then store in an airtight container until ready to serve.

When ready to serve, sprinkle a layer of chocolate crumbs over each chocolate mousse and gently drop 1 or 2 spoonfuls of blood orange jelly on top. Serve immediately.

DESSERTS

SPICED CHOCOLATE CREAM WITH CARAMEL RICE CRISPIES

This is a grown-up take on my favourite guilty pleasure: chocolate cornflake clusters. Growing up, I used to make them with my mum and each time they were ready, I'd eat about fifteen of them in a row until I felt sick. This dessert is a little more sophisticated but it will please adults and children alike.

SERVES 4–6

For the spiced chocolate cream
450ml double cream
60g caster sugar
2 whole cardamom pods, lightly crushed
¼ teaspoon ground cinnamon
a pinch of sea salt
4 large egg yolks
200g dark chocolate (at least 65 per cent cocoa solids), roughly broken up

For the caramel rice crispies
butter, for greasing
220g fondant icing sugar
80ml water
160g crisped rice cereal
100g black and white sesame seeds

First, make the caramel rice crispies. Grease a deep 30 x 20cm baking tray with butter. Put the fondant sugar and water into a saucepan placed over a medium heat. Stir to dissolve the sugar then leave it to boil for 5 minutes until it turns to a light caramel. Pour in the crisped rice and sesame seeds. Carefully fold the dry ingredients into the hot caramel then quickly pour the combined mixture into the prepared tray. Gently press down the mixture with a wet spatula to spread it out evenly and into all corners. Leave to cool completely, by which time the mixture will have set. Cut into desired shapes then store in an airtight container until ready to serve.

Heat the double cream, sugar, cardamom pods, cinnamon and salt in a heavy-based saucepan, until just below boiling point.

Beat the egg yolks in a large bowl, and add the hot cream slowly, whisking all the time.

Return the mixture to a clean pan and heat gently until thickened (it's ready when the mixture coats the back of a wooden spoon). Set aside to infuse for 15 minutes.

Meanwhile, place the chocolate in a heatproof bowl and set the bowl on top of a pan of barely simmering water to melt.

Remove the cardamom pods from the custard and stir in the melted chocolate. Divide into bowls and chill in the refrigerator for at least 30 minutes. Serve with the caramel rice crispies.

CREAMED RICOTTA AND STRAWBERRY PEPPER COMPOTE ON THYME SOURDOUGH TOASTS

I first had a combination of strawberries, ricotta and thyme as a savoury crostini in a Shanghai restaurant opened by Jean-Georges Vongerichten. It was a fantastic starter but I was convinced that it would make an equally beautiful summery dessert.

SERVES 4

For the strawberry pepper compote
250g caster sugar
juice of ½ lemon
250g strawberries, hulled and halved
¼ teaspoon cracked black pepper

For the creamed ricotta
250g ricotta
2 tablespoons double cream

For the thyme sourdough
olive oil
a few sprigs of thyme, leaves stripped
4 thick slices of sourdough
sea salt

To serve
200g fresh strawberries, hulled and sliced
2–3 tablespoons Stock Syrup (see page 231)

To make the compote, put the sugar and lemon juice into a pan and place over a medium–high heat. Give it a stir and continue to heat until the sugar has dissolved. Add the strawberries and pepper and simmer for 5 minutes until the strawberries are soft but still holding their shape. Take the pan off the heat. Skim the scum from the surface of the compote then leave to cool completely in the pan.

For the creamed ricotta, in a bowl whisk together the ricotta and the cream until combined.

For the thyme sourdough, heat a thin layer of olive oil in a wide frying pan over a medium–low heat then add the thyme. After 30–60 seconds, when the thyme has imparted a lovely fragrance, add the sourdough slices to the pan. Increase the heat to medium–high and toast the bread for about 1½–2 minutes on each side, until golden brown. Remove from the pan and sprinkle with a little sea salt.

To serve, spread the toasts with the creamed ricotta then spoon over some strawberry compote. Toss the sliced strawberries with a little stock syrup then use to garnish each slice of toast. Serve immediately.

SOCIAL SUPPERS

BLOOD ORANGE GRANITA WITH CRÈME CHANTILLY AND CANDIED LIME

This is the definitive dessert for a dinner party because it is so easy to make and assemble and the results are fabulous. It is also great for serving a large crowd – just double or triple the recipe. I guarantee that everyone will enjoy this. You may end up with a little extra candied lime zest. If so, use it to top your breakfast yoghurt or plain vanilla ice cream.

SERVES 4–6

75g caster sugar
75ml water
juice of 12 blood oranges (about 1 litre of juice)
200ml Champagne (or dry sparkling wine)

For the candied lime
2 unwaxed limes
50g caster sugar
125ml water

For the crème Chantilly
200ml double cream
25g icing sugar
1 vanilla pod, split in half, seeds scraped out with a knife

For the granita, put the sugar and water into a small saucepan and stir over a medium heat to dissolve the sugar. Simmer for a couple of minutes then pour into a large bowl and leave to cool completely. Add the orange juice and Champagne to the syrup. Stir well then pour the mixture into a large, shallow, freezerproof container. Seal and freeze for an hour, then remove and stir the ice crystals around the edge of the container with a fork. Repeat the freezing and stirring until the entire mixture consists of ice crystals. Freeze until ready to serve.

Prepare the candied lime. Thinly slice off the zest of the limes without taking in any white pith. If you do get some white pith on the zest, slice it off with a small sharp knife. Stacking a few at a time, thinly slice the zest into thin matchstick strips. Put these into a small saucepan and cover with cold water. Bring to the boil then immediately drain the zest and return to the pan. Add the sugar and water and bring to a simmer, stirring to help the sugar dissolve. Simmer over a medium heat for 1–1¼ hours until the zest is soft. Remove the pan from the heat and leave to cool completely. Drain the lime pieces and spread out on a piece of kitchen paper to dry.

For the crème chantilly, put the cream, icing sugar and vanilla seeds into a large bowl. Whisk to soft peaks then set aside.

To serve, spoon the crème Chantilly into chilled bowls and top with the granita. Decorate with the candied lime and serve immediately.

APPLE AND BLACKBERRY CRUMBLE

I love crumbles and this one has been on our Pollen Street Social menu for the longest time. We serve the dessert in a fun way at the restaurant. Our waiters will bring out all the components and assemble the dessert tableside in a counter-intuitive manner. The mascarpone and cinnamon ice cream is placed at the bottom of each bowl and this is followed by the apple and blackberry compote and crumble. Saying that, it is delicious whichever way you plate it.

SERVES 4

For the marinated apple wedges
125g caster sugar
75ml cider
½ vanilla pod, split in half lenghtways, seeds scraped out with a knife
1 large (or 2 medium) apple(s), peeled, cored and sliced into thin wedges

For the apple and blackberry compote
1kg Bramley apples (about 5 or 6), peeled, cored and roughly chopped
a squeeze of lemon juice
60–100g caster sugar, to taste
1 vanilla pod, split in half, seeds scraped out with a knife
100g blackberries

For the crumble
45g softened butter
45g demerara sugar
45g caster sugar
45g ground almonds
45g plain flour
20g blanched hazelnuts, coarsely chopped
20g blanched almonds, coarsely chopped

To serve
a handful of blackberries
a few sprigs of lemon thyme, leaves only
Mascarpone and Cinnamon Ice Cream or Vanilla Ice Cream (both recipes page 231) or crème fraîche

First, prepare the marinated apple slices. Put the sugar into a heavy-based saucepan and place the pan over a medium–high heat. As the sugar begins to melt around the edges, tilt the pan slightly from side to side to encourage the sugar to melt evenly. When the caramel has turned to a terracotta colour, stand back and pour in the cider, taking care, as the hot caramel will spit and splutter upon contact with the cold liquid. If the caramel hardens at this point, stir it over a medium heat to melt it down again. Add the vanilla pod and seeds and boil for a few minutes to allow the flavours to infuse, then take the pan off the heat.

Place the apple wedges into a bowl and pour over the caramel. Leave to cool completely, then cover with cling film and chill overnight.

To make the apple and blackberry compote, put three-quarters of the diced apple in a heavy-based pan and the remainder in a bowl of water with a squeeze of lemon juice. Add the sugar, vanilla seeds and pod, and a few tablespoons of water to the pan then cook over a low heat for about 10 minutes, until the apples are soft. Drain and stir in the reserved diced apple and cook for another 5 minutes until the pieces are just tender but still holding their shape. Transfer to a bowl and leave to cool before folding through the blackberries. If making ahead, cool completely then cover and chill until needed.

For the crumble, preheat the oven to 150°C/Gas Mark 2. Place all the ingredients in a large mixing bowl and stir together until combined. Spread the mixture on to a lightly greased baking tray and bake for 20 minutes until lightly golden brown and crisp. Leave to cool and store in an airtight container if making in advance.

When ready to serve, warm the apple compote in a pan and the crumble in a low oven, as necessary. Spoon the compote into shallow serving bowls. Arrange a few slices of marinated apple next to the compote, draining off the excess caramel (save the caramel to drizzle over ice cream or yoghurt). Top the compote with the warm crumble then scatter over some fresh blackberries and lemon thyme leaves. Add a scoop of ice cream or crème fraîche on the side, as wished, and serve immediately.

DESSERTS

SOCIAL SUPPERS

RICE PUDDING WITH OAT CRUMBLE BISCUIT

This is a really wintry dessert that you can serve either warm or cold. The rice pudding is served with goat's milk, giving it a distinctive richness. This is offset by a slightly salty oat crumble which adds texture to the rice pudding. For a truly indulgent treat, we top our rice pudding with goat's milk ice cream, but you can leave it out to keep things simple. This recipe will yield more oat crumble than you need, but you can use up any leftovers by serving alongside a simple ice cream.

SERVES 4–6

For the rice pudding

175g pudding rice
1 litre goat's milk
70g caster sugar, or to taste
1 vanilla pod, split in half, seeds scraped out with a knife
75ml double cream, softly whipped

For the oat crumble biscuit

90g unsalted butter, softened
40g caster sugar
30g clear honey
½ teaspoon fine sea salt
½ vanilla pod, split in half, seeds scraped out with a knife
135g plain flour
1 teaspoon bicarbonate of soda
60g rolled oats

To serve

Goat's Cheese Ice Cream (see page 180) (optional)

If you have time, soak the rice in cold water overnight. Drain and put into a heavy-based saucepan with the milk, sugar and vanilla seeds. Bring to a simmer, stirring to dissolve the sugar. Cook very slowly for 45–60 minutes until the rice is tender, or cooked to your liking. Be sure to stir the mixture from time to time, as the rice may catch and burn on the bottom of the pan. Taste and add a bit more sugar if you prefer it sweeter. When ready, remove the pan from the heat, cover with a lid and leave to stand for 15–20 minutes. Give it a stir every once in a while to prevent a skin from forming on top as it cools.

To make the oat biscuit, preheat the oven to 140°C/Gas Mark 1. Put the butter, sugar, honey, salt and vanilla seeds into the bowl of a stand-alone mixer fitted with the beater attachment. Beat until the mixture is light, fluffy and well combined. Tip in the remaining ingredients and mix on a low speed until the dough comes together. Do not overmix or the biscuits will be tough.

Roll the dough out into a rough rectangle between two large sheets of baking parchment – it should be about 1cm thick. Use the baking parchment to transfer the dough to a baking sheet. Remove the parchment and bake for about 15 minutes, then lower the oven temperature to 70°C/Gas Mark ¼ (the lowest gas mark) and bake for another 15 minutes until the biscuit is cooked and golden all over. Remove from the oven and leave to cool completely. Break into large pieces and store in an airtight container.

To serve, whip the double cream in a small bowl to soft peaks. Fold this into the rice pudding then divide between serving bowls. Crumble some oat biscuits on top and add a scoop of the goat's cheese ice cream, if using. Serve at once.

MASCARPONE MOUSSE TARTS WITH POACHED RHUBARB AND RHUBARB SORBET

This sophisticated dessert is a cross between a tartlet and a millefeuille. It looks nothing like a child's pudding but one bite and I'm instantly reminded of my childhood. The 'mousse' is actually a mascarpone panna cotta cut neatly into rounds to fit between layers of puff pastry discs. The rhubarb has been gently poached in a gorgeous ginger and grenadine syrup and the rhubarb sorbet is beautiful, both in the way it is presented and in the way it tastes.

SERVES 4
(WITH EXTRA SORBET)

2 large or 3 small gelatine leaves
250ml whole milk
1 vanilla pod, split in half, seeds scraped out with a knife
60g caster sugar
3 medium egg yolks
200g mascarpone
300g puff pastry
250ml double cream
icing sugar, to dust
shredded mint leaves, to decorate (optional)

For the rhubarb sorbet
500g rhubarb, trimmed and chopped
zest and juice of 1 orange
zest and juice of 2 lemons
25g peeled and finely grated ginger
400ml water
250g caster sugar
100ml grenadine

For the poached rhubarb
4–5 stalks of rhubarb
50g pickled ginger, sliced
75g granulated sugar
60ml grenadine

First, make the rhubarb sorbet. Put all the ingredients into a pan and place over a medium heat. Stir to dissolve the sugar, then simmer for about 10–12 minutes until the rhubarb is very soft. Transfer the rhubarb and its juices to a food processor and blend to a purée. Pass the purée through a fine sieve and push down with the back of a wooden spoon or a ladle to extract as much juice as possible. Leave to cool completely, then pour the purée into the bowl of an ice-cream machine and churn until almost set. Transfer to a freezerproof container and freeze for at least 4 hours or overnight until the sorbet is set. (If you don't have an ice-cream machine, freeze the sorbet in a suitable container for a couple of hours then stir the ice crystals with a fork to break them down. Freeze again and repeat the process 2 or 3 more times.)

To make the mascarpone mousse, soak the gelatine leaves in a bowl of cold water. Put the milk and vanilla pod and seeds into a saucepan and bring to a simmer.

Meanwhile, whisk the sugar and egg yolks together, then very slowly incorporate the hot milk, whisking the whole time. Return the combined mixture to the saucepan and stir frequently over a medium–low heat until the mixture begins to thicken to a custard that lightly coats the back of a spoon. Drain and squeeze out the excess water from the gelatine leaves and add these to the pan. Stir to dissolve. Pass the custard through a fine sieve into a shallow container. Fold through the mascarpone then cover with cling film and chill for a few hours.

Preheat the oven to 190°C/Gas Mark 5. Roll out the puff pastry to 2–3mm thick on a lightly floured surface. Use an 8cm pastry cutter to cut out 12 discs of puff pastry. Put the pastry discs on a baking sheet lined with baking parchment or a silicone mat. Prick each pastry disc all over with a fork. Lightly grease another baking sheet and gently place this on top of the first to hold down the pastry discs (be careful though, you don't want to weigh them down so much that the discs lose their shape). Bake for 15 minutes, then gently remove the top baking sheet and evenly dust the pastry discs with icing sugar. Return to the oven and bake for another 5–10 minutes until golden and crisp. Remove from the oven and leave to cool completely.

Next, prepare the poached rhubarb. Cut the rhubarb into 8cm lengths. If they're very thick, halve them lengthways into batons about 5mm thick. Place in a bowl with the pickled ginger. Put the sugar and 200ml water in a small pan and dissolve over a medium heat. Add the grenadine and bring to the boil. Add the rhubarb and ginger and leave to simmer for 3 minutes, then remove from the heat and let the rhubarb steep until it cools completely.

To assemble, place a pastry disc on each serving plate. Use the pastry cutter to stamp out neat rounds of the mousse. Place these on top of the plated pastry bases. Repeat with another layer of pastry and mousse and top with a pastry disc. The tarts should have two layers of mascarpone mousse sandwiched between three pastry discs. Drain and neatly pile a few rhubarb batons alongside the tart then decorate with the shredded mint leaves, if using. Finally, place neat scoops of rhubarb sorbet on top of and alongside the tarts. Serve at once.

DESSERTS

SOCIAL SUPPERS

TARTE TATIN WITH CLOTTED CREAM ICE CREAM

I often play with classic dishes, deconstructing them to create a modern presentation or adding different flavours or textures to give them an interesting twist. But I know to leave a recipe alone when it is as perfect as this traditional apple tarte Tatin. The clotted cream ice cream is gorgeously creamy, but you could simply serve the tarte Tatin with a good vanilla ice cream to save time.

SERVES 4
(WITH EXTRA ICE CREAM)

3 or 4 Pink Lady apples
180g puff pastry
50g unsalted butter
50g caster sugar

For the clotted cream ice cream
670ml whole milk
100g caster sugar
30g liquid glucose
5 medium egg yolks
100g clotted cream

First, peel the apples neatly, then cut into quarters and remove the cores. Trim the edges of each apple quarter to neaten the sides. Arrange the apple quarters in a single layer on a plate lined with kitchen paper. Place the plate in the refrigerator, uncovered, for 12 hours or overnight. (This will help to dry out the apples so that their juices will not dilute the caramel during cooking.) Do not worry if the apples turn brown as they will be covered with dark caramel later on.

Next, make the ice cream. Put the milk into a heavy-based saucepan, along with the sugar and liquid glucose. Stir over a low heat to dissolve the sugar. Meanwhile, put the egg yolks into a large bowl and beat lightly. Once the sugar has dissolved, take the pan off the heat. Slowly add the warm milk to the eggs, whisking continuously as you do so.

Once everything is combined, return the mixture to the pan and stir over a low heat until the custard begins to thicken. When it's ready the custard should lightly coat the back of a spoon and you should be able to draw a line across it. Transfer the custard to a large bowl and leave to cool completely. Give it a stir every once in a while to prevent a skin from forming as it cools. Once cool, whisk in the clotted cream, using a beater or hand blender. Cover with cling film and chill for a few hours.

Pour the cold custard into the bowl of an ice-cream machine and churn until it has thickened and is beginning to set. Transfer to an airtight container and freeze for at least 2 hours or until the ice cream is firm. (If you don't have an ice-cream machine, freeze the custard in a suitable container for 90 minutes then stir the ice crystals with a fork to break them down. Freeze again and repeat the process 2 or 3 more times.)

To make the Tatin, put a small 20cm ovenproof frying pan into the freezer. Roll out the puff pastry between two sheets of baking parchment, into a circle slightly larger than the pan. Put the pastry circle into the freezer for 30 minutes.

Remove the cold pan and pastry circle from the freezer. Thinly slice the butter and arrange a neat layer on the base of the pan. Sprinkle the sugar evenly over the butter. Remove the apple quarters from the refrigerator. Place 2 of the apple quarters, skinned side down, in the middle of the pan, then neatly arrange the remaining quarters around them. Overlap them slightly to fit in as many as possible.

Remove the baking parchment from the puff pastry and lay the pastry over the apples. Use your fingers to gently press the edges of the pastry down along the edges of the pan and over the apples so that the contours are visible. (If the pastry is frozen hard, leave it for a few minutes to thaw out before doing this.) Prick the pastry well with a fork to allow the steam to escape during the cooking. Chill for about 10 minutes or until you are ready to cook.

Preheat the oven to 180°C/Gas Mark 4. Place the pan over a high heat and let the butter and sugar caramelise to a rich, dark golden colour. As the butter and sugar begin to melt, swirl the pan a few times so that the rim of the puff pastry becomes caramelised as well. Carefully put the pan into the oven and bake for about 25–30 minutes, until the pastry is golden and crisp. Remove from the oven and let the tarte rest for a few minutes before inverting on to a plate. Serve with scoops of the clotted cream ice cream.

ALMOND, PRUNE AND RUM TART

Brioche-based tarts are a little tricky to manage, but they are a delightful change from the usual shortcrust or puff pastry bases. This prune and rum tart is absolutely delicious and it is one of my favourite classic desserts. I doubt you will have any, but should you find yourself with some leftover tart, keep it in an airtight container in a cool part of the kitchen. It should keep well for a few days.

SERVES 8

For the prune and almond filling
250g pitted prunes
60ml rum
150ml orange juice
250g caster sugar
240g unsalted butter
2 medium eggs, plus 1 medium egg yolk
10g plain flour
240g ground almonds

For the brioche pastry
225g strong white flour
½ teaspoon fine sea salt
40g caster sugar
8g fresh yeast (or half a 7g dried active yeast sachet)
30ml tepid whole milk
100g unsalted butter, softened, plus extra to brush
2 large eggs, lightly beaten
¼ teaspoon ground nutmeg
1 teaspoon ground cinnamon
1 medium egg, to glaze

To serve
Clotted cream (optional)

First, soak the prunes in the rum and enough orange juice to cover for at least an hour or overnight.

To make the pastry, sift the flour and salt into the bowl of a stand-alone electric mixer fitted with a dough hook. Stir in 10g of the sugar and make a well in the centre. Dissolve the yeast in the milk and add to the bowl along with the butter and eggs. Run the machine on a low speed to incorporate the ingredients and keep it running until the dough is soft and sticky. Increase the speed and mix until the dough comes together and leaves the sides of the bowl. It should look rather smooth and elastic.

Remove the bowl from the machine and cover it with a lightly oiled piece of cling film. Chill and let the dough rise in the refrigerator for about 8 hours or overnight, until it doubles in volume.

When you're ready to assemble and bake the tart, place a baking sheet in the middle shelf of the oven and preheat the oven to 160°C/Gas Mark 3.

Roll out the pastry thinly on a lightly floured surface to a wide circle. Drape it over a rolling pin and lay it over a 23–24cm loose-bottomed tart tin, leaving a rim of dough overhanging the sides. Gently push the dough into the edges of the tart tin, then trim off the excess dough to neaten the top. Mix the remaining 30g of sugar with the cinnamon together in a small bowl.

Beat the egg for the glaze, then brush the base and sides of the pastry with it, before dusting with the cinnamon sugar.

Drain the prunes, reserving the marinade, and arrange them evenly over the base of the tart.

For the rest of the filling, cream the sugar and butter with an electric beater until the mixture is light and fluffy. Gradually beat in the eggs and egg yolk. Fold in the flour, ground almonds and 3 tablespoons of the prune marinade. Spoon the almond filling over the prunes and level the top with a spatula. Put the tart tin on the preheated baking sheet and bake for around 1 hour and 15 minutes, until the pastry is risen and the top is golden brown.

Remove from the oven and brush with the remaining prune marinade. Leave to cool completely before turning out on to a serving plate. Slice and serve with dollops of clotted cream, if you wish.

SPICED MELON SOUP WITH GINGER SORBET AND BASIL

This is one of the most refreshing desserts you can have. When honeydew melon is in season, I serve the spiced melon soup in a small chilled glass as a palate cleanser in-between courses. It is an ideal dessert for people with dairy and wheat intolerances and a lovely way to get your fruit intake for the day. It is also a great way to use up over-ripe melons.

**SERVES 4
(WITH EXTRA SORBET)**

*1 cantaloupe melon, halved and deseeded
200g fresh pineapple cubes
20g ginger, peeled and chopped
50g caster sugar
a handful of small basil leaves, to garnish*

For the ginger sorbet
*250g granulated sugar
2 tablespoons liquid glucose
400ml water
20g peeled and chopped ginger
1 tablespoon lemon juice*

First, make the ginger sorbet. Put the sugar, liquid glucose and water in a saucepan and stir over a medium–high heat until the sugar has dissolved. Let the syrup boil for a few minutes, then take the pan off the heat. Add the ginger and lemon juice to the syrup and leave to cool completely.

Strain the syrup through a fine sieve into a jug. Pour 50ml of the syrup into a bowl and set aside. Pour the rest into the bowl of an ice-cream machine. Churn until the sorbet is softly set. Transfer the sorbet to a freezerproof container and seal. Freeze for at least 4 hours or overnight, until set. (If you don't have an ice-cream machine, freeze the sorbet for a couple of hours, then remove and stir to break down the ice crystals. Return to the freezer and repeat 2 or 3 more times.)

Cut the melon flesh into eighths and remove the skins. Finely slice 2 wedges of melon into long strips and place them in a wide, shallow bowl. Pour over the reserved syrup from the sorbet to marinate the melon slices. Roughly chop the remainder of the melon and put into a blender along with the pineapple, ginger and sugar. Blend to a fine and smooth soup. Pass the soup through a fine sieve into a bowl. Cover with cling film and chill until needed.

To serve, arrange the marinated melon slices on the base of chilled, shallow soup bowls. Place a neat scoop of ginger sorbet into each bowl then pour in enough melon soup to come halfway up the sides of the sorbet. Garnish with the basil leaves and serve at once.

SUMMER FRUIT COOKED IN LIQUORICE WITH FROMAGE BLANC SORBET

Liquorice may not be an obvious pairing for soft fruit, but believe me they work really well together. The liquorice imparts a sweet aniseed note to the poached fruit which is lovely and refreshing. Instead of summer berries and stone fruits, you could poach citrus fruits, apples or pears in the same manner during the colder months.

SERVES 4
(WITH EXTRA SORBET)

750g summer fruits, such as berries, cherries and stone fruit, stoned (or use citrus segments in winter)

For the poaching stock

500g caster sugar
500ml boiling water
4 sticks of liquorice (I use the Panda brand), chopped into small pieces
80ml crème de cassis

For the fromage blanc sorbet

200g caster sugar
3 tablespoons liquid glucose
300ml water
3 tablespoons lemon juice, to taste
130g full-fat cream cheese
130g fromage frais

First, make the sorbet. Put the sugar, liquid glucose, water and lemon juice into a saucepan and stir over a medium–high heat until the sugar has dissolved. Whisk in the cream cheese and fromage frais. Remove the pan from the heat then strain the mixture through a fine sieve into a wide bowl. Leave to cool completely, then pour the mixture into the bowl of an ice-cream machine and churn until softly set. Scrape the sorbet into a freezerproof container, seal and freeze for at least 4 hours. (If you don't have an ice-cream machine, freeze the sorbet in a suitable container for a couple of hours then stir the ice crystals with a fork to break them down. Freeze again and repeat the process 2 or 3 more times.)

Meanwhile, make the poaching stock. Put 200g of the sugar into a heavy-based pan and place over a high heat. As the sugar begins to melt around the edges of the pan, swirl the pan slightly until all the sugar has melted. Continue to heat until the caramel is a deep golden brown. Pour in the water, standing back, as the hot caramel will splutter and spit upon contact with the water. If the caramel hardens, stir it over a medium heat until it dissolves again. Add the remaining sugar and liquorice and stir to dissolve. Boil for a few minutes then pour in the crème de cassis and simmer for a few more minutes to allow the flavours to infuse. Finally, scoop out any pieces of liquorice that haven't dissolved.

If you are using stone fruits, slice them into bite-sized pieces. Berries, such as raspberries, blackberries and blueberries, can be left whole. If using strawberries, hull them. If you're using citrus fruits, peel and cut them into segments. Keep the softer fruits, such as berries, separated from firmer stone fruits.

Put the firmer prepared fruit into the hot poaching syrup and poach over a low heat for 1–2 minutes, depending on how soft they are. Transfer the poached fruits and poaching stock to a large bowl, add the softer fruit and allow to cool completely. (This can be done 1–2 days in advance, which gives the flavours plenty of time to infuse.) Strain the fruit once cool.

To serve, arrange the poached fruits in individual serving bowls, then add a scoop of sorbet and serve immediately.

DESSERTS

SOCIAL SUPPERS

SLOE GIN AND ORANGE CURD ICE CREAM WITH SOFT BLACKBERRIES AND SHORTBREAD

This may look like a plain vanilla ice cream but beyond its creamy appearance, it has lovely complex flavours from sloe gin and orange curd. It is absolutely delicious with my orange-flavoured shortbread and macerated blackberries.

SERVES 6

For the sloe gin and orange curd ice cream
325g orange curd (shop-bought is fine)
300ml crème fraîche
300g natural yoghurt
150ml sloe gin

For the shortbread
160g unsalted butter
75g caster sugar, plus extra to sprinkle
250g plain flour, plus extra to dust
a pinch of fine sea salt
finely grated zest of 1 orange
1 vanilla pod, split in half, seeds scraped out with a knife

For the soft blackberries (optional)
300g ripe blackberries
50g icing sugar

First, make the ice cream. Combine the orange curd, crème fraîche, yoghurt and sloe gin in the bowl of an ice-cream machine. Give the mixture a stir then churn until it is almost set. Transfer the ice cream to a freezerproof container, cover and freeze for at least 4 hours until set. (If you do not have an ice-cream machine, freeze the mixture in a suitable container for 90 minutes then stir the ice crystals that are beginning to form. Return to the freezer and repeat this process 2 or 3 times.)

Next, make the shortbread. In a large bowl, beat the butter and sugar until the mixture is light and creamy. Sift the flour and salt into a separate bowl then stir in the orange zest and vanilla seeds. Fold the dry mixture into the creamed butter until well combined. Gather the dough and flatten into a disc. Wrap the dough with cling film and let it rest in the refrigerator for at least 30 minutes.

Preheat the oven to 180°C/Gas Mark 4. Line a baking sheet with baking parchment. Dust a little flour on a work surface and roll out the dough evenly to a thickness of about 4mm. Cut out neat shapes, such as triangles or rectangles, and sprinkle over a little caster sugar. Carefully transfer the squares to the lined baking sheet. Bake for 12–15 minutes, until the shortbread is lightly golden. Turn off the oven and partially open the oven door. Leave the shortbread in the open oven for a few minutes before removing the baking sheet. Let the shortbread cool completely then store in an airtight container, if not serving immediately.

For the blackberries, put the berries, sugar and 2 tablespoons of water into a small saucepan. Place the pan over a low–medium heat and slowly warm the blackberries, stirring gently all the time. As soon as the blackberries begin to soften, transfer them to a bowl and leave to cool completely.

To serve, place neat scoops of orange curd ice cream into chilled bowls and spoon over the softened blackberries, if using. Serve immediately with the shortbread squares.

ELDERFLOWER AND VANILLA PANNA COTTA WITH PEACH, RASPBERRY AND THYME

The elderflower season is so short, you may miss it if you blink an eyelid. However, if you do find yourself some fresh elderflowers, try making some cordial and then this fragrant panna cotta. It is superb with delicate peaches and raspberries or any other soft summer fruit.

SERVES 6

4 small gelatine leaves
500ml double cream
350ml whole milk
100g caster sugar
2 vanilla pods, split in half, seeds scraped out with a knife
juice of ½ lemon
100ml elderflower cordial

For the marinated peaches
4 firm but ripe peaches, peeled and very finely sliced (ideally using a mandolin)
1 vanilla pod, split in half, seeds scraped out with a knife
500ml Stock Syrup (see page 231)

For the peach purée
2 firm but ripe peaches, peeled, stoned and roughly chopped
2 tablespoons icing sugar
juice of ½ lemon
juice of ½ orange

To serve
80g raspberries, frozen for at least 24 hours
a few sprigs of thyme, leaves picked

Soak the gelatine leaves in a shallow bowl of cold water. Put the double cream, milk and sugar into a saucepan with the vanilla pods and seeds. Bring the creamy milk to a simmer, stirring initially to help the sugar dissolve. When the sugar has dissolved, add the lemon juice and elderflower cordial and take the pan off the heat. Fish out the vanilla pods then strain the hot mixture through a fine sieve into a bowl. Squeeze out the excess water from the gelatine leaves and add them to the creamy milk. Stir until dissolved. Set the bowl over a larger bowl half-filled with iced water. Stir frequently as the mixture cools and begins to thicken – this helps to distribute the vanilla seeds evenly through the mixture, otherwise they tend to sink to the bottom. When the mixture has thickened slightly but is not yet set, pour it into 6 shallow bowls and chill for at least 4 hours or until set.

For the marinated peaches, use a 2–3cm round cutter to stamp the peach slices into neat round discs, reserving the peach trimmings for later. Arrange the discs in one even layer in a large, clean, resealable bag. Add the vanilla pod and seeds to the stock syrup and pour this into the bag. Seal the bag, squeezing out as much air as possible, then leave to infuse in the refrigerator for at least 6 hours, preferably overnight.

To make the peach purée, put the peach trimmings into a food processor. Add the chopped peach, sugar and lemon and orange juices. Blend to a smooth purée. Depending on the sweetness of the peaches, add a little more sugar as necessary. Put the purée into a small saucepan and place over a medium heat until the purée thickens and reduces a little. Pour into a squeezy bottle or piping bag and refrigerate until needed

To serve, drain the marinated peach discs and arrange them on top of each panna cotta, then squeeze, pour or pipe a little peach purée over each slice. Remove the raspberries from the freezer and chop finely with a sharp knife. Sprinkle a little of the chopped raspberries over each pudding, decorate with thyme leaves and serve.

DESSERTS

ROASTED PINEAPPLE WITH LONG PEPPERCORNS, MANGO AND LYCHEE SORBET

This fruity dessert is deliciously light and refreshing and it is an ideal way to end an Asian meal or a particularly rich and heavy Western one. Pairing mild spices like these long peppercorns with fruit is not a new concept. In fact, many people have come round to the idea of serving strawberries with pepper and this is no different. I do like to use long peppercorns (also known as Sarawak peppercorns, which hail from East Malaysia) as they are mild and fragrant and they work really well with fruit. The lychee sorbet is cool and uplifting, but if you are pressed for time, you can serve the roasted pineapples with a spoonful of crème fraîche or shop-bought mango sorbet or vanilla ice cream.

SERVES 6

130g caster sugar
1 teaspoon golden syrup
65ml water
1 large ripe pineapple, peeled, cored and sliced into 6 rings
1 vanilla pod, split in half, seeds scraped out with a knife
1 tablespoon long Sarawak (or regular) peppercorns, lightly crushed
2 tablespoons dark rum
4 tablespoons unsalted butter
a pinch of sea salt

For the lychee sorbet
100g liquid glucose
2 x 565g can of lychees in syrup

To serve
2 ripe Alphonso mangoes, peeled, stoned and diced

First, make the lychee sorbet. Tip the liquid glucose, lychees and 150ml of the syrup into a blender and blend until smooth. Strain the mixture through a fine sieve into the bowl of an ice-cream machine, pressing down on the pulp to extract as much juice as possible. Churn the mixture until it is just thick and almost firm. It should have the consistency of a soft sorbet. Transfer the mixture to a freezerproof container and freeze for a few hours or until completely frozen. (If you do not have an ice-cream machine, strain the mixture straight into a freezerproof container, seal and freeze for about 1½ hours until it is partially frozen around the edges. Stir the ice crystals into the still-liquid centre. Cover and freeze for another 1½ hours. Repeat twice more until the mixture is smooth and completely frozen.)

For the pineapple, preheat the oven to 180°C/Gas Mark 4. Put the sugar, golden syrup and water into a heavy-based ovenproof pan and stir over a low heat until the sugar has dissolved. Increase the heat and let the syrup boil until it turns to a medium-brown caramel. It should take about 7 minutes or so, but do swirl the syrup every once in a while to prevent it from catching and burning in various spots.

Meanwhile, place the pineapple rings in a single layer in a deep ovenproof tray.

Once the caramel has reached a nice brown colour, take the pan off the heat and carefully add the vanilla pod and seeds and peppercorns. Pour the caramel over the sliced pineapple and place the tray into the hot oven and roast for about 30–35 minutes, turning the pineapple rings over every 10 minutes.

Once the pineapples are golden brown and tender, remove the pan from the oven. Use a slotted spoon to transfer the pineapple rings to a plate then cover with a piece of kitchen foil. Make a sauce with the caramel in the pan by removing the vanilla pod, then whisking in the rum, butter and salt. Continue to stir until the sauce is smooth and glossy.

To serve, place a roasted pineapple ring in the middle of each plate and fill the centre with the diced mango. Spoon over the spiced caramel sauce and then top with a neat scoop of lychee sorbet. Serve immediately.

SMOKED BACON AND PEACH CORNBREAD WITH CANDIED PECAN AND MAPLE CREAM

This is an interesting dessert that was inspired by a Southern American 'soul food' lunch I once had in New York City. Before the waitress brought our dishes to the table, she served us a basket of warm bacon cornbread that was so good I could not stop eating it. Americans like their cornbread sweet and salty and I thought it made the base for a lovely dessert. Here, I'm making and serving my cornbread with bacon, maple syrup and pecans – all the typical ingredients of an American brunch.

SERVES 4

3 rashers of thin smoked streaky bacon, roughly chopped
90g plain flour
60g caster sugar
½ teaspoon fine sea salt
2 teaspoons baking powder
½ teaspoon bicarbonate of soda
190g cornmeal
2 large eggs
3 tablespoons clear honey
1 tablespoon molasses
180ml buttermilk
125ml whole milk
60g dried peaches or apricots, chopped

For the candied pecans and maple cream
110g caster sugar
110ml water
30g pecan nuts (about 18–20)
vegetable oil, for frying
300ml double cream, whipped
20ml maple syrup

In a non-stick pan set over a medium–high heat, fry the bacon for 4–6 minutes until golden brown and crisp. Drain on a plate lined with kitchen paper and set aside.

Preheat the oven to 160°C/Gas Mark 3. Butter and flour a 20cm square baking tin. Sift the flour, sugar, salt, baking powder and bicarbonate of soda into a large bowl. Add the cornmeal to the bowl and stir well. In another bowl, whisk the eggs together with the honey, molasses, buttermilk and whole milk until well combined. Pour half of the wet mixture into the dry ingredients and fold until the mixture is smooth, then add this mixture to the remaining wet ingredients and fold until just incorporated. Finally, fold in the crisp bacon and the dried peaches.

Pour the mixture into the prepared tin and bake for about 25–30 minutes, rotating the tin towards the end of cooking if one side is browning too quickly. The cornbread is ready when a skewer inserted into the centre comes out clean. Remove the cornbread from the oven and leave to cool on a baking rack. Once cool, run a thin knife along the edges of the tin to release the cornbread before tipping it out on to a chopping board. Cut the cornbread into squares or thick slices to serve.

For the candied pecans, put the sugar and water into a small saucepan and stir over a medium heat. Once the sugar has dissolved, bring to a simmer, then add the pecans and cook for a few minutes. Drain the pecans and spread them out on a tray lined with a large sheet of baking parchment.

Heat 2–3cm of vegetable oil in a frying pan until hot. When the oil appears to be simmering, carefully add the candied pecans and fry for 2 minutes until they are just golden brown. Lift them out with a slotted spoon and drain on another tray lined with baking parchment. Leave to cool completely then roughly chop three quarters of the pecans (reserving the remainder for garnish).

Whip the cream then stir through the maple syrup and fold in the chopped nuts.

To serve, warm the cornbread in a low oven for a few minutes, then place two slices on each serving plate and add a large dollop of the maple cream. Finally, grate over the reserved candied pecans and serve at once.

SOCIAL SUPPERS

BAKED VANILLA CHEESECAKE WITH PRUNES IN ARMAGNAC

I love all kinds of cheesecake, from the light, gelatine-set ones to the heavy and dense baked American-style cheesecakes. Here, I'm teaming a rich baked cheesecake with a French classic of prunes soaked in Armagnac. Try to use Agen prunes, which have the best flavour.

SERVES 8–12

140g digestive biscuits
90g unsalted butter, plus extra to grease
2 large eggs, plus 3 large yolks
180g caster sugar
500g cream cheese
180ml double cream
finely grated zest and juice of 1 lemon
½ vanilla pod, split in half, seeds scraped out with a knife
40g cornflour

For the prunes in Armagnac
250g dried pitted prunes
300ml water
50g caster sugar
1 Earl Grey teabag
½ vanilla pod, split in half, seeds scraped out with a knife
185ml Armagnac

Start with the prunes. Check the prunes to make sure that all the stones are removed, then set aside. Bring the water to the boil in a small saucepan. Add the sugar and teabag and stir until the sugar has dissolved. Simmer for 1 minute then take the pan off the heat. Leave the teabag to infuse for 8–10 minutes before discarding it. Add the prunes and vanilla pod and seeds to the Earl Grey syrup in the pan. Bring back to the boil then remove the pan from the heat. Carefully transfer the hot prunes and syrup to a clean jar (or bowl) then pour in the Armagnac. Stir well and leave to cool completely. Cover the jar and leave the prunes to macerate overnight in the refrigerator. The next day, if you find the syrup too thin, strain it, place in a saucepan and bubble to reduce to a syrupy consistency, then pour it back over the plumped-up prunes.

Preheat the oven to 180°C/Gas Mark 4. Butter the base and sides of a 20cm springform cake tin and line the base and sides with baking parchment.

Put the digestive biscuits into a clean plastic bag, seal and crush them with a rolling pin. Melt the butter in a small saucepan. Tip the crushed biscuits into a mixing bowl then pour in the melted butter and mix well. Press the mixture evenly over the base of the prepared cake tin. Bake for about 8–10 minutes until the base is lightly toasted and golden brown. Remove the tin and place it on a wire rack to cool while you prepare the filling.

In a large bowl, whisk the eggs, egg yolks and sugar, using an electric beater, until the mixture has doubled in volume. Add the cream cheese, double cream, lemon zest and juice, vanilla seeds and cornflour and beat on a low speed until the mixture is well combined. Take care not to overbeat, as the filling should be smooth and light. Spread the cream cheese filling over the biscuit base and level the top. Bake for 20–30 minutes. For a soft and creamy centre (and to prevent large cracks), take the cheesecake out of the oven when it still has a slight wobble in the middle when you gently shake the tin. Let it cool on a wire rack for a few minutes. Run a thin sharp knife around the cheesecake then release the catch and lift up the ring. Leave the cheesecake to cool completely on the wire rack.

Once cool, run a palette knife along the metal base of the cheesecake to loosen it from the baking parchment then slide the cheesecake on to a serving plate. Serve with the Armagnac soaked prunes.

basics

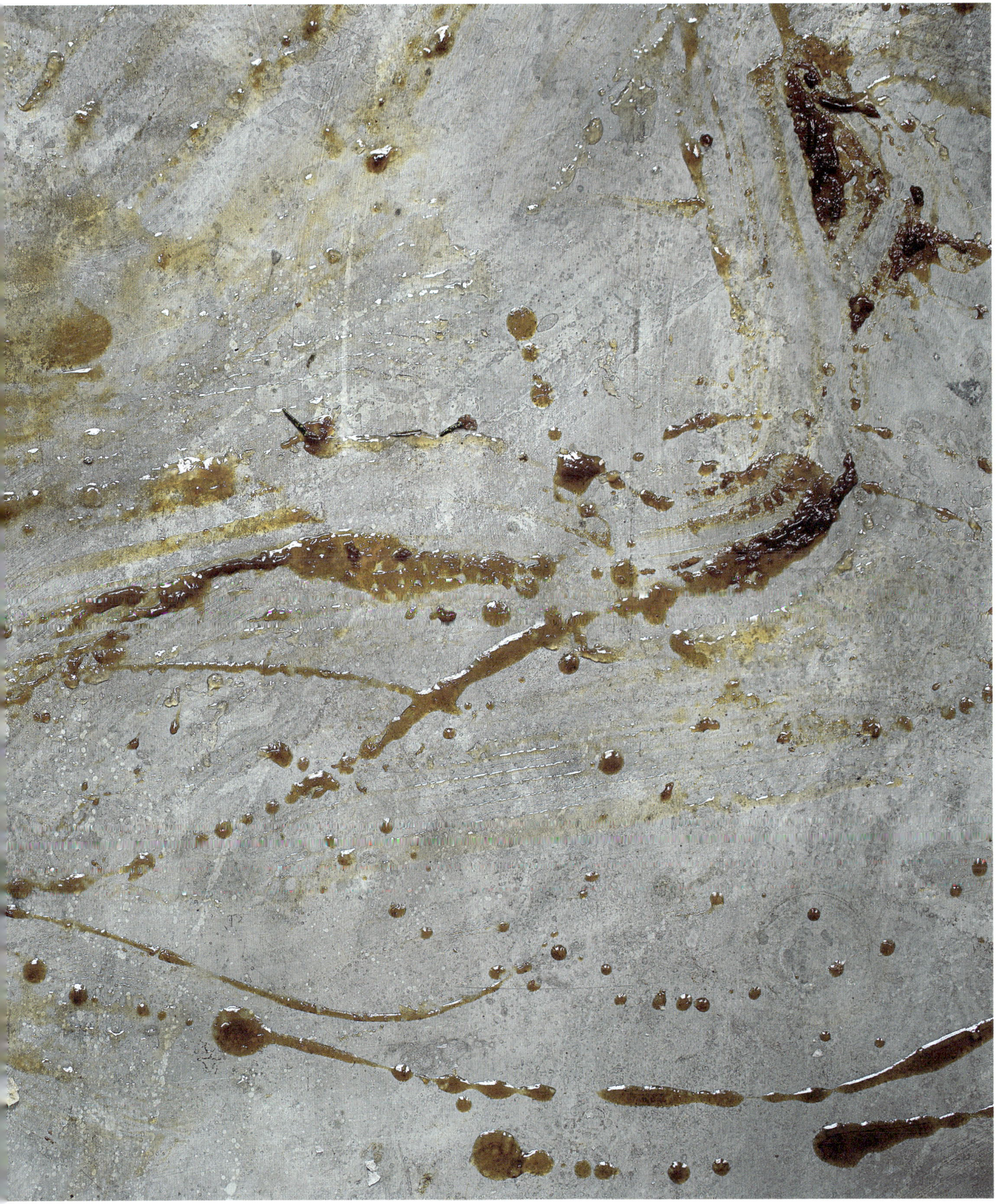

BASICS

218/ CHICKEN STOCK **218/** BROWN FISH STOCK **219/** VEGETABLE STOCK
219/ VEAL/BEEF STOCK **220/** DUCK JUS **221/** DASHI (JAPANESE STOCK)
221/ HERB OIL **222/** BASIC VINAIGRETTE **222/** SHALLOT VINAIGRETTE
223/ YUZU WASABI DRESSING **223/** VIETNAMESE DRESSING **224/** MAYONNAISE
224/ AÏOLI **225/** COLESLAW **225/** TAPENADE **226/** TOMATO SAUCE

226/ SPICY TOMATO SAUCE **226/** TOMATO FONDUE **227/** PARSLEY PURÉE
227/ PICCALILLI **228/** CREAMY MASHED POTATOES **228/** CHUNKY CHIPS
229/ CONFIT SHALLOTS **229/** PIZZA DOUGH **230/** HOME-MADE GRANOLA
230/ CONFIT LEMON STRIPS **231/** STOCK SYRUP **231/** VANILLA ICE CREAM
231/ MASCARPONE CINNAMON ICE CREAM

CHICKEN STOCK

MAKES ABOUT 1.5–2 LITRES

1.5 kg chicken carcass
about 3 litres cold water
1½ celery stalks, trimmed and roughly chopped
white of 1 leek, roughly chopped
2 onions, peeled and roughly chopped
¼ head of garlic, unpeeled
a sprig of thyme

Place the chicken carcass in a large stock pot and pour in just enough cold water to cover. Bring to the boil and skim off the scum that rises to the surface. Turn the heat down to as low as possible. Add all the remaining ingredients, making sure they are all fully submerged in the water. Let the stock simmer for 3–4 hours then pass it through a muslin-lined sieve. Discard the solids. Divide the stock into smaller portions and freeze in suitable containers.

VARIATION
To make brown chicken stock, preheat the oven to 180°C/Gas Mark 4. Take the chicken carcass and chop the bones into smaller pieces, then place on a roasting tray, drizzling over a couple of tablespoons of olive oil, and roast for 20–30 minutes until they are golden brown. Meanwhile, fry the celery, leeks and garlic in a little olive oil until golden brown. Add to a large stock pot, add the browned chicken bones and cover in about 3 litres of water, and then cook, skim and finish as per the recipe above.

BROWN FISH STOCK

MAKES ABOUT 1.5 LITRES

1.5 kg white fish bones (such as turbot, haddock, brill or halibut), washed
1 onion, peeled and roughly chopped
1 leek, peeled, trimmed and roughly chopped
1 celery stalk, trimmed and roughly chopped
1 small fennel bulb, roughly chopped
3 cloves of garlic, peeled
2 tablespoons olive oil
300ml white wine
1 bay leaf
a sprig of thyme
a few parsley stalks
10 white peppercorns
1 lemon, sliced
2 litres cold water

Preheat the oven to 180°C/Gas Mark 4. If you're using the heads of the fish for the stock, remove the eyes and gills. Chop the bones into smaller pieces then place on a roasting tray with a little drizzle of oil. Roast for 20–30 minutes until they are golden brown.

In a large pot, sweat the onion, leek, celery, fennel and garlic in a little olive oil for 4–5 minutes. Pour in the wine and let boil until reduced to a syrupy glaze. Add the herbs, peppercorns, lemon slices and browned fish bones to the pot. Cover with water and bring to a simmer, skimming off the scum that rises to the surface. Gently simmer for 20 minutes then let it cool and allow the stock to settle before straining it through a muslin-lined sieve. Divide the stock into smaller portions and freeze in suitable containers.

VEGETABLE STOCK

MAKES ABOUT 1.5 LITRES

5 carrots, trimmed and roughly chopped
2 onions, trimmed and roughly chopped
2 celery stalks, trimmed and roughly chopped
1 leek, trimmed and roughly chopped
1 litre cold water
a few sprigs each of basil, chervil and chives
½ head of garlic, unpeeled
2 star anise
6 coriander seeds
6 white peppercorns
6 pink peppercorns
200ml dry white wine
1 lemon, cut into wedges

Put the carrots into a stockpot, followed by the onions, celery and leek. Cover with the cold water and bring to the boil. Lower the heat and allow to simmer for 8 minutes. Add the herbs, garlic and spices to the pot, ensuring they are totally submerged in the water. Simmer for a further 2 minutes then add the white wine and lemon wedges. Turn off the heat and leave to cool completely.

Chill for 24 hours, dividing the stock into smaller batches if the stockpot does not fit into your refrigerator.

Pass the stock through a muslin-lined sieve and discard the vegetables, herbs and spices. Freeze in smaller portions if not using at once.

VEAL/BEEF STOCK

MAKES ABOUT 1.5–2 LITRES

1.5kg veal or beef bones
75ml olive oil
1 large onion, peeled and roughly chopped
2 large carrot, peeled and roughly chopped
2 celery stalks, peeled and roughly chopped
¼ head of garlic, unpeeled
1½ tablespoons tomato purée
150ml port
150ml Madeira
5 litres cold water
a sprig of thyme
1 bay leaf

Preheat the oven to 220°C/Gas Mark 7. Roast the bones for about 1–2 hours until they are golden brown.

Heat the oil in a large stockpot and add the vegetables and garlic. Stir frequently over a medium heat until the vegetables are lightly golden. Add the tomato purée and stir for another 2–3 minutes. Pour in the port and Madeira and let the liquid boil vigorously until reduced to a sticky glaze.

Add the browned bones to the pot, leaving behind the excess fat. Pour over the cold water to cover and bring to a gentle simmer. Skim off any scum that rises to the surface. Add the herb sprigs and leave the stock to simmer for 5–6 hours.

Strain the stock through a muslin-lined sieve into a clean pan. Return to the heat and boil until reduced by half. Cool and freeze in batches if not using immediately.

DUCK JUS

MAKES ABOUT 600ML

2–3 tablespoons olive oil
500g duck wings, jointed (or duck bones, chopped into smaller pieces)
1 onion, peeled and quartered
1 carrot, peeled and roughly chopped
white of 1 leek, roughly chopped
¼ head of garlic
a small bunch of thyme
2 bay leaves
5 white peppercorns
a pinch of rock salt
1 teaspoon tomato purée
175ml dry white wine
500ml Chicken Stock (see page 218) (or duck stock if you have any)
500ml Veal Stock (see page 219)

Heat a wide heavy-based pan over a high heat until hot. Add a thin layer of olive oil to the pan followed by the duck wings. In batches, fry the wings for about 2 minutes on each side until they are golden brown all over. Transfer to a large plate and set aside.

Add a little more oil to the pan then tip in the vegetables, thyme and bay leaves. Stir and fry for 6–8 minutes, stirring occasionally, until the vegetables are golden brown. Add the peppercorns, a little pinch of rock salt and the tomato purée then stir over a high heat for a couple of minutes. Pour in the white wine and let it boil until reduced to a syrupy consistency. Return the wings to the pan and add the chicken and veal stocks. Bring to the boil then reduce the heat and let the stocks simmer for 40–45 minutes until the sauce is flavourful.

Strain the sauce through a fine sieve into a clean saucepan and discard the solids. If you prefer the sauce thicker, boil it until reduced to a syrupy consistency. Taste and adjust the seasoning. Keep warm or reheat before serving.

DASHI (JAPANESE STOCK)

MAKES ABOUT 1 LITRE

10g kombu (Japanese dried kelp)
1 litre water
10g katsuobushi (bonito fish flakes)

Put the kombu and water into a saucepan and leave to soak for about 30 minutes.

Place the pan over a medium–low heat and bring to a simmer. Simmer for 10 minutes then add the katsuobushi and turn off the heat. Leave the stock to infuse for 10 minutes, by which time the fish flakes would have sunk to the base of the pan. Strain the stock through a fine sieve. If not using immediately, keep the cooled dashi in the refrigerator and use within a few days or freeze in smaller portions and keep for up to 1 month.

HERB OIL

MAKES ABOUT 150ML

2 large bunches of herbs (such as mint, parsley, chives and basil)
1 teaspoon bicarbonate of soda
150ml olive or vegetable oil

Bring a large pan of water to the boil. Prepare a large bowl of iced water on the side. Pick the herb leaves and discard the stems. Add the bicarbonate of soda to the boiling water and stir. Blanch the herb leaves for 30 seconds until the leaves are bright green. Drain and immediately plunge into the iced water. Once cooled, drain and squeeze the blanched leaves or pat dry with kitchen paper. Put the leaves and oil into a blender and blend for a minute or two. Transfer to a bowl and leave to infuse for 1 hour. Strain the oil through a muslin-lined fine sieve into a jug. Using a funnel, pour the herb oil into a sterilised jar or squeezy bottle. Refrigerate and use within a few weeks.

VARIATION
To make Chilli Oil, very gently heat 225ml of olive or vegetable oil in a small saucepan with 4 teaspoons of dried chilli flakes and 1–2 whole dried chillies for 3–4 minutes. Watch the pan, as you do not want the chilli flakes to burn. Leave to cool slightly, then pour into sterilised bottles or jars using a funnel. Add the whole chillies and chilli flakes as well. Seal and keep in a cool, dark place. The oil should keep in the refrigerator for up to a week.

BASIC VINAIGRETTE

MAKES 350ML

50ml white wine vinegar
300ml extra-virgin olive oil
sea salt and freshly ground black pepper

Put all the ingredients into a measuring jug and whisk well. If you have a hand-held stick blender, use it to blend the dressing until emulsified. Pour into a sterilised bottle or jar and chill. This can be stored in the refrigerator for a few weeks; shake well before each use.

SHALLOT VINAIGRETTE

MAKES 300ML

75ml light olive oil
75ml rapeseed oil
50ml white wine vinegar
25g Dijon mustard
40g clear honey
3 tablespoons wholegrain mustard
3 tablespoons Confit Shallots (see page 229)
sea salt and freshly ground black pepper

Put all the ingredients into a clean jar or bowl. Whisk to combine then season to taste with salt and pepper. Cover and refrigerate. Use within a few weeks. Shake well before each use.

YUZU WASABI DRESSING

MAKES ABOUT 225ML

2 tablespoons wasabi paste
1 tablespoon clear honey
1 tablespoon dark soy sauce
1 tablespoon lime juice
50ml yuzu (or lemon) juice
100ml sesame oil
1 tablespoon black mustard seeds
sea salt and freshly ground black pepper

Whisk together all the ingredients and season well to taste. Store in a clean, sterilised jar and keep refrigerated for up to 2 weeks.

VIETNAMESE DRESSING

MAKES ABOUT 400ML

5 teaspoon sesame oil
4 shallots, peeled and finely chopped
1 small garlic clove, peeled and finely chopped
15g fresh ginger, peeled and grated
3 red chillies, deseeded and finely chopped
50ml mirin
1 tablespoon palm sugar, or to taste
50ml lime juice
125ml rice wine vinegar
60ml soy sauce
5 teaspoons fish sauce
1 small bunch of coriander, leaves only, finely chopped

Gently heat the sesame oil in a saucepan and add the shallot, garlic, ginger and chilli. Stir well and sweat the vegetables over a medium–low heat for 8–10 minutes, until the shallots are soft. Pour in the mirin and increase the heat slightly. Stir and simmer the mixture until it has reduced by half. Add the sugar, lime juice and vinegar and stir until the sugar is dissolved. Simmer for a few minutes then add the soy sauce and fish sauce. Taste and adjust the seasoning to your liking, adding a bit more sugar, lime juice or soy sauce as necessary. Take the pan off the heat and leave to cool. (If making ahead, pour the hot mixture into sterilised jars, seal and leave to cool completely. Refrigerate and use within a few weeks.) Stir the chopped coriander into the sauce a few minutes before you are ready to serve.

MAYONNAISE

MAKES ABOUT 275ML

2 large egg yolks
1 teaspoon Dijon mustard, or to taste
250ml vegetable oil
2 teaspoons lemon juice (or white wine vinegar), or to taste
sea salt and freshly ground white pepper

Put the egg yolks in a small food processor with the mustard and a little seasoning. Blend until the mixture is thick and smooth. With the motor running, very slowly trickle in the oil – the mixture should be thick and creamy. If it curdles, transfer the mixture to a jug and add another egg yolk to the bowl of the food processor. Start again by blending the egg yolk with the curdled mixture. Mix in the lemon juice and adjust the seasoning with a little more salt and pepper. Thin it down with a tablespoon or two of warm water if you prefer it to have a lighter consistency.

AÏOLI

MAKES ABOUT 200ML

2 garlic cloves, peeled and finely crushed
2 medium egg yolks
a small pinch of saffron threads
75ml olive oil
75ml vegetable oil
1 teaspoon white wine vinegar, or to taste
sea salt

Put the garlic, egg yolks and saffron into a food processor and blitz to a thick paste. Put both oils into a measuring jug. With the motor running, trickle the oils into the food processor and blend until all the oil has been incorporated and you get a thick sauce. (If the sauce splits, transfer it to a jug then put another egg yolk or two in the food processor. Whizz until thick then slowly blend in the split sauce.) Season the sauce to taste with the vinegar and some salt and pepper. Transfer to a bowl, cover and chill until ready to use. Store any left over in the refrigerator for up to 3 days.

COLESLAW

SERVES 6–8

½ white cabbage (about 450g), trimmed and finely shredded
1 tablespoon caster sugar
1 small carrot, peeled and shredded
1 small red onion, peeled and shredded
4 tablespoons Mayonnaise (see page 224)
a pinch of cayenne pepper
small splash of cider vinegar, to taste
2 teaspoons wholegrain mustard
sea salt and freshly ground black pepper

Place the cabbage into a large bowl. Mix the sugar with a pinch of salt and add this to the cabbage. Toss to mix and leave for an hour, by which time the cabbage will have released some of its moisture. Tip the cabbage into a large colander and rinse well under cold running water (about 3–4 minutes). Drain thoroughly and pat dry with a clean kitchen towel, then place in a large bowl.

Add the shredded carrot and onion to the bowl of cabbage then stir in enough mayonnaise to coat the vegetables evenly. Add the cayenne pepper, vinegar, mustard and salt and pepper to taste. Mix well then cover the bowl with cling film and refrigerate until ready to serve. (This coleslaw is best made a day in advance of when you need it.)

TAPENADE

MAKES ABOUT 270G

200g pitted black olives
40g anchovy fillets in olive oil, drained
20g capers, drained and rinsed
1 garlic clove, peeled
1 tablespoon olive oil, plus extra to drizzle

Put all the ingredients into a food processor and blend until smooth. Spoon into a sterilised jar and cover with a thin layer of olive oil to help preserve the tapenade. Chill and use within 2 weeks.

TOMATO SAUCE

MAKES 800ML

60ml olive oil
2 small onions, finely chopped
2 garlic cloves, finely chopped
2 x 400g can whole plum tomatoes
3 tablespoons tomato purée
sea salt and freshly ground black pepper

Put the olive oil, onions, garlic and a pinch each of salt and pepper into a large pan. Stir and gently sweat the onions over a low–medium heat for 10–12 minutes until they are really soft. Add the tomatoes and tomato purée. Roughly break up the tomatoes in the pan using a spatula or spoon and then simmer for about 20 minutes until the sauce has thickened to a chutney-like consistency. Taste and adjust the seasoning. Leave to cool. Transfer to clean jars or a large bowl, cover and refrigerate until ready to serve. Use within 1 week.

SPICY TOMATO SAUCE

MAKES ABOUT 400ML

500g vine-ripened tomatoes, cut into wedges
olive oil, to drizzle
80g caster sugar
2 teaspoons sea salt
1 teaspoon white peppercorns
500ml tomato juice
3–4 garlic cloves, peeled and chopped
½ bunch of basil
a few dashes Tabasco sauce

Preheat the oven to 180°C/Gas Mark 4. Put the tomatoes on to a lightly oiled shallow baking tray and toss with a drizzle of olive oil and the sugar, salt and white peppercorns. Spread them out on the tray and place in the oven for 1 hour, stirring the mixture once or twice. The tomatoes will be soft and slightly caramelised. Add the tomato juice, garlic and basil to the tray and stir to mix. Return the tray to the oven for 30 minutes.

Transfer the mixture to a food processor and blend to a smooth purée. Pass the purée through a fine sieve into a saucepan. Season to taste with salt, pepper and a few dashes of Tabasco. (If not using immediately, put the sauce into a sterilised jar and refrigerate. It keeps well for 2 weeks.)

TOMATO FONDUE

MAKES ABOUT 215G

500g vine-ripened tomatoes, peeled, deseeded and finely chopped
2 tablespoons olive oil
3 shallots, peeled and finely chopped
1 garlic clove, peeled and finely chopped
a sprig of thyme
1 bay leaf
sea salt and black pepper
1 tablespoon tomato purée
1–2 tablespoons Basic Vinaigrette (see page 222)
pinch of caster sugar (optional)

Bring a pot of water to the boil. Lightly score the top and base of the tomatoes with a sharp knife. Blanch them in a the hot water for a minute then drain and refresh under cold running water. Peel off the skins then cut into quarters and remove the seeds. Finely chop the flesh.

Heat a pan with the oil and sauté the shallots, garlic, thyme and bay leaf for 3–4 minutes until the shallots begin to soften. Stir in the tomato purée and sauté for another 2 minutes. Tip in the tomatoes and cook over a medium–high heat for 10–12 minutes until the tomato juices have cooked off and the pan is quite dry. Stir in the vinaigrette then taste and season with salt, pepper and a pinch of sugar. For a smooth sauce, pass the mixture through a fine sieve. Cool and keep chilled in a clean jar. Use within a week.

PARSLEY PURÉE

MAKES ABOUT 120ML

2 large bunches of curly parsley
100ml vegetable oil
sea salt and freshly ground black pepper

Bring a pan of water to the boil. Have ready a bowl of iced water. Pick the leaves from the parsley and set the stalks aside. Blanch the stalks for 5–6 minutes, until they begin to wilt, then add the leaves and blanch the leaves for a minute or two, just until they become bright green. Drain and refresh in the iced water, reserving some of the hot water from the pan.

Squeeze out the excess water from the parsley then place in a blender with the oil and some seasoning. Blend to a smooth purée, adding a splash of the hot water as necessary to thin down the mixture. The purée will keep for a few days if refrigerated in a clean, sealed jar. Alternatively, freeze in ice cube trays, as you'll likely use small quantities at a time.

PICCALILLI

MAKES ABOUT 900G

750g cauliflower, cut into florets
275ml white wine vinegar
150ml malt vinegar
100g caster sugar
1 teaspoon ground turmeric
15g dry English mustard
1½ tablespoons cornflour, mixed with
  2–3 tablespoons water
150g silverskin onions
150g cornichons, drained and diced
fine sea salt

Spread the cauliflower florets out on a large tray and sprinkle with fine sea salt. Cover with cling film and leave in a cool part of the kitchen overnight.

The next day, rinse and drain the cauliflower in a colander. Put the white wine and malt vinegars into a wide pot and boil for 10–15 minutes until reduced by one quarter. Mix the sugar, turmeric and mustard together then add to the pot. Stir until the sugar has dissolved. Simmer for a few minutes. Pour in the cornflour and water mixture and let it boil for another 4–5 minutes to cook out the cornflour.

Tip in the cauliflower and onions and stir well. Simmer for 2 minutes then take the pan off the heat and add the cornichons. Give the mixture a good stir. Spoon into sterilised jars and seal immediately. Try not to use metal-topped jars, as the vinegar will rust the metal. Best left to mature for a few weeks before serving.

CREAMY MASHED POTATOES

SERVES 4–6

1kg Ratte potatoes
350ml whole milk
250ml double cream
100g butter
sea salt

Put the potatoes into a large pan of cold salted water. Bring the water to the boil then turn down the heat to a simmer. Gently simmer for 20–30 minutes until the potatoes are tender. There should be no resistance when you pierce the middle of a potato with a sharp knife. Once the potatoes are ready, remove the pan from the heat. Peel 3 or 4 potatoes at a time then immediately push them through a potato ricer. Continue until all the potatoes have been peeled and mashed. For a very fine mash, push the mashed potatoes through a fine sieve.

Put the milk, cream and butter into a saucepan and gently heat until the butter has melted. Slowly add the milk to the potatoes, stirring well, until the desired consistency is reached. Season to taste with a little more salt. Serve while still warm.

CHUNKY CHIPS

SERVES 4

vegetable fat, for deep-frying
850g large potatoes, peeled and cut into 1cm-thick chips
salt

Heat the vegetable oil in a deep-fat fryer or other suitable deep, heavy-based pan to 130°C. Fry the chips in batches for 5 minutes, or until cooked all the way through, but not browned. Remove the chips with a slotted spoon and drain on a tray lined with several layers of kitchen paper. Set aside until you're almost ready to serve.

When you're ready to cook, heat the oil to 180°C (if you don't have a sugar thermometer, test it by dropping a small piece of bread into the hot oil – it should sizzle vigorously). Deep-fry the chips in several batches for 2–3 minutes until they are evenly golden brown and crisp. Remove and drain on a tray lined with kitchen paper. Sprinkle with a little salt and keep warm while you continue frying the rest of the chips. Serve hot and crisp.

CONFIT SHALLOTS

MAKES ABOUT 450G

9 large banana shallots, peeled and finely chopped
a sprig of thyme
a pinch of sea salt
200ml extra-virgin olive oil

Place the shallots and thyme in a saucepan and sprinkle with a pinch of sea salt. Cover the shallots with the olive oil then place the pan over a medium heat. As soon as the oil begins to simmer, turn the heat down to low and slowly cook for 30–40 minutes until the shallots are very tender. Cool in the oil and keep chilled in a clean jar if not using immediately.

PIZZA DOUGH

**MAKES 2 LARGE OR
4 SMALL (20CM) PIZZAS**

400g strong white flour
1 teaspoon sea salt
25g dried yeast or 7g dried active yeast
250g tepid water

Mix the flour and salt in a large bowl. In a separate small bowl, dissolve the yeast in the tepid water. Leave the yeast to activate for a few minutes until the mixture becomes frothy. Add this to the flour then knead the dough for about 4 minutes, until it is smooth, soft and elastic. Gather the dough into a ball and place it in a lightly oiled bowl. Cover the bowl with an oiled piece of cling film and leave to rise for an hour or two before using to make pizzas.

HOME-MADE GRANOLA

MAKES 500G

60g pecans, roughly chopped
50g blanched hazelnuts, roughly chopped
250g rolled oats
50g desiccated coconut
½ teaspoon ground cinnamon
3 tablespoons clear honey
3 tablespoons maple syrup
2 tablespoons vegetable or groundnut oil
50g golden raisins, roughly chopped
50g dried cherries
50g dried apricots, coarsely chopped

Preheat the oven to 180°C/Gas Mark 4.

Put the pecans and hazelnuts into a large bowl and combine with the oats, coconut and cinnamon. Make a well in the centre of the dry mixture and add the honey, maple syrup and oil. Mix well then spread the mixture out on a baking tray. Place the tray in the oven and bake for about 10 minutes then give the granola a stir and return to the oven for another 10 minutes until it is nicely toasted and golden brown. Remove from the oven and stir in the dried fruit, breaking up any large pieces of the granola, if you wish. Cool completely and store in an airtight container until ready to eat.

CONFIT LEMON STRIPS

MAKES ABOUT 100G

3 lemons
125g granulated sugar
125ml water

Bring a small pan of water to the boil and have a bowl of iced water ready on the side. Carefully pare the zest of the lemons using a vegetable peeler or a sharp paring knife, keeping the strips of even thickness. If there is any white pith on the lemon peel, use a small sharp knife to remove it. Stack a few lemon peels together and slice them lengthways into thin matchsticks. Repeat with the remaining strips.

Blanch the peel in the boiling water for a few seconds, then remove with a slotted spoon and refresh in the iced water. Repeat twice more, then drain well. This process should help to remove the bitterness from the peel.

Put the sugar and water into the saucepan over a high heat and stir until the sugar has dissolved. Simmer for a few minutes before adding the lemon strips. Bring back to a simmer, and gently cook the lemon peel for about 1–1½ hours, until tender.
It is quite possible that the sugar may start to crystallise. In order to stop this from happening make sure you do not stir the lemon and keep brushing the sides of the pan with water. Remove the pan from the heat and allow the lemon strips to cool in the sugar syrup. Store in a clean sterilised jar and refrigerate if not using immediately. The lemon should keep well for a few weeks.

STOCK SYRUP

MAKES ABOUT 750ML

500g caster sugar
500ml water
squeeze of lemon juice (optional)

Stir the sugar and water in a saucepan over a low heat to dissolve the sugar. Increase the heat and bring to the boil. Boil for a few minutes and let the syrup thicken slightly. Cool and keep chilled if not using immediately – you can store it for up to 3 weeks in the refrigerator.

VARIATION:
For a light stock syrup, reduce the sugar quantity by half.

VANILLA ICE CREAM

MAKES ABOUT 600ML

250ml double cream
250ml whole milk
2 vanilla pods, split in half, seeds scraped out with a knife
4 large egg yolks
100g caster sugar

Pour the double cream, milk, vanilla pod and seeds into a heavy-based saucepan. Gradually bring the liquid to the boil over a medium–low heat.

Meanwhile beat the egg yolks and sugar together in a mixing bowl. As soon as the creamy milk begins to bubble up the sides of the pan, take it off the heat and slowly trickle it into the sugary eggs, whisking the whole time. When fully incorporated, pour the mixture into a clean saucepan and stir with a wooden spoon over a medium–low heat until the mixture thickens enough to thinly coat the back of the spoon. Pass the custard through a fine sieve into a wide bowl and leave to cool, stirring every once in a while to prevent a skin from forming. Pour the custard into the bowl of an ice-cream machine and churn until thick and almost set. Transfer to a freezerproof container and freeze until needed. (If you do not have an ice-cream machine, freeze the mixture in a suitable container for 90 minutes then stir the ice crystals that are beginning to form. Return to the freezer and repeat this process 2 or 3 times.)

MASCARPONE CINNAMON ICE CREAM

MAKES ABOUT 1 LITRE

250g mascarpone
250ml double cream
250ml whole milk
½ cinnamon stick
100g caster sugar
1 teaspoon ground cinnamon
6 medium egg yolks

Put the mascarpone, cream, milk and cinnamon stick in a heavy-based saucepan and slowly bring to a simmer. As soon as the liquid begins to boil, turn off the heat and leave the flavours to infuse for 20 minutes.

Whisk the sugar, ground cinnamon and egg yolks together in a large bowl until pale and creamy. Strain the creamy milk through a fine sieve into the bowl. Gradually whisk the strained liquid into the egg mixture until fully incorporated. Return the combined mixture to the pan and stir over a low heat until thickened to a light custard. It should lightly coat the back of a wooden spoon. Strain the custard again through a fine sieve into a bowl.

Set the bowl of custard over a larger bowl of iced water and leave to cool, stirring occasionally to prevent a skin from forming on the surface. Pour the cooled mixture into an ice-cream machine and churn until almost firm. Transfer to a freezerproof container, cover and freeze until ready to serve. (If you do not have an ice-cream machine, freeze the mixture in a suitable container for 90 minutes then stir the ice crystals that are beginning to form. Return to the freezer and repeat this process 2 or 3 times.)

INDEX

a

aïoli 70, 114, 224
almonds:
Almond, Prune and Rum Tart 200
cake with honey 179
anchovies:
with Caesar salad 42
with fried eggs, black pudding and capers 16
apples:
Apple and Blackberry Crumble 192
with crab salad 63
with pork cheeks and polenta 120
salad with kohlrabi, whisky walnut and sea trout 55
Tarte Tatin 199
Armagnac: with prunes 211
artichokes: baby violet with tomatoes and broad beans 29
asparagus:
with braised lamb neck 151
with halibut, potatoes and shrimps 92
salad with crab and radishes 60
salad with sea trout 107
aubergines: with tuna salad 44
avocado:
purée with wasabi 47
salad with Baby Gem, orange and carrot 38

b

Baby Violet Artichokes with Datterini Tomatoes and Broad Beans 29
bacon:
cornbread with peaches 209
jam with mushrooms on toast 28
lardo di colonnata with cod 95
with Roquefort and Iceberg salad 41
smoky with burger and onion chutney 147
Baked John Dory with Red Onions, Tomatoes and Rosemary Potatoes 106
Baked Vanilla Cheesecake with Prunes in Armagnac 211
Basic Vinaigrette 222
basil:
pizza with poached egg 84
with spiced melon soup 201
B.B.L.T. (Belly, Brioche, Lettuce and Tomato) 117
beans: with pork belly and black pudding 123; *see also* broad beans; haricot beans
beef:
burger with bacon and onion chutney 147
Côte de Boeuf with Herb Salsa 143
garlic herb with kohlrabi remoulade 137
rib-eye steaks with chimichurri sauce 134
steak tartare with quail's egg and radish salad 75
stock 219
beetroot:
cured sea trout with horseradish cream 51
with roast venison 158
with loin of venison 156
salad with goat's cheese mousse 34
spiced with roasted duck 162
biscuits:
milk 180
Oat Crumble 195
shortbread 205
black pudding:
with fried eggs, capers and anchovies 16
with honey-roast ham hock 126
with potato and parsley soup 18
with roasted pork belly 123
blackberries:
crumble with apple 192
with gin and orange curd ice cream 205
Blood Orange Granita with Crème Chantilly and Candied Lime 191
bone marrow:
with braised ox cheeks 140
with gentleman's relish and onions on toast 78
Braised Lamb Neck, Peas, Broad Beans, Asparagus and Creamed Wild Garlic 151
Braised Ox Cheeks, Carrots, Bone Marrow, Sourdough Crumbs and Horseradish Pomme Purée 140
Braised Oxtail with Pasta 139
Braised Pork Belly with Chorizo and Pepper Purée and Spiced Onions 121
Braised Pork Cheeks with Honey, Soy and Crisp Shallots 118
bread:
garlic toast with fish stew 114
sauce with roast pheasant 165
smoked bacon and peach cornbread 209
Spanish tomato with sardines 49
sugared with chocolate ganache 185
thyme sourdough toasts 189
toast with bone marrow, gentleman's relish and onions 78
toast with crab mayonnaise 64
toast with sea urchin, goat's cheese and peppers 72
toast with wild mushrooms 28
brioche:
B.B.L.T. 117
grilled with lemon curd and yoghurt sorbet 170
broad beans:
with baby artichokes and tomatoes 29
with braised lamb neck 151
with goat's cheese, peas, mint and ham 26
broccoli: with smoked salmon pizza 90
Brown Fish Stock 218
Brown Sugar Tart with Black Sesame Crumble and Crème Fraîche Sorbet 174
Brussels sprouts: with roast squab 160
bulgur wheat: with curried monkfish 102
Burrata and Figs with Truffle Honey 22

c

cabbage:
braised with loin of venison 156

pesto with mint 152
see also red cabbage
cakes:
Carrot 177
Honey and Almond 179
Pistachio and Olive Oil 176
capers: with fried eggs, black pudding and anchovies 16
caramel: rice crispies with chocolate cream 188
carrots:
with braised ox cheeks 140
Carrot Cake with Cream Cheese Sorbet 177
with roasted duck 162
salad with avocado, Baby Gem and orange 38
cauliflower:
risotto with crayfish 110
sautéed with curried monkfish 102
celeriac: cream soup with rabbit confit 21
Cep Mushroom Pizza with Balsamic Onion Chutney, Mascarpone and Parmesan 86
Chargrilled Rib-Eye Steaks with Chimichurri Sauce 134
Chargrilled Sole with Scottish Cockles 109
cheese:
Burrata and Figs with Truffle Honey 22
Cheddar toasties with potato and parsley soup 18
cream cheese sorbet 177
creamed burrata with spring vegetable tartine 25
fromage blanc sorbet 202
Gruyère with smoked haddock gratin 101
Manchego with smoked haddock tortilla 100
Parmesan with corn on the cob and chilli 33
Roquefort and Iceberg Salad with Alsace Bacon 41
with smoked salmon and broccoli pizza 90
see also goat's cheese; mascarpone
cheesecake: vanilla with prunes 211

Chicken Stock 218
chillies:
with corn on the cob and Parmesan 33
with razor clams and chorizo 59
chives: with confit tuna and piperade 46
chocolate:
Ganache with Spanish Olive Oil and Sugared Bread 185
Mousse, Blood Orange Jelly and Chocolate Crumbs 186
Spiced Cream with Caramel Rice Crispies 188
chorizo:
purée with pork belly 121
with razor clams, coriander and chilli 59
with roast cod and haricot beans 96
Spanish Breakfast 14
Chunky Chips 228
chutneys:
balsamic onion 86
balsamic onion with burger and bacon 147
smoked tomato 113
cinnamon: mascarpone ice cream 231
cockles: with chargrilled sole 109
coconut: wafers with Thai rum ice cream 183
cod:
with lentils and lardo di colonnata 95
roasted with haricot beans, chorizo and tomato 96
with spiced potted rice 97
Confit Lemon Strips 230
Confit Tuna with Piperade and Chives 46
coleslaw 225
coriander:
apple and crab salad 63
with razor clams and chorizo 59
Cornish Cod with Braised Lentils and Lardo di Colonnata 95
Cornish Fish Stew with Garlic Toast and Aïoli 114
Côte de Boeuf with Herb Salsa, Courgette Frites and Ceps 143
courgettes:

flowers stuffed with goat's cheese 63
frites with côte de boeuf 143
crab:
mayonnaise with bitter leaves 64
salad with asparagus 60
salad with apple 63
crayfish: risotto with cauliflower 110
cream:
Chantilly with blood orange granita 191
Chantilly with pistachio and olive oil cake 176
clotted ice cream 199
cream cheese: sorbet 177
Creamed Ricotta and Strawberry Pepper Compote on Thyme Sourdough Toasts 189
Creamy Mashed Potatoes 155, 228
crème fraîche: sorbet 174
Crisp Lamb's Tongue with Mint Gribiche 76
cucumber: pickled with salmon 'crudo' 47
Curried Monkfish with Sautéed Cauliflower and Bulgur Wheat 102

d

Dashi (Japanese Stock) 221
dressings:
Basic Vinaigrette 222
Caesar 42
pine nut 34
Shallot Vinaigrette 222
sherry 44
Vietnamese 66, 223
Yuzu Wasabi 223
duck:
roasted with carrots, turnips and beetroot 162
jus 220

e

eggs:
fried with black pudding, capers and anchovies 16
pizza with basil 84
quail's with steak tartare 75
Spanish Breakfast 14
Elderflower and Vanilla Panna Cotta with Peach, Raspberry and Thyme 206

f

fennel: pickled with scallop ceviche 56
figs: with burrata and truffle honey 22
Fine de Claire Oysters with Vietnamese Dressing 66
fish:
brown stock 218
Chargrilled Sole with Scottish Cockles 109
Curried Monkfish with Sautéed Cauliflower and Bulgur Wheat 102
Halibut with Parsley Potatoes, Shrimps and Asparagus 92
John Dory with Red Onions, Tomatoes and Rosemary Potatoes 106
Red Mullet Pizza 89
Salmon 'Crudo' with Pickled Cucumber and Avocado Purée 47
sardines with Spanish tomato bread 49
sea bass pastrami with gazpacho garnish 50
Sea Bream with Morecambe Bay Shrimps, Sautéed Kale, Samphire and Mustard Velouté 105
Smoked Salmon, Broccoli and Sairass Cheese Pizza 90
stew with garlic toast and aïoli 114
see also anchovies; cod; sea trout; seafood; smoked haddock; tuna
Fried Eggs with Black Pudding, Capers and Anchovies 16
Fried Ox Tongue with Mushrooms and Peas 77
fruit:
Burrata and Figs with Truffle Honey 22
mango with roasted pineapple 208
Passion Fruit Ice Cream 184
rhubarb sorbet 196
Spiced Melon Soup 201
strawberry Eton Mess 173
summer cooked in liquorice 202
see also apples; blackberries; lemons; oranges; peaches; pears; pineapple; prunes; strawberries

g

game *see* pheasant; venison
Gariguette Strawberry Eton Mess 173
garlic:
creamed with braised lamb neck 151
herb beef with kohlrabi remoulade 137
roasted potatoes with parsley and brava sauce 32
toast with fish stew 114
ginger: sorbet 201
goat's cheese:
with peas, broad bean, mint and ham 26
ice cream with honeycomb and milk biscuit 180
mousse with beetroot salad 34
with sea urchin and peppers on toast 72
Stuffed Courgette Flowers with Apple and Crab Salad 63
with winter vegetable salad 37
granola 165, 230
Griddled Corn on the Cob with Parmesan and Chilli 33
Grilled Brioche with Lemon Curd and Yoghurt Sorbet 170

h

Halibut with Parsley Potatoes, Morecambe Bay Shrimps and Asparagus 92
ham:
hock with pigs' ears, black pudding and piccalilli 126
Serrano with goat's cheese, peas, broad beans and mint 26
haricot beans:
braised with roast cod 96
with pork chops 130
with pork shanks 129
with smoked haddock gratin 101
Herb-Roasted Sea Trout with Pink Fir Apple Potatoes, Samphire and Asparagus Salad 107
herbs:
chives with tuna and piperade 46
oil 221
salsa with côte de boeuf 143
see also basil; coriander; mint; parsley; rosemary; thyme
honey:
with braised pork cheeks 118
with burrata and figs 22
cake with almonds 179
honeycomb with goat's cheese ice cream 180
Honey-Roast Ham Hock with Crisp Pigs' Ears, Black Pudding and Piccalilli 126
horseradish:
cream with beetroot-cured sea trout 51
pomme purée with ox cheeks 140

i

ice cream:
clotted cream 199
goat's cheese 180
mascarpone cinnamon 231
Passion Fruit 184

Sloe Gin and Orange Curd 205
Thai rum 183
vanilla 231

j

jellies:
blood orange 186
honey 179
John Dory: with red onions, tomatoes and rosemary potatoes 106

k

kale: with sea bream and shrimps 105
kohlrabi:
remoulade with garlic herb beef 137
salad with apple, whisky walnut and sea trout 55

l

lamb:
braised neck with peas, broad beans and asparagus 151
roast rack with olive jus and mashed potatoes 155
roast with rosemary rub 148
slow-roasted shoulder with autumn vegetables 152
lamb's tongue: with mint gribiche 76
Langoustines with Pickled Vegetables and Peas 65
lemons:
candied with quail and pear salad 73
confit strips 230
confit with scallop ceviche 56
curd with grilled brioche 170
lentils: braised with cod 95
lettuce:
Baby Gem with avocado, orange and carrot salad 38
B.B.L.T. 117
Caesar salad with anchovy 42
Iceberg with Roquefort salad 41
lime: candied with blood orange granita 191
liquorice: with summer fruit 202
Little Social Burger with Smoky Bacon and Balsamic Onion Chutney 147
Little Social Steak Tartare with Quail's Egg and Radish Salad 75
Loin of Venison with Beetroot and Venison Sauce and Braised Cabbage 156
London Honey and Almond Cake with Honey Jelly 179
lychees: sorbet 208

m

mango: with roasted pineapple 208
maple syrup: pecan cream 209
mascarpone:
with cep mushroom pizza 86
ice cream with cinnamon 231
mousse tarts with poached rhubarb 196
mayonnaise 224
aïoli with Cornish fish stew 114
crab with bitter leaves on toast 64
squid ink aïoli 70
meat:
Meatballs with Tomato Sauce 144
Rabbit Confit with Celeriac Cream Soup 21
see also beef; game; lamb; offal; pheasant; pork; venison
melon: spiced soup 201
meringue: Strawberry Eton Mess 173
milk:
biscuit with goat's cheese ice cream 180
mousse 184
mint:
with goat's cheese, peas, broad beans and ham 26
gribiche with lamb's tongue 76
pesto with cabbage 152
Mixed Beetroot Salad with Goat's Cheese Mousse and Pine Nut Dressing 34
monkfish: curried with cauliflower and bulgur wheat 102
mousse:
chocolate 186
mascarpone tarts 196
milk 184
Mrs. Tee's Wild Mushrooms on Toast with Bacon Jam 28
mushrooms:
ceps with côte de boeuf 143
with fried ox tongue 77
pizza with onion chutney, mascarpone and Parmesan 86
roasted ceps, green vegetables and octopus 69
sautéed with pork belly 124
on toast with bacon jam 28

n

nuts:
pecan and maple cream 209
pine nut dressing 34
Pistachio and Olive Oil Cake 176
walnut, kohlrabi, apple, whisky and sea trout salad 55
see also almonds

o

oats: crumble biscuit 195
octopus: with roasted ceps and green vegetables 69
offal:
braised ox cheeks 140
Braised Oxtail with Pasta 139
Fried Ox Tongue with Mushrooms and Peas 77

lamb's tongue with mint gribiche 76
pigs' ears with ham hock 126
see also bone marrow
oils: herb 220
olive oil:
bread with chocolate ganache 185
cake with pistachio 176
olives:
jus with roast rack of lamb 155
tapenade 225
tapenade with red mullet pizza 89
onions:
with bone marrow and gentleman's relish 78
chutney with burger and bacon 147
chutney with cep mushroom pizza 86
spiced with pork belly 121
see also red onions; shallots; spring onions
oranges:
Blood Orange Granita 191
curd ice cream with sloe gin 205
jelly with chocolate mousse 186
salad with avocado, Baby Gem and carrot 38
ox cheeks: braised with carrot and bone marrow 140
ox tongue: with mushrooms and peas 77
oxtail: braised with pasta 139
oysters: with Vietnamese dressing 66

p

parsley: with garlic-roasted potatoes and brava sauce 32
potatoes with halibut and shrimps 92
purée 227
soup with potato and black pudding 18
pasta: with braised oxtail 139
Passion Fruit Ice Cream with Milk Mousse and Confetti Fruit 184
Pastrami of Sea Bass with Gazpacho Garnish 50

peaches:
cornbread with bacon 209
with elderflower and vanilla panna cotta 206
pears:
poached with roast venison 158
salad with quail and candied lemon 73
peas:
with braised lamb neck 151
with fried ox tongue 77
with goat's cheese, broad beans, mint and ham 26
with langoustines and pickled vegetables 65
pecan nuts: maple cream 209
peppers:
piperade with confit tuna 46
purée with pork belly 121
roast with suckling pig 131
with sea urchin and goat's cheese on toast 72
pheasant: roast with pumpkin, bread sauce and granola 165
Piccalilli 126, 227
pine nuts: dressing with beetroot salad and goat's cheese mousse 34
pineapple:
with roast suckling pig 131
roasted with long peppercorns 208
Pistachio and Olive Oil Cake with Gariguette Strawberries and Crème Chantilly 176
pizza:
cep mushroom with onion chutney 86
dough 229
poached egg and basil 84
red mullet with tapenade and vegetables 89
smoked salmon, broccoli and cheese 90
Poached Egg and Basil Pizza 84
polenta: with pork cheeks and apple 120
pork:
B.B.L.T. (Belly, Brioche, Lettuce and Tomato) 117
braised belly with chorizo and pepper purée 121

braised cheeks with honey, soy and crisp shallots 118
cheeks with soft polenta and apple 120
chops with haricot beans and tomato sauce 130
pulled with coleslaw 116
shanks with haricot beans 129
slow-roasted belly with black pudding 123
suckling pig with pineapple and peppers 131
tamarind-glazed belly with red cabbage and mushrooms 124
see also bacon; black pudding; chorizo; ham
potatoes:
Chunky Chips 228
Creamy Mashed 228
creamy mashed with rack of lamb 155
crushed with roasted pork belly 123
dauphinois with roast lamb 148
garlic-roasted with parsley and brava sauce 32
horseradish pomme purée 140
parsley with halibut and shrimps 92
rosemary with John Dory, red onions and tomatoes 106
salad with sea trout 107
soup with parsley 18
poultry:
Chicken Stock 218
quail, candied lemon, pear and sourdough crumb salad 73
roast duck with carrots, turnips and beetroot 162
roast squab with Brussels sprouts and red cabbage 160
prawns: burger with squid and tomato chutney 113
prunes:
almond and rum tart 200
in Armagnac with vanilla cheesecake 211
Pulled Pork Sandwiches with Coleslaw 116
pumpkin: with roast pheasant 165

q

quail:
salad with lemon, pear and sourdough crumb 73

r

Rabbit Confit with Celeriac Cream Soup and Rabbit Floss 21
radishes:
with crab and asparagus salad 60
salad with steak tartare 75
raspberries: with elderflower and vanilla panna cotta 206
Razor Clams with Chorizo, Coriander and Chilli 59
red cabbage:
braised with pork belly 124
braised with roast squab 160
Red Mullet Pizza with Tapenade and Provençal Roast Vegetables 89
red onions: with John Dory and tomatoes 106
rhubarb: sorbet 196
rice: Cauliflower and Crayfish Risotto 110 spiced potted with cod 97
Rice Pudding with Oat Crumble Biscuit 195
ricotta: creamed with strawberry pepper compote 189
Roast Anjou Squab with Yakitori of Innards and Brussels Sprouts and Braised Red Cabbage 160
Roast Caesar Salad with White Anchovies 42
Roast Cod with Braised Haricot Beans, Chorizo and Tomato 96
Roast Rack of Lamb with Spice Olive Jus and Creamy Mashed Potatoes 155
Roast Venison and Beetroot with Poached Pears 158
Roasted Ceps, Pistou of Green Vegetables and Paprika Octopus 69
Roasted Duck Breast with Carrots, Turnips and Honey and Spiced Beetroot 162
Roasted Pineapple with Long Peppercorns, Mango and Lychee Sorbet 208
Roquefort and Iceberg Salad with Warm Croutons and Alsace Bacon 41
rosemary:
potatoes with John Dory 106
rub with roast lamb 148
rum: almond and prune tart 200

s

salads:
apple and coriander crab 63
avocado, Baby Gem, orange and carrot 38
beetroot with goat's cheese mousse 34
Caesar with white anchovy 42
coleslaw with pulled pork sandwiches 116
crab and asparagus with radishes 60
kohlrabi, apple, whisky walnut and sea trout 55
potato, samphire and asparagus with sea trout 107
Quail, Candied Lemon, Pear and Sourdough Crumb 73
Roquefort and Iceberg with bacon 41
seared tuna with miso aubergines 44
winter vegetable with goat's curd 37
Salmon 'Crudo' with Pickled Cucumber and Wasabi and Avocado Purée 47; *see also* smoked salmon
Salt and Pepper Squid with Squid Ink Aïoli 70
samphire:
salad with sea trout 107
with sea bream and shrimps 105
sardines: with Spanish tomato bread 49
sauces:
brava with garlic-roasted potatoes 32
bread 165
chimichurri 134
duck jus 220
spicy tomato 130, 226
tomato 144, 226
venison 156
Scallop Ceviche with Pickled Fennel and Lemon Confit 56
sea bass: pastrami with gazpacho garnish 50
Sea Bream with Morecambe Bay Shrimps, Sautéed Kale, Samphire and Mustard Velouté 105
sea trout:
beetroot-cured with horseradish cream 51
herb-roasted with potato, samphire and asparagus salad 107
kohlrabi, apple, whisky and walnut salad 55
Sea Urchin, Goat's Cheese and Peppers on Toast 72
seafood:
cockles with chargrilled sole 109
crayfish and cauliflower risotto 110
Langoustines with Pickled Vegetables and Peas 65
octopus with roasted ceps and green vegetables 69
oysters with Vietnamese dressing 66
Razor Clams with Chorizo, Coriander and Chilli 59
Scallop Ceviche with Fennel and Lemon Confit 56
Sea Urchin, Goat's Cheese and Peppers on Toast 72
see also crab; shrimps; squid
Seared Tuna Salad with Miso Aubergines and Sherry Dressing 44
sesame seeds: crumble with brown sugar tart 174
shallots:
Confit 229
crisp with braised pork cheeks 118
Vinaigrette 222
shrimps:

with halibut, potatoes and asparagus 92
with sea bream, kale and samphire 105
Simple Roast Leg of Lamb with Rosemary Rub and Potato Dauphinois 148
Sloe Gin and Orange Curd Ice Cream with Soft Blackberries and Shortbread 205
Slow-roasted Pork Belly with Black Pudding, Crushed Potatoes and Green Beans 123
Slow-Roasted Lamb Shoulder with Autumn Vegetables and Cabbage and Mint Pesto 152
Smoked Bacon and Peach Cornbread with Candied Pecan and Maple Cream 209
smoked haddock:
gratin with haricot beans and Gruyère herb crust 101
with Manchego and spring onion tortilla 100
Smoked Salmon, Broccoli and Sairass Cheese Pizza 90
sole: chargrilled with cockles 109
sorbet:
Blood Orange Granita 191
cream cheese 177
crème fraîche 174
fromage blanc 202
ginger 201
lychee 208
rhubarb 196
strawberry 173
yoghurt 170
soups:
celeriac cream with rabbit confit 21
Potato and Parsley with Black Pudding 18
Spiced Melon 201
soy sauce: with braised pork cheeks 118
Spanish Breakfast 14
Spanish Tomato Bread with Sardines 49
'Spanish-Style' Roast Suckling Pig with Candied Pineapple and Roast Peppers 131

Spiced Chocolate Cream with Caramel Rice Crispies 188
Spiced Melon Soup with Ginger Sorbet and Basil 201
Spiced Potted Rice with Cod 97
Spiced Roast Pheasant with Pumpkin, Bread Sauce and Home-Made Granola 165
Spicy Tomato Sauce 226
spring onions: with smoked haddock tortilla 100
Spring Vegetable Tartine with Creamed Burrata 25
squab: roast with Brussels sprouts and red cabbage 160
squid:
burger with prawn and tomato chutney 113
with squid ink aïoli 70
Stock Syrup 231
stocks:
brown fish 218
chicken 218
dashi (Japanese) 221
veal/beef 219
vegetable 219
strawberries:
Eton Mess 173
pepper compote with creamed ricotta 189
with pistachio and olive oil cake 176
Summer Fruit Cooked in Liquorice with Fromage Blanc Sorbet 202
sweetcorn: on the cob with Parmesan and chilli 33

t

Tamarind-Glazed Pork Belly with Braised Red Cabbage and Sautéed Mushrooms 124
Tapenade 89, 225
Tarte Tatin with Clotted Cream Ice Cream 199

tarts (savoury): spring vegetable with burrata 25
tarts (sweet):
Almond, Prune and Rum 200
brown sugar 174
mascarpone mousse 196
Tarte Tatin 199
Thai Rum Ice Cream with Coconut Wafers 183
thyme:
with elderflower and vanilla panna cotta 206
sourdough toasts 189
tomatoes:
with baby artichokes and broad beans 29
B.B.L.T. 117
bread with sardines 49
fondue 226
with John Dory and red onions 106
with roast cod and haricot beans 96
sauce 226
sauce with meatballs 144
smoked chutney 113
spicy sauce 226
Tartare 31
tuna:
confit with piperade and chives 46
salad with aubergine and sherry dressing 44
tartare 'D.I.Y.' 45
turnips: with roasted duck 162

V

vanilla:
cheesecake with prunes 211
ice cream 231
panna cotta with elderflower 206
Veal/Beef Stock 219
vegetables:
artichokes with tomatoes and broad beans 29
aubergines with tuna salad 44

autumn with roast lamb shoulder 152
broccoli with smoked salmon pizza 90
Brussels sprouts with roast squab 160
celeriac soup 21
Corn on the Cob with Parmesan and
 Chilli 33
green beans with pork belly 123
kale with sea bream and shrimps 105
Piccalilli 126, 227
pickled fennel with scallop ceviche 56
pickled with langoustines 65
piperade with confit tuna 46
pumpkin with roast pheasant 165
roasted with red mullet pizza 89
Spring Vegetable Tartine with Burrata 25
stock 219
turnips with roasted duck 162
winter salad with goat's curd 37
see also asparagus; beetroot; broad beans;
 cabbage; carrots; cauliflower; courgettes;
 kohlrabi; mushrooms; onions; peas;
 peppers; potatoes; radishes
venison:
with beetroot and venison sauce 156
roast with beetroot and pears 158
Vietnamese dressing 223

W

walnuts: kohlrabi, apple, whisky and sea
 trout salad 55
wasabi:
dressing 223
purée with avocado 47
watercress: with garlic herb beef 137
whisky: kohlrabi, apple, walnut and sea
 trout salad 55
Winter Vegetable Salad with Goat's Curd
 37
yoghurt: sorbet with grilled brioche 170
Yuzu Wasabi Dressing 223

ACKNOWLEDGEMENTS

I would like to thank Jon Croft for creating my first ever Social Book and having the faith in me to deliver a great product. I would like to thank Meg Avent for persevering with me and for always giving me a nudge to hurry up (I'm always notoriously late). Art director and designer Matt Inwood, for a beautiful book, for always being really humorous on location when we were shooting and generally for just being a good support. Alice Gibbs, for her constant perseverance and for her endless patience. Without Alice none of this would have happened. She's the one who pulled all of this together and made it all work and she's been an absolute dream to work with – thank you, Alice.

Thank you to Imogen Fortes, for being the editor and making all this into beautiful text and for overseeing the project. John Carey, who does all of my photography for the restaurants and for the websites and now for the book: I am inspired by your photography and creativity every time we work together. I would like to thank Emily Quah and Nicole Herft for doing all of the recipe testing and making it all come together at such speed: without you guys it wouldn't have been possible. Props stylist Jo Harris, for framing the food to look even better than it already is. Zoe Ross, for her diligent proofing of the book. To Kathi Grilz, for helping with the actual writing of the recipes.

Thank you to my executive team: Irha Atherton, Michael West, Sarah Hutchins and Anne-Marie Kinane for getting this project off the ground and for keeping everything running smoothly. I would also like to say a massive thank you to Cary Docherty and Dominique Park for helping me to do the photo shoots, for always making sure the preparation was done immaculately and for helping me deliver a great book: your support was invaluable.

Thank you to the chefs from all my London restaurants. To Paul Hood at Social Eating House – thanks mate for all your support and for sending the food over for the shoots. To Phil Carmichael, for helping with the produce and for delivering such a great restaurant at Berners Tavern. To Ross Bryans, Alex Craciun, Paul Walsh and all the team at Pollen Street Social for holding the fort for me and allowing me the time to go off and shoot this book.

Thank you to all my chefs abroad. In Singapore, to Colin Buchan at Pollen and to Andrew Walsh at Esquina and Keong Saik Snacks. In Hong Kong, to Chris Whitmore, Andres Lara and Nathan Green of 22 Ships and Ham & Sherry; and in Shanghai to Scott Melvin and Kim Lyle at Table 1 and The Commune Social. Thank you for your inspiration and for helping me to pull all of these recipes together and for making my working life such a dream.